ECONOMIC GROWTH ISSUES

ECONOMIC GROWTH ISSUES

L. A. FINLEY
EDITOR

Nova Science Publishers, Inc.
New York

For permission to use material from this book please contact us:
Telephone 631-231-7269; Fax 631-231-8175
Web Site: http://www.novapublishers.com

LIBRARY OF CONGRESS CATALOGING-IN-PUBLICATION DATA
Available upon request

ISBN 1-59454-555-3

Published by Nova Science Publishers, Inc. ✦ New York

CONTENTS

PREFACE

By "economic growth" economists mean, in the first place, annual increases in the nation's total output of goods and services—its national product. Maintaining rapid economic growth depends increasingly on productivity gains, particularly in the service sector. Economic growth and the productivity are impacted by individual enterprises, industrial sectors and the wider economy. The standard of living of a country is profoundly effected by economic growth and productivity. One of the key questions within the debate on economic growth and productivity is the effect of information technology on the system. This new book presents leading edge research on this exciting topic.

The role of learning and R&D in economic development in an endogenous growth model is addressed in chapter 1. When human capital is below a threshold level, the model predicts that skills are accumulated as the only growth-generating activity, whereas both innovation activities and learning drive growth above this level. Hence, an endogenous regime shift is triggered when the level of human capital reaches the threshold level, because it becomes profitable to innovate. The transitional dynamics of the model is determined to study development of important variables. The calibrated growth rate from the model is compared to estimated trend rates of growth for the US economy. It is found that the growth predictions of the model are well in accordance with US growth experience from 1870 to 1989.

The empirical economic growth literature has generally ignored spatial interdependence across countries. The role of a country's geographic location is an empirical issue that has been taken into consideration just only recently. Chapter 2 uses spatial econometric techniques with spatially lagged dependent variables and spatially lagged errors to estimate an economic growth model that includes cross-country interdependence, in which a country's economic growth depends on the growth rate of its neighbors. Based on a sample of 98 countries over three decades (1965-1975, 1975-1985, 1985-1995) and using several tests to explore and evaluate spatial dependence we find some interesting results. In particular, spatial relationships across countries are quite relevant. A country economic growth is indeed affected by the performance of its neighbors and then influenced by its own relative geographical position. This result suggests that the spillover effects among countries are important for growth. Consequently, our results indicate that spatial interrelation across countries can not be ignored in the analysis of economic growth. Ignoring such relationships can result in significant model misspecification, omitted variables problem and can underestimate spillover effects and externalities across economies.

In chapter 3, the authors develop a simple endogenous growth model with two competing production technologies and productivity spillover effects between firms that use the same technology. Investments are directed to the technology with highest current and future returns. Since current investments increase future returns through spillovers, the economy will usually lock in, specializing in one of the two technologies. In the case that the economy has selected a highly pollutant technology, sustainable growth requires a transition towards the clean technology. We analyze the scope for (environmental) policies that induce such a transition.

The imperative of the state, irrespective of its organization, is to provide law and order, contract enforcement, and property rights. The government provides the foundation for markets to function and for society to prosper. A common thread in any government is that, for a given society, the state holds a monopoly over most of its services. Although the state may choose not to exploit this market power, the public agents that represent the state within the aggregate production process, necessarily will. Chapter 4 presents a macroeconomic framework that explicitly considers the local monopoly power of public agents. In the context of a representative agent model, I consider a private sector production function versus a public sector production function in which both sectors compete over labor and capital. Estimates are made of the productivity of private versus public capital, of private versus public labor, and of public infrastructure within the private sector production function. The theoretical implications of decentralized public agents are then analyzed within an endogenous growth framework. The results suggest that the elasticity of public infrastructure is significantly lower than previous estimates. They also confirm that the elasticity of private infrastructure is country specific. The theoretical results suggest that decentralization of public agents which, intuitively is greater in less developed countries than industrialized ones, is associated with steeper growth paths that lead to lower steady state capital labor ratios and per capita consumption levels. This implies that shocks to less developed countries have more dramatic effects but shorter life spans than shocks to industrialized countries, or more simply, business cycles in developing countries are shorter but more volatile."Sure there are dishonest men in local government. But there are dishonest men in national government too." - Richard M. Nixon [1913-1994]

The decline in the service flow from a stock of capital goods with age, due to the physical retirement of capital units and the gradual loss of efficiency of each unit remaining, can be described by survival curves and efficiency curves. Chapter 5 discusses the relationship between the retirement process of the capital, as formalized by these curves, and the average retirement rate, and how this relationship is affected by changes in the investment growth path. The effect of changes in the survival and efficiency curves on the age distribution of the capital goods, those existing as well as those retired in each period, is also considered. The authors next reconsider the relationship between these curves and the vintage prices of capital under neo-classical assumptions about perfect second-hand markets and malleability, using duality between quantities and prices. Three examples with parametric survival and efficiency curves are presented. The retirement rate is a declining function of the growth rate of investment (except in the exponential decay case) and quite sensitive to this growth rate over a reasonable interval. Approximating the retirement rate by the inverse of the capital's maximal life-time or twice this value ('double declining balance') will frequently produce very inaccurate results. The response of the capital/investment ratio and the retirement/investment ratio to changes in the investment growth rate and in the curvature of the survival function is also investigated. Concavity of the survival and efficiency curves may be compatible with convexity of the age-price profile. This approach for making inference on survival and efficiency functions from vintage price data is contrasted with the frequently cited Hulten-Wykoff approach. The estimates give evidence less strongly in favour of convex efficiency and survival curves than is often believed.

Chapter 6 begins by posing the question of what is the relationship between telecommunications investment and regional economic development. After providing a theoretical basis for each of the three potential relationships, i.e., growth causes investment, investment causes growth, and growth and investment are jointly determined, the authors review the statistical methodology involved in testing for Granger causality and look at some recent applications in the development economics literature. Next, they present results from three different causality analyses. First, they present the results of causality tests performed on a panel of six states from the southern Unites States over the year 1983 - 1992. Next, a straightforward application of causality testing using fifty years of data (1947-1996) for the United States is presented. The third analysis employs time series data from 25 OECD countries for the years 1980 – 1996. The results of these distinct analyses are consistent and indicate that economic growth causes telecommunications investment but not conversely.

In: Economic Growth Issues
Editor: L. A. Finley, pp. 1-22

ISBN 1-59454-555-3

Chapter 1

CHARACTERISTICS OF GROWTH-GENERATING PROCESSES: R&D AND LEARNING

Anders Sørensen
Johns Hopkins University

ABSTRACT

The role of learning and R&D in economic development is addressed in an endogenous growth model. When human capital is below a threshold level, the model predicts that skills are accumulated as the only growth-generating activity, whereas both innovation activities and learning drive growth above this level. Hence, an endogenous regime shift is triggered when the level of human capital reaches the threshold level, because it becomes profitable to innovate. The transitional dynamics of the model is determined to study development of important variables. The calibrated growth rate from the model is compared to estimated trend rates of growth for the US economy. It is found that the growth predictions of the model are well in accordance with US growth experience from 1870 to 1989.

Keywords: Growth, R&D, Education, Regime shift

1. INTRODUCTION

This chapter offers a theory of development that describes the relationship between productivity improvements through human capital accumulation and productivity gains obtained through R&D. The main finding is that R&D is unprofitable for low levels of human capital, whereas the activity becomes profitable when human capital reaches a threshold level. Hence, an endogenous regime shift takes place from a situation without R&D to a situation with R&D. The result is driven by the interaction of two relationships. First, human capital is important for the size of domestic markets. Second, in order to cover innovation costs a critical market size is required for activities based on new inventions.

Market size is important for R&D because agents have the alternative option of investing in human capital. For low levels of human capital the return to innovation will be lower than the return to investing in learning. Therefore, no R&D takes place. Over time human capital increases, thereby expanding the market size such that R&D becomes profitable at some point in time. As a consequence, the model predicts that learning is relatively important for productivity improvements at low levels of human capital, whereas R&D is relatively important for higher levels. In other words, the characteristics of growth-generating processes change over time.

The motivation for the analysis is the observation that economic growth appears to undergo different phases. In recent empirical studies, trend rates of economic growth per capita change significantly between different periods of time, see Ben-David and Papell (1995), Crafts and Mills (1996), and Raj (1992). In Ben-David and Papell (1995) it is found that the trend rate of growth increases between World War One and World War Two in the 16 developed countries in the analysis. An explanation for the changing growth rate is that the characteristics of growth-generating processes change. Crafts (1997) argues that productivity improvements through learning were far more important in the British Economy than those obtained through investments in R&D from around the Industrial Revolution until World War One. After World War One R&D investments have been of main importance.

To investigate whether the above explanation for the U.K. seems to be appropriate for other developed countries, different indicators of productivity improvements through R&D and learning are presented. The indicators are R&D expenditures relative to economic output and the number of researchers as a proportion of total employment. Furthermore, the share of GDP growth that is explained by education activities is used to measure the importance of learning as a growth-generating activity.

It is evident from Table 1 that there has been a large increase in resources devoted to R&D after the interwar period; and that R&D makes up a significant share of economic activities today. Before World War Two almost no resources were devoted to R&D. The overall impression is that the importance of R&D activities has increased significantly in the second half of the twentieth century.

Table 1: R&D Expenditures and Employment of Researchers in Manufacturing

Germany		Britain		USA	
R&D / Value added	Researchers / Employment	R&D / Net output	Researchers / Employment	R&D / Net output	Researchers / Employment
-	-	0.43 (1934)	0.03 (1933)	-	0.17 (1933)
-	-	0.43 (1938)	0.07 (1938)	0.98 (1937)	0.29 (1940)
0.58 (1950)	-	-	0.07 (1945–46)	-	0.32 (1946)
1.40 (1959)	-	3.49 (1959)	0.57 (1959)	5.82 (1959)	1.31 (1959)
1.96 (1964)	1.29 (1964)	4.40 (1964)	-	-	-
3.08 (1969)	1.70 (1969)	3.40 (1968)	2.69 (1968)	-	-
3.88 (1975)	1.92 (1975)	3.50 (1975)	2.42 (1975)	-	-
5.72 (1983)	-	4.79 (1983)	3.66 (1983)	5.96 (1981)	-
6.91 (1989)	3.29 (1989)	4.77 (1989)	3.55 (1989)	7.33 (1987)	-

Notes: Years of measurement in brackets.
Source: Broadberry and Wagner (1996).

The data presented in Table 1 is only available for Germany, Britain, and the United States. However, a similar pattern is found by Maddison (1991) for the economy as a whole in France, Germany, Japan, Netherlands, U.K., and the United States.

Table 2 shows the share of GDP growth accounted for by education activities. This share tends to fall over time in all countries except in the Netherlands and the United States[1], suggesting that the relative importance of productivity improvements through education has fallen during the twentieth century.

Table 2: Growth of Labor Quality due to Education, 1913-87

	Growth rate (% p.a.)			Share of GDP Growth (%)		
	1913-50	1950-73	1973-87	1913-50	1950-73	1973-87
France	0.52	0.56	0.80	32	8	26
Germany	0.35	0.27	0.15	19	3	6
Japan	0.87	0.74	0.64	27	6	25
Netherlands	0.38	0.62	0.80	12	9	32
U.K.	0.47	0.29	0.47	26	7	19
U.S.A.	0.59	0.68	0.63	15	13	18

Source: Maddison (1991)
Notes: Growth of labor quality due to education is calculated on the basis of average years of schooling in primary, secondary, and higher education. In order to derive joint factor input, the labor growth is given a weight of 0.7. The share of GDP growth is calculated as 0.7 times labor growth in relation to GDP growth.

The support for decreasing importance of productivity improvements through learning is mixed. It is important, however, to emphasize that the applied measure is crude even though it is descriptive. First of all, it is based on data on years of schooling and not a more subtle measure of human capital. Furthermore, formal education is not a perfect measure of learning activities, since it does not include all relevant effects.

In spite of measurement problems, the observations in the two tables support to some degree the view that productivity improvements through learning were more important than those obtained through investments in R&D in the earlier stages of capitalist development, whereas productivity improvements obtained through R&D have been of main importance in the second half of the twentieth century. The present analysis offers an explanation for this phenomenon.

The model follows Romer (1990) extended with human capital accumulation. Designs for complementary intermediates are developed in an R&D sector. The patents to these designs are sold to intermediate firms that issue shares to finance initial capital. Final goods are produced by using intermediates and human capital. The technology is such that higher human capital creates higher demand for intermediates and thereby larger intermediate markets. The model also includes a learning sector in which skills are accumulated. Income is either used for consumption or is invested in shares in intermediate firms.

As mentioned, an endogenous regime shift takes place in the model since R&D becomes profitable for a threshold of human capital. To understand this, consider the conditions for

[1] Ho and Jorgenson (2001) analyze quality improvements of the U.S. workforce. By applying data from this paper it is found that the share of GDP growth explained by education seems to be constant over time for U.S.A.

R&D to take place. To start activities in the intermediate sector, entrant firms acquire patents to designs at prices equal to unit costs in R&D, issuing shares to finance these fixed setup costs. However, consumption and the derived demand for intermediates are low when the level of human capital is low, implying that the profit from innovation is low relative to the fixed setup cost. This depresses the rate of return on shares, and hence households gain a higher rate of return from investing in learning only and restrain from investing in shares. Therefore, share prices are relatively low when human capital is low, implying that the price intermediate firms are able to pay for patents falls short of unit costs in R&D. Consequently, market-driven R&D is unprofitable and innovation activities are absent. Yet, households still invest in shares in existing intermediate firms. Over time human capital increases. This increases the size of intermediate markets and thereby the value of intermediate firms. At some point in time R&D becomes profitable and the activity becomes present in the economy.

The idea that market size is important for economic development goes back to Adam Smith and is often stressed in the literature, see among others Fleming (1955), Krugman (1993), and Murphy et al. (1989*a, b*). The underlying framework in these papers is that producers decide whether to adopt modern increasing returns technologies or to use old-fashioned constant returns to scale technologies. The implementation of the modern technology requires a large market size relative to fixed setup costs as in the present analysis. Two outcomes are possible in this framework: an underdeveloped economy with low income, and an industrialized economy with high income. This is similar to the present analysis since the technology in final goods production exhibits constant returns when R&D is absent and increasing returns when R&D is present.

Zilibotti (1995) analyzes the transition to long run equilibrium. As in the above mentioned contributions a poverty trap and an industrialized equilibrium are identified. It is found that two otherwise identical economies can end up in different equilibria. In the present model it is also possible that the economy ends up in a zero growth equilibrium if the adjustment elapses along an underdevelopment saddle-path. This aspect is not analyzed further since the focal point is changing characteristics of growth-generating processes rather than industrialization.

The relation between market size and human capital accumulation in determining structural shifts is emphasized in Temple and Voet (1998) and Goodfriend and McDermott (1995). Temple and Voet (1998) modify the framework of Murphy et al. (1998*a, b*) such that the advanced technology is adopted when human capital reaches a threshold level. In their analysis, however, human capital is exogenously given, whereas the incentive to invest in learning drives the regime shift presented in this chapter. Goodfriend and McDermott (1995) analyze the development process in the pre-industrial period where growth is driven by expanding population. In the industrialized period growth is driven by human capital accumulation. A common characteristic of these contributions is the focus on industrialization. The focus of the present analysis is economic progress after industrialization has occurred.

The growth rate of the model is calculated over time from a relatively low initial stock of human capital. In order to determine the transitional dynamics, a numerical algorithm is employed. This is the Time-Elimination Method by Mulligan and Sala-i-Martin (1991). The calibrated growth rate from the model is compared to estimated trend rates of growth for the United States. It is found that the growth predictions of the model is consistent with US growth experience for the period from 1870 to 1989 as presented in Crafts and Mills (1996). This supports the endogenous growth model applied in the chapter including convergence of the growth rate to the steady state level from below. This result contradicts predictions of the neoclassical growth model with convergence to the steady state growth rate from above.[2]

In the next section the production side of the economy is described, while the third section describes the household optimization problem. In the fourth section the result that R&D activities are absent for low levels of human capital is derived. In the fifth section the transitional dynamics of the model is determined. Therefore, it becomes possible to investigate when it is profitable to perform R&D activities and when it is not. Furthermore, comparative statics are discussed. In the sixth section the growth experience of the United States is compared to the growth predictions of the model. The seventh section concludes. The model is solved in an appendix.

2. Production Side

In this section the production side of the economy is described. The underlying framework follows Romer (1990).

2.1. Final Goods Sector

Final goods are produced according to

$$y=\left[\int_0^n x(j)^\alpha dj\right]h_y^{1-\alpha}\ ,\ 0<\alpha<1, \tag{1}$$

with $j\in[0,n]$. y is the quantity of final goods, $x(j)$ is the quantity of intermediate variety j, h_y is human capital used in the sector, n is the stock of different intermediate designs, and α is the capital share. The quantity of physical capital equals $\int_0^n x(j)dj$, whereas effective physical capital is given by the square bracket in (1). Consequently, the larger the number of intermediate designs, the higher is the productivity of a given physical capital level.

The demand for the j'th intermediate variety and human capital equals

$$x(j)=\left(\frac{\alpha}{p(j)}\right)^{\frac{1}{1-\alpha}}h_y \tag{2}$$

[2] Romer (1986) argues that the economic growth rate increases over time, suggesting that the relationship between growth and the stage of development is positive.

$$h_y = \frac{(1-\alpha)y}{w}, \tag{3}$$

respectively, assuming perfect competition and profit maximizing behavior. It is assumed that a unit of physical capital is fully depreciated within one time period, implying that $p(j)$ is the price of one unit intermediate variety j. w is the wage rate of one unit of human capital.

2.2. Intermediate Sector

To start activities an intermediate firm issues shares in order to finance the patent that is required for production. It is assumed that profit is paid to shareholders as dividends. Furthermore, property rights are completely secured by patents and monopolistic competition applies. An intermediate firm possesses the property right to intermediate variety j and produces by transforming final goods to intermediates. The profit,

$$\pi(j) = (p(j) - 1)x(j),$$

is maximized subject to (2), resulting in the intermediate price of $p(j) = \overline{p} = 1/\alpha$. This also implies a market-clearing quantity

$$x(j) = \overline{x} = \alpha^{\frac{2}{1-\alpha}} h_y \tag{4}$$

and a profit level, $\pi(j) = \overline{\pi}$. The intuition for (4) follows (1): an increase in the level of human capital in final goods production shifts the marginal product schedule out for given level of intermediates. As a result, demand for the single intermediate variety increases for unchanged intermediate price.

By substituting (1) and (4) into (3), the wage rate is found to be:

$$w = \alpha^{\frac{2\alpha}{1-\alpha}}(1-\alpha)n \tag{5}$$

The usual non-arbitrage condition for financial capital applies:

$$r_f = \frac{\dot{p}_n}{p_n} + \frac{\overline{\pi}}{p_n}, \tag{6}$$

where r_f is the rate of return on shares in intermediate firms and p_n is the patent price. A dot above a variable indicates a time derivative. r_f is given by a dividend plus a capital gain.

2.3. R&D Sector

Human capital and general knowledge are employed in the production of new designs. The innovation process generates new general knowledge as a by-product, so n is used interchangeably for the number of designs and the stock of knowledge. The development in the stock of designs is assumed to follow:

$$\dot{n} = Dnh_R. \tag{7}$$

D is a productivity parameter and h_R is human capital employed in R&D.

R&D activities are present, i.e. $\dot{n} > 0$, when innovators are able to cover unit costs. The profit is zero due to perfect competition implying that the patent price can be derived to $p_n = w/Dn$. In the opposite case, where innovators are unable to cover unit costs or equivalently when the patent price falls short of unit costs, $p_n < w/Dn$, no R&D activities will be carried out, i.e. $\dot{n} = 0$.

In the case with R&D, the patent price is constant which becomes evident by substituting the wage rate in (5) into the expression for p_n, i.e. $\dot{p}_n = 0$. This implies that the rate of return on shares can be expressed as

$$r_f = \frac{\bar{\pi}}{p_n} = \alpha D h_y. \tag{2.6$'$}$$

One important characteristic is evident from (2.6′). The higher the level of human capital in final goods production, the higher is the rate of return on shares. In other words, the larger the size of the market for an intermediate variety, the larger is the profit in the matching firm, and thereby the larger is the incentive to innovate.

3. Consumption and Education

In this section the household side of the economy is described. The model includes an education sector in which skills are accumulated, such that time spent in learning competes with time spent on the job. Hence, agents either work or spend time in education and forego current consumption to take advantage of future consumption possibilities. The adding of the education sector is an extension of Romer (1990).

The household sector is characterized by a representative household with an infinite time horizon. Preferences are described by the isoelastic utility integral

$$U = \int_0^\infty e^{-\rho t} \frac{c^{1-\theta} - 1}{1-\theta} dt. \tag{8}$$

$\rho > 0$ is the rate of time preference, $\theta > 0$ is the inverse intertemporal elasticity of substitution, and c is consumption of final goods. U is maximized subject to two restrictions: the learning technology and the budget constraint.

Skills are accumulated in an education sector according to

$$\dot{h} = Bl^{\gamma} h_e^{1-\gamma} - \delta h. \tag{9}$$

h is total human capital, h_e is human capital devoted to education, l is infrastructural services used in the education sector, δ is a depreciation parameter of human capital, B is a productivity parameter, and γ is the capital share. The gross accumulation, $\dot{h} + \delta h$, exhibits positive and diminishing marginal productivity with respect to human capital, which implies that human capital formation is bounded. l is exogenous and assumed equal to one without loss of generality.[3]

The budget constraint is given by:

$$\dot{f} = wh_s + r_f f - c, \tag{10}$$

where f is financial capital and h_s is human capital supplied to the labor market.

In the following u denotes the share of human capital used in education. Hence, $h_e \equiv uh$ and $h_s \equiv (1-u)h$. u and c are treated as control variables, f and h as state variables, and a and b as co-state variables (shadow prices of income and human capital, respectively). Let $V \equiv b/a$ be the shadow price of human capital in units of final goods.

The optimal division of human capital between learning and production is determined by the first-order condition for u:

$$w = V(1-\gamma)B(uh)^{-\gamma}. \tag{11}$$

The left hand side of the equation is given by the marginal product of human capital in production, which equals the wage rate. The right hand side is given by the marginal product of human capital in education measured in units of final goods. Hence, human capital is divided between learning and production activities such that the marginal products in the two activities are equal.

The Keynes-Ramsey rule applies to the rate of return to shares:

$$r_f = -\frac{\dot{a}}{a}, \tag{12}$$

which follows from the first-order condition for f.

---

[3] The learning technology is similar to that applied in Lucas (1988), Mulligan and Sala-i-Martin (1993), Barro and Sala-i-Martin (1995), among others. Contrary to these contributions human capital formation is bounded in the present analysis. This follows the concept of human capital discussed by Romer (1990).

The rate of return to the marginal unit of human capital in education is determined by substituting (11) into the first-order condition for h and applying the definition of V:

$$r_e \equiv \left[(1-\gamma)B(uh)^{-\gamma} - \delta\right] + \frac{\dot{V}}{V} = -\frac{\dot{a}}{a}. \tag{13}$$

This rate of return is referred to as the rate of return to education, r_e. r_e is composed of the marginal product of human capital in education net of depreciations and the rate of change in the value of human capital. The Keynes-Ramsey rule also applies to r_e.

It is clear from (12) and (13) that the rate of return to education equals that of shares, $r = r_f = r_e$. If this condition is not fulfilled but $r_f > r_e$ applies, the return to savings can be increased for unchanged total savings. To understand this imagine that one unit human capital is reallocated from the learning sector to the production side. According to (11) the wage rate is equal to the marginal product of human capital in learning. In other words, the return to savings increases by $(r_f - r_e)w$ because the additional wage income is invested in shares. The reallocation of human capital closes the gap between the two rates of return and continues until $r_f = r_e$. A similar argument holds for the case where $r_f < r_e$.

Finally, the growth rate in consumption is derived to

$$g_c = \frac{1}{\theta}(r - \rho) \tag{14}$$

by applying the first-order condition of c and $r = r_e = r_f = -\dot{a}/a$. g_c indicates the growth rate of c.

The number of designs is assumed to be positive without R&D activities. This is interpreted as the presence of exogenous discoveries before time 0 leading to $n_0 > 0$. Since intermediate firms exist when no R&D activities are present shares are traded between households. However, no new shares are issued due to the absence of R&D.

The equilibrium conditions for the n intermediate markets and the final goods market are already imposed on the model. Furthermore, a share ϑ of human capital on the production side is employed in final goods production, whereas the rest is employed in R&D. ϑ adjusts such that wage rates are equal in R&D and final goods production. Finally, the patent market clears according to Walras' Law. In the following $v = (1-u)\vartheta$ denotes the share of human capital in final goods production and u is the share of human capital in education.

4. The Regime Shift

In the previous sections it was found that the rate of return on shares in intermediate firms is positively related to human capital in final goods production when R&D activities are present. Furthermore, the learning technology exhibits diminishing returns to human capital. Consequently, it is expected that R&D activities are absent for low levels of human capital. Under such circumstances, growth is generated by learning only. In this section it is shown that R&D is absent if human capital is below a threshold level or equivalently if the size of intermediate markets is below a critical level. The result is established in two propositions. In the first it is shown that R&D is unprofitable for low levels of human capital. In the second the threshold level of human capital is determined. In the following the case without R&D is referred to as Regime 1, whereas the case with R&D is referred to as Regime 2. The solution to the model is derived in the appendix.

Proposition 1. (Rates of Return) The rate of return in Regime 1 exceeds that of Regime 2 for $h \to 0$.

Proof. Proposition 1 is proven by showing that:

$$r_1 \geq r_{1|\min} > r_{2|\max} \geq r_2 \text{ for } h \to 0.$$

r_1 and r_2 are equilibrium rates of return in Regime 1 and Regime 2, whereas $r_{1|\min}$ and $r_{2|\max}$ are the minimum and the maximum rate of return for the two regimes.

The equilibrium rate of return in Regime 1 equals:

$$r_1 = \frac{\theta u}{\theta u + \gamma(1-u)}\left(B(uh)^{-\gamma} - \delta - \rho\right) + \rho - \frac{\gamma\theta\delta}{\theta u + \gamma(1-u)},$$

which is derived by (5), (11), (13) and (16) The minimum rate of return $r_{1|\min}$ is derived by choosing the value of u that minimizes the above rate of return for a given level of human capital. This value is referred to as $u_{\min}$. The lower limit of $u_{\min}$ is $u_{|\dot{h}=0}$ since $\dot{h} \geq 0$ has to be fulfilled for h below the steady state value. If this is not the case the adjustment path is unstable. Below three potential candidates for $u_{\min}$ is analyzed. These are $u_{\min} = u_{|\dot{h}=0}, u_{|\dot{h}=0} < u_{\min} < 1$, and $u_{\min} = 1$.

(i) The rate of return for $u_{|\dot{h}=0}$ is derived to:

$$r_1 = \frac{\theta(1-\gamma-\underline{u})\delta + \gamma(1-\underline{u})\rho}{\theta\underline{u} + \gamma(1-\underline{u})}, u_{|\dot{h}=0} \equiv \underline{u} = \left(\frac{\delta}{B}\right)^{\frac{1}{1-\gamma}} h^{\frac{\gamma}{1-\gamma}},$$

by (9)

(ii) It can be shown that $\partial^2 r_1/\partial u^2 < 0$ for $\partial r_1/\partial u = 0$ when $u_{|\dot{h}=0} < u < 1$. This implies that no interior local minimum value of r_1 exists, which thereby rules out the candidate.

(iii) The rate of return for $u=1$ equals:

$$r_1 = Bh^{-\gamma} - (1+\gamma)\delta.$$

This candidate is ruled out for $h \to 0$ since $r_1 \to \infty$ for this value.

The consequence of (i)-(iii) is that $u_{\min} = u_{|\dot{h}=0}$ for $h \to 0$ and thereby that $r_{1|\min} \to (\rho + \theta\delta(1-\gamma)/\gamma) > 0$ for $h \to 0$.

The rate of return in Regime 2, $r_2 = \alpha D h_y$, is below the rate of return where all human capital is allocated to final goods production, i.e. $r_{2|\max} = \alpha D h$. For $h \to 0$, $r_{2|\max} \to 0$. Consequently, $r_1 > r_2$ for $h \to 0$, which proves the proposition.■

Proposition 1 implies that the rate of return in Regime 1 exceeds that of Regime 2 for low levels of human capital. Consequently, the economy is in Regime 1 for low human capital. In other words, share prices are of such a size that the price intermediate firms are able to pay for patents cannot cover unit costs in R&D implying that the activity is unprofitable.

Proposition 2. (Optimal Timing) The shift from Regime 1 to Regime 2 takes place for $r_1 = r_2$. The condition is satisfied for the threshold level of human capital $\overline{h} > 0$ for which R&D is profitable.

Proof. Proposition 2 is derived by determining the trigger point in time, T, for the regime shift. The utility function in (8) is rewritten to

$$U = \int_0^T e^{-\rho t} \frac{c_1^{1-\theta} - 1}{1-\theta} dt + \int_T^\infty e^{-\rho t} \frac{c_2^{1-\theta} - 1}{1-\theta} dt.$$

The optimal consumption in Regime 1, c_1, is determined by (16), whereas optimal consumption in Regime 2, c_2, is determined by (17). Hence, R&D is unprofitable when c_1 applies and profitable when c_2 applies. The choice of *T* that maximizes *U* requires that consumption is independent of regime type:

$$c_1(T) = c_2(T)$$

By using (14) the consumption level is rewritten to

$$c(t) = c(0)\exp\left[\int_0^t \frac{r(\tau)-\rho}{\theta} d\tau\right].$$

Since the economy is in Regime 1 from 0 to T and $c_1 = c_2$ at time T, it is clear that $r_1 = r_2$ at time T. The level of human capital at time T, $h(T)$, is defined as the threshold level $\bar{h}$.■

Proposition 2 implies that the rate of return for Regime 1 must equal the rate of return for Regime 2 at the trigger point in time. The equality of the rates of return in the two regimes implies that share prices attain such a size that unit costs in R&D are recovered, i.e. R&D is profitable and the regime shift takes place.

The adjustment over time from an initial situation of low human capital to the endogenous regime shift is described on the basis of three time trends in Regime 1, see the appendix. These are a falling rate of return, rising profits in intermediate firms and rising asset prices. Consequently, two opposite effects are in force in Regime 1. Over time the rate of return decreases, whereas profits increase which rises the value of intermediate firms and thereby share prices. For some level of human capital share prices reach a size for which unit costs of R&D are covered. This implies that R&D becomes profitable and the regime shift takes place. For this level of human capital the rates of return in the two regimes are equal.

5. Simulation of the Model

In this section the transitional dynamics of the model is derived to study development of important variables. The applied method is the "Time-Elimination Method", see Mulligan and Sala-i-Martin (1991). The rates of return in the two regimes are derived as a function of the state variable, h. Hence, the threshold level of human capital, i.e. $h(T) = \bar{h}$, is determined where the condition for optimal timing is fulfilled.

The remaining of this section is divided in five subsections. First, the choice of parameter values applied in the simulations is discussed. Second, the rate of return to investments in the two regimes are derived as functions of the human capital level. The derivation is performed by using the solution of the model (see Equations (16) and (17) of the appendix), and the condition that the rates of return is equal in the two regimes at the trigger point of time. Third, the optimal allocation of human capital between sectors are derived. Fourth, the growth rate is simulated as a function of human capital and time, and fifth, comparative statics for $\bar{h}$ and T are discussed.[4]

5.1. Parameter Values

The baseline values for the parameters are chosen according to existing literature on calibration of endogenous growth models. Hence, $\theta = 2$, $\rho = 0.03$, $\delta = 0.05$, and $\alpha = 0.5$. The parameters that describe the technologies in growth-generating sectors are chosen somewhat more arbitrary. It is believed that education uses human capital more

[4] The stability of the model is studied in Sørensen (1999). Here it is shown that there exist one and only one equilibrium with positive long run growth for $\theta \geq 1$. This equilibrium is saddle path stable.

intensive than final goods production, such that $(1-\gamma) > (1-\alpha)$. As a consequence, γ is chosen to 0.15. Furthermore, D is chosen to 1. The last parameter, B, is chosen to be close to 0.09 implying that the steady-state growth rate equals 2% and the steady-state rate of return is 7%. In the baseline case, $u^* = 0.50$, $v^* = 0.43$, and $h^* = 0.28$.

5.2. Rates of Return

In Figure 1 the rates of return in the two regimes are shown as functions of human capital. The downward sloping r_1-curve illustrates the rate of return when the economy is in Regime 1 where only education drives economic growth. When the level of human capital increases the rate of return to education, r_e, falls due to diminishing marginal product in the learning technology.

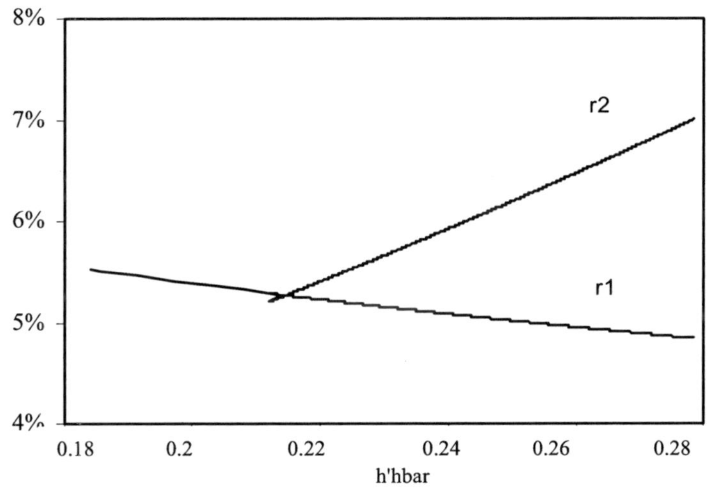

Figure 1: Rates of returns in the two regimes

The r_2-curve shows the rate of return in Regime 2, where both education and R&D generate growth. The slope of the r_2-curve is positive due to the relation between the level of human capital and market size for intermediate goods. Hence, the higher is the level of human capital the larger is profits in the single intermediate firm and thereby the higher is the rate of return on shares. The rate of return to education equals that of shares due to arbitrage.[5]

It is evident from the figure that it is optimal to restrain from investing in shares in intermediate firms when h is below $\bar{h}$, because the rate of return is higher in the alternative regime where only human capital accumulation drives growth. This implies that the R&D sector is inactive in the economy. When the level of human capital is equal to or above the threshold level, $\bar{h}$, it is optimal for households to invest in shares implying that the R&D sector is active. Consequently, it is optimal to assign all growth-generating resources to education for $h < \bar{h}$ and wait to be active in innovation until the demand for the single intermediate variety is so high that investments in new intermediate firms are attractive.

5.3. Optimal Allocation of Human Capital

The shares of human capital in final goods production, education, and R&D as functions of the human capital level are shown in panels $a-c$ of Figure 2. It is evident from panel a and b that $0 < u < 1$ and $0 < v < 1$ for all levels of human capital, implying that final goods production and learning activities always are present. This is not the case for R&D activities since no human capital is devoted to the R&D sector for $h < \bar{h}$ $(1-u-v=0)$, whereas the share of human capital in R&D is positive for $h \geq \bar{h}$. This is seen from panel c.

The curves presented in Figure 2 are generated as the net result of an income effect, a relative profitability effect, and an intertemporal substitution effect. First of all, as h rises over time, the wealth of the representative household increases. Because households prefer to smooth consumption, they feel able to forego larger amounts of consumption by investing more heavily in education and financial capital as their level of wealth and consumption increases. *Ceteris paribus*, this income effect tends to raise the share of human capital used in education, u, and the share of human capital employed in R&D, $1-u-v$, at the expense of human capital allocated to final goods production, v.

Second, an increase in h causes an increase in the demand for intermediates which in turn raises the demand for new designs, thereby drawing human capital into innovation activities away from the other sectors. This effect stemming from an increased profitability of R&D clearly increases $1-u-v$.

Third, the rate of return to education changes when h increases. On the one hand, the marginal product of h in education is diminishing and thereby the growth rate of human capital. On the other hand, the lower marginal product results in a higher value of human capital, see (11). This is the intertemporal substitution effect. If the former effect is dominated by the latter the rate of return to education increases. In this case, households are induced to forego more current consumption by spending more time in education to take advantage of the improved future consumption possibility. Under these circumstances the effect works positively on u. Conversely, the opposite scenario applies if the rate of return to education falls, implying a negative effect on u.

From the above discussion the total effect on v and u from a rising h seems theoretical ambiguous. In Regime 1 below the threshold level of human capital, $\bar{h}$, the relative profitability effect is absent. It is seen from Figure 2 panel b that the income effect dominates when h is relatively small, such that the share of human capital in education

---

[5] The share of human capital in R&D equals zero in Regime 2 when $h = h'$ implying that $\vartheta = 1$ is a restriction for $h < h'$.

increases in h. When h is relatively large the intertemporal substitution effect dominates implying that the opposite situation applies.

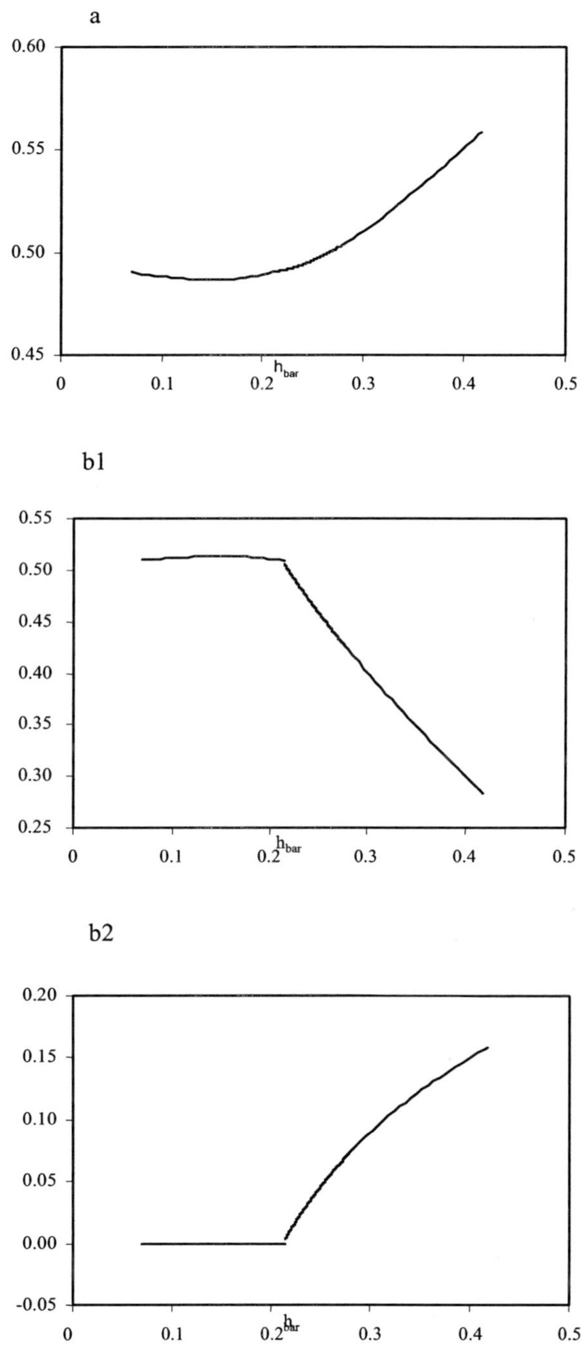

Figure 2a) Share of Human Capital in Final Goods, ν, b) Share of Human Capital in Education, u, c) Share of Human Capital in R&D, 1-u-ν

When the level of human capital is above the threshold level, $\bar{h}$, the economy is in Regime 2. It is clear from panel a that the share of human capital allocated to final goods production is increasing in the level of human capital, implying that the share allocated to investment activities is falling. At the same time it is evident from panel b and c that the profitability effect is relatively strong since the share of human capital in R&D increases in h, whereas it decreases in education.

5.4. The Growth Rate

In Figure 3, the growth rates of output, g_y, is illustrated for different levels of human capital. It is seen that g_y decreasing in h when education drives growth ($h < \bar{h}$). When innovation activities are present ($h \geq \bar{h}$), g_y increases in h. g_y is constant when $h = h^*$, since there is constant returns to n, i.e. the number of intermediate varieties. This is the factor that is accumulated in steady-state, which implies that the growth process is driven by R&D alone in the long run. The intuition for the look of the curve follows that of the rate of return in Figure 1.

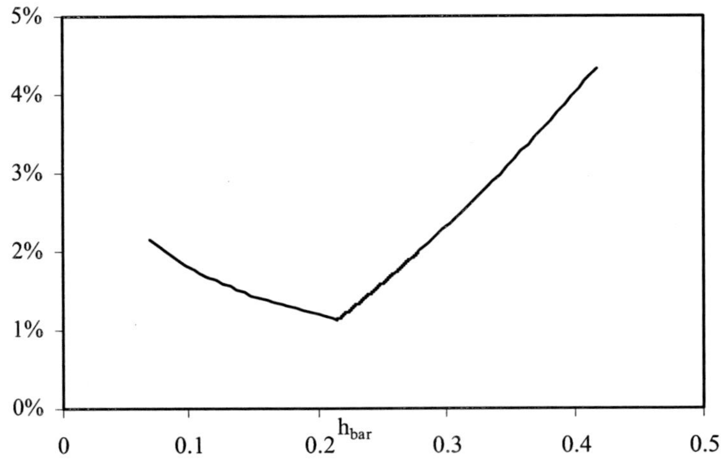

Figure 3: Growth rate, g_y

Figure 4 shows the adjustment of the economy from an initial level of human capital of one quarter of the steady-state level. The starting year of the adjustment can be thought of as early industrialization. g_y is falling for a long time since the stock of human capital is growing and the economy is in Regime 1. At some point in time ($T = 65$) the economy shifts from Regime 1 to Regime 2, because it becomes profitable to innovate. As a consequence of the regime shift, g_y starts to increase. After a long transition in Regime 2 (165 periods) g_y (approximately) equals the steady-state level of 2%.

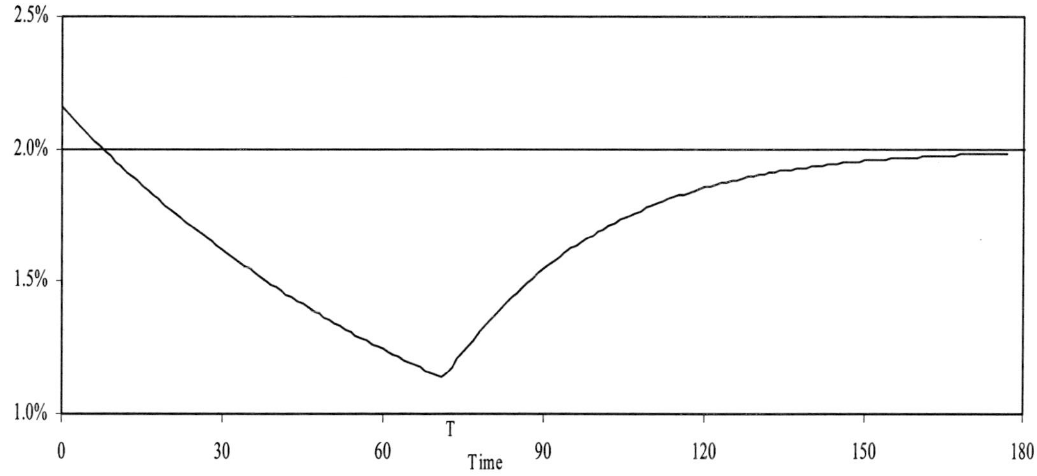

Figure 4: The development in the grow rate over time (g_y)

One important characteristic of the model is evident from Figure 4: the growth rate converges to the steady state level from below. This challenges the predictions of many other growth models where the growth rate converges to the long run level from above, see Barro and Sala-i-Martin (1995) for an overview. The reasonability of this prediction is discussed to some extent in the next section.

5.5. Comparative Statics

It is of interest to investigate the sensitivity of the threshold level of human capital and the trigger point in time with respect to the parameters of the model.

Table 3 Sensitivity of $\bar{h}$ and T

	Education			Other		Preferences	
	γ	B	δ	α	D	ρ	θ
$\bar{h}$	+	+	-	-	-	-	-
T	-	-	+	-	-	+	+

It is evident from Table 3 that an improved learning technology (larger γ, larger B, or lower δ) leads to a higher threshold level of human capital and a lower trigger point in time, an improvement of technologies of other sectors (higher α or D) leads to a lower threshold level of human capital and a lower trigger point in time. Finally, a less patient representative household (higher ρ or θ) results in lower threshold level of human capital and higher trigger point in time.

6. Predictions of the Model and Empirical Findings

In this section the predictions of the model are discussed in relation to empirical findings. The main message of this chapter is that the relative importance of growth-generating processes change over time. Therefore, the model predicts a structural change when the economy shifts from Regime 1 to Regime 2. This is consistent with recent empirical studies where breaks in growth rates are found to exist, see Ben-David and Papell (1995), Crafts and Mills (1996), and Raj (1992). In Table 4, the results in Ben-David and Papell (1995) are reported.

Table 4: Estimated Trend Rates of Growth in Real GDP per Capita.

% p.a.	Period	Year of break	Pre-break	Post-break
Canada	1870-1989	1928	2.19	2.77
France	1870-1989	1939	1.20	3.80
Germany	1870-1989	1946	1.25	2.66
Italy	1870-1989	1945	0.68	2.33
Japan	1885-1989	1944	1.92	6.12
U.K.	1870-1989	1918	1.18	1.89
U.S.A.	1870-1989	1929	1.65	2.09

Source: Ben-David and Papell (1995)

The important message in Table 3 is that economic growth undergo different phases. This result contradicts with the Kaldor's (1961) stylized fact' that the growth rate remains steady over time.

In the model the closed economy assumption is applied, which has two implications: transfer of technology between countries is excluded by construction and the market for new innovations is constituted of the home market. This corresponds fairly well to the characteristics of the US economy, since it has been the world economic leader since late 1800s, see Nelson and Wright (1992). As a consequence, technology improvements are mainly attributed to R&D performed within the country, because there is no technological gap that can be closed to other countries. Hence, technological spill-overs from other countries to the US economy are limited. Furthermore, the US economy can to some degree be treated as a closed economy in the sense that the market for new inventions approximately is constituted by the domestic market.[6] Therefore, the results of the model will be discussed in relation to the United States in the remaining of this section.

It is interesting to compare estimated trend rates of growth for the US economy to the calibrated growth rate in Figure 4. In Table 5 average growth rates for the growth profile in Figure 4 are calculated and compared to estimated trend rates of growth for the USA.

6 The ratio of mercandise exports to GDP in the USA at current market prices is equal to 6.1 in 1913, 3.6 in 1950, 8.0 in 1973, and 5.7 in 1987, see Maddison (1991).

Table 5: Calculated and Estimated Trend Rates of Growth in GDP per Capita for the US Economy

% p.a.	1870-1914	15-19	20-39	40-50	51-73	74-89
Estimates	1.70	1.58	0.86	3.76	1.54	1.89
Calculation	1.66	1.32	1.21	1.37	1.65	1.84

Source: Crafts and Mills (1996), own calculations

The estimated trend rates of growth originates from the unrestricted segmented trend model in Crafts and Mills (1996). It is evident that the estimated trend rates of growth and the calculated average growth rates are quite similar. This supports the endogenous growth model applied in this chapter; including convergence of the growth rate to the steady state level from below. This latter result contradicts predictions of the neoclassic growth model with convergence of the steady state growth rate from above.

7. Conclusion

The model presented in this chapter combines two complementary reasons for economic growth. These are learning and innovation. The production side of the model is vertically disintegrated: the early stage of the line is an R&D sector that develops designs to complementary intermediates. Patents to these designs are sold to intermediate firms that issue shares to finance initial capital. The latest stage of the line is a final goods sector that uses intermediates and human capital. This structure follows Romer (1990). However, as an extension the model also includes an education sector in which skills are accumulated.

One important result is found in the chapter: it is not profitable to perform R&D in an economy at a low stage of development. The reason is that the rate of return to investments is higher when learning alone drives growth, than in the presence of both growth-generating activities. Hence, education alone drives growth when the skill level is relatively low, whereas both learning and innovation are present after human capital has reached a threshold level.

The endogenous regime shift can be given an interesting economic interpretation since it can be viewed as a process of maturing markets. The economy becomes ready to innovate at a trigger point in time because private households accumulate skills. That is, the market size for the single intermediate variety increases, since production factors expand. Hence the growth process changes to encompass R&D as well as learning at the point in time it becomes profitable to innovate. The accumulation of human capital still contributes to economic growth in the transition from the regime shift until steady state is reached. In the long run equilibrium, however, economic growth is driven solely by R&D and education only serves to offset the depreciation of existing human capital.

The predictions of the model are compared to empirical findings. This comparison is quite favorable to the model developed in this chapter. It is found that estimated trend rates of growth from Crafts and Mills (1996) and the calculated average growth rates are quite similar. Furthermore, the prediction that R&D activities arc present only above a critical stage of development and that growth-generating processes change over time seem to be supported by empirical studies. Finally, some support for the prediction that the importance of human capital accumulation for economic growth declines over time is established.

A. APPENDIX: SOLUTION OF THE MODEL

The solution of the model is given by (5), (6), (7), (9), (10), (11), (12), (13), (14), and the two transversality conditions $\lim_{t\to\infty}\left[a(t)\,f(t)\right]=0$ and $\lim_{t\to\infty}\left[b(t)\,h(t)\right]=0$.

(10) is rewritten by using $f=np_n$, (4), (5), (6), and (7):

$$c=\alpha^{\frac{2\alpha}{1-\alpha}}(1-\alpha^2)nh_y \tag{15}$$

In Regime 1, the conditions that $\dot{n}=0$ and $h_s=h_y$ are taken into account, whereas $\dot{p}_n=0$ and $h_s=h_y+h_R$ together with $p_n=w/D_n$ are taken into account in Regime 2.

The steady state equilibrium is unique and stable for $\theta\geq 1$ if it exists. For $\theta<1$ there is at least one stable steady state equilibrium if any exist. In the present analysis it is assumed that $(1-\gamma)^{1-\gamma}B\left(\alpha D\left(\rho+\gamma\delta\right)/\delta\rho\right)^{\gamma}>\rho+\delta$, which secures the existence of a stable steady state equilibrium and rules out possible poverty traps. In Sιιrensen (1999) these issues are investigated further.

The equilibrium in Regime 1 is expressed as:

$$\begin{aligned}\dot{u}/u&=\left(1-u\right)((1-\frac{1}{\theta u+\gamma\left(1-u\right)})B(uh)^{-\gamma}+\frac{\rho+\delta-(\theta-\gamma)\delta}{\theta u+\gamma\left(1-u\right)})\\ \dot{h}/h&=Bu^{1-\gamma}h^{-\gamma}-\delta\end{aligned} \tag{16}$$

besides (15). (16) is derived by using $\dot{n}=0$.

The equilibrium in Regime 2 is expressed as:

$$\begin{aligned}\dot{u}/u&=\left(D\alpha vh-D(1-u-v)h-\left(1-\gamma\left(1-u\right)\right)B(uh)^{-\gamma}+(1+\gamma)\delta\right)/\gamma\\ \dot{v}/v&=(D\alpha vh-\rho)/\theta-Bu^{1-\gamma}h^{-\gamma}+\delta-D(1-u-v)h\\ \dot{h}/h&=Bu^{1-\gamma}h^{-\gamma}-\delta,\end{aligned} \tag{17}$$

besides (15). (17) is derived by using $\dot{p}_n=0$

Below three time trends for Regime 1 are derived:

(1) r_1 depends on u and h and changes according to:

$$\frac{dr_1}{dh}=\frac{\partial r_1}{\partial u}u'(h)+\frac{\partial r_1}{\partial h}=-\frac{\gamma\theta}{\theta u+\gamma(1-u)}\frac{u}{h}\left(B(uh)^{-\gamma}+\frac{(\dot{u}/u)^2}{(1-u)(\dot{h}/h)}\right)$$

where $\dot{u}/u$ and $\dot{h}/h$ are given in (16). Hence, $dr_1/dh<0$ for $\dot{h}>0$.

(2) It is relevant to ask whether $r_1<\rho$ which implies $g_{c_1}<0$, see (14), is a possible outcome. Imagine that $r_1=r_2<\rho$ applies for $h=\overline{h}$. This implies that $g_{c_2}<0$ and $\dot{h}_y/h_y<0$ since $\dot{n}/n>0$, see (15). According to (2.6′) r_2 falls over time as a result, which makes g_{c_2} to fall. A negative and falling g_{c_2} is not in accordance with steady state equilibrium with positive long run growth. Consequently $r_1>\rho$ and $r_2>\rho$ apply. Since $g_c=\dot{\pi}/\pi$ (see (4) and (17)) profits in intermediate firms rise over time in Regime 1.

(3) It is known that p_n has to increase in Regime 1 until $p_n=w/Dn$ for regime shift. To determine the sign of $\dot{p}_{n_1}$ imagine that it is negative. In this case $p_{n_1}<0$ which is seen by applying (6) and the facts that $\dot{r}_1<0$ and $\dot{\pi}_1>0$. The former fact follows from $dr_1/dh<0$ and $\dot{h}>0$, whereas the latter follows from $g_{c_1}=\dot{\pi}_1/\pi_1$. Consequently, no regime shift takes place and the economy adjusts to stationary state in Regime 1. However, $p_{n_1}>w/Dn$ in stationary state if $(1-\gamma)^{1-\gamma}B(\alpha D(\rho+\gamma\delta)/\delta\rho)^{\gamma}>\rho+\delta$ applies implying that $\dot{p}_{n_1}>0$.

References

[1] Barro, R.J. and X. Sala-i-Martin (1995), '*Economic Growth*', New York: McGraw-Hill.

[2] Ben-David, D. and D.H. Papell (1995), 'The Great Wars, the Great Crash, and Steady State Growth: Some New Evidence about an old Stylized Fact', *Journal of Monetary Economics*, 36, 453-475

[3] Broadberry, S.N. and K. Wagner (1996), 'Human Capital and Productivity in Manufacturing During the Twentieth Century: Britain, Germany and the United States', in B. van Ark and N.F.R. Crafts (Eds.), Quantitative Aspects of Postwar European Economic Growth, Cambridge: Cambridge University Press.

[4] Crafts, N.F.R and T.C. Mills (1996), 'Europe's Golden Age: an Econometric Investigation of Changing Trend Rates of Growth', in B. van Ark and N.F.R. Crafts (Eds.), Quantitative Aspects of Postwar European Economic Growth, Cambridge: Cambridge University Press.

[5] Crafts, N.F.R. (1997), 'Endogenous Growth: Lessons for and from Economic History', in David M. Kreps and Kenneth Wallis (Eds.), Advantages in Economics and Econometrics: Theory and Applications, Seventh World Congress, Vol II, Cambridge.

[6] Fleming, M. (1955), 'External Economies and the Doctrine of Balanced Growth', *Economic Journal*, 241-256

[7] Goodfriend, M. and J. McDermott (1995) 'Early Development', *American Economic Review*, 85 (1), 116-33.

[8] Ho, M. S. and D. W. Jorgenson (2001), 'The Quality of the U.S. Work Force, 1948-95', Working Paper Harvard University

[9] Kaldor, N. (1961), 'Economic Growth and Capital Accumulation', in F. Lutz and D.C. Hague, eds., The Theory of Capital (Macmillian, London)

[10] Krugman, P. (1993), 'Toward a Counter-Counterrevolution in Development Theory', *Proceedings of the World Bank Annual Conference on Development Economics 1992*, 15-61

[11] Lucas, R.E. Jr. (1988), 'On the Mechanics of Economic Development', *Journal of Monetary Economics*, 22 (1), 3-42.

[12] Maddison, A. (1991), *'Dynamic Forces in Capitalist Development'*, Oxford: Oxford University Press

[13] Mulligan, C.B., and X. Sala-i-Martin (1991), 'A Note on the Time-Elimination Method for Solving Recursive Dynamic Economic Models', NBER Technical Working Paper Series no. 116.

[14] Mulligan, C.B., and X. Sala-i-Martin (1993), 'Transitional Dynamics in Two-Sectors Models of Endogenous Growth', *The Quarterly Journal of Economics*, 108 (3), 737-73.

[15] Murphy, K.M., Shleifer, A., Vishny, R.W. (1989*a*), 'Income Distribution, Market Size, and Industrialization', *Quarterly Journal of Economics*, 104, 537-564

[16] Murphy, K.M., Shleifer, A., Vishny, R.W. (1989*b*), 'Industrialization and the Big Push', *Journal of Political Economy*, 97, 1003-1026

[17] Nelson, R.R. and G. Wright (1992), 'The Rise and Fall of American Technological Leadership', *Journal of Economic Literature*, 30, 1931-1964

[18] Raj, B. (1992), 'International Evidence of Persistence in Output in the Presence of an Episodic Change', *Journal of Applied Econometrics*, Vol. 7, 281-293

[19] Romer, P.M. (1986), 'Increasing Returns and Long-Run Growth', *Journal of Political Economy*, 94 (5), 1002-37

[20] Romer, P.M. (1990), 'Endogenous Technological Change', *Journal of Political Economy*, 98 (5), part II, S71-S102.

[21] Solow, R. (1956), 'A Contribution to the Theory of Economic Growth', *Quarterly Journal of Economics*, 70, 65-94

[22] Sørensen, A. (1999), 'R&D, Learning, and Phases of Economic Growth', *Journal of Economic Growth*, 4(4), 429-445

[23] Temple, J. and H.-J. Voth (1998), 'Human Capital, Equipment Investment, and Industrialization', *European Economic Review*, 42, 1343-1362

[24] Zilibotti, F. (1995), 'A Rostovian Model of Endogenous Growth and Underdevelopment Traps', *European Economic Review*, 39, 1569-1602

In: Economic Growth Issues
Editor: L. A. Finley, pp. 23-51
ISBN 1-59454-555-3

Chapter 2

SPATIAL DEPENDENCE AND ECONOMIC GROWTH: EVIDENCE FROM A PANEL OF COUNTRIES

María Teresa Ramírez [*, 1] ***and Ana María Loboguerrero*** [#, 2]
*Central Bank of Colombia
#Inter-American Development Bank

ABSTRACT

The empirical economic growth literature has generally ignored spatial interdependence across countries. The role of a country's geographic location is an empirical issue that has been taken into consideration just only recently. We use spatial econometric techniques with spatially lagged dependent variables and spatially lagged errors to estimate an economic growth model that includes cross-country interdependence, in which a country's economic growth depends on the growth rate of its neighbors. Based on a sample of 98 countries over three decades (1965-1975, 1975-1985, 1985-1995) and using several tests to explore and evaluate spatial dependence we find some interesting results. In particular, spatial relationships across countries are quite relevant. A country economic growth is indeed affected by the performance of its neighbors and then influenced by its own relative geographical position. This result suggests that the spillover effects among countries are important for growth. Consequently, our results indicate that spatial interrelation across countries can not be ignored in the analysis of economic growth. Ignoring such relationships can result in significant model misspecification, omitted variables problem and can underestimate spillover effects and externalities across economies.

Keywords: Economic growth, Interdependence, Spatial proximity, Spatial econometrics.

---

[1] E-mail: mramirgi@banrep.gov.co, FAX: (+571) 342 1804, Phone: (+571) 343 0564
[2] E-mail: ANAMARIALO@Contractual.IADB.ORG

1. INTRODUCTION

The relationship between economic growth and its determinants has been studied extensively in the economic literature. So far there is some agreement regarding the factors that determine growth. A large number of empirical studies, using cross-country data sets, have found that economic growth is related to initial income, human capital, investment, physical infrastructure and institutions. However, the role of geography in economic growth is an empirical issue that has been taken into consideration just recently. Some authors like, Sachs and Warner (1995), Gallup, Sachs and Mellinger (1999), Hall and Jones (1999), Sachs (2001), and McArthur and Sachs (2001)[3] have used indicators such as climate, landlocked, distance from the equator, absolute value of latitude, land area, tropics, among others, in order to demonstrate that geography, is an element that affects economic growth in the long run.

Interactions among countries are also important in explaining economic growth. Countries can interact strongly with each other through channels such as trade, technological diffusion, capital inflows, and common political, economic and social policies. In such cases, externalities can spillover the limits among countries, contributing in the explanation of growth. Trade is a typical example of interdependence among countries. Agreements among neighboring economies, such as the Andean Pact, NAFTA, MERCOSUR and the European Economic Union (EEU), among others, have been designed to promote trade and, consequently, growth. Technological diffusion between neighboring economies may be even more important. According to Ciccone (1997), the aggregate level of technology in each country may not only rely on externalities originated by capital accumulation within the country, but also on the aggregate level of technology of its neighbors.

Evidence of spatial relationship across geographically close economies can also be taken from the recent contagion literature. Calvo and Reinhart (1996) argue that one channel in which contagion can be spread among regions is through technological factors and/or political instability. This way, a shock in any country can alter not only its own fundamentals but also those of its neighbors, and consequently have an impact on its neighbors' economic performance. Spatial dependence may also be influenced by the political stability of the region. For instance, foreign investment decisions towards a country may depend on both the internal country's conditions and the region's political stability. Then, there are issues that make investors do not discriminate between different macroeconomic fundamentals among countries. According to the authors, even if the fundamentals of a country have not been affected by a shock that occurs in a neighboring country, it is probable that this country will observe a reduction of foreign investment because investors tend to classify all countries that are located close to the economy that suffers from the adverse shock, as risky.

Spatial proximity is an issue that has just been recently considered in the empirical growth literature that pool data for large samples of countries. For instance, Chua (1993) states that countries can gain from increase economic activity in their neighboring countries. Barro and Sala i Martin (1995) measure economic effects from neighboring countries by adding to the growth equation the weighted average of the logarithm of per capita GDP of the

---

[3] McArthur J. and J. Sachs (2001) made a comment on Acemoglu, D, S. Johnson and J. A. Robinson (2000)'s paper. The latter authors suggest that variations in the levels of economic development are correlated to weak institutions but not to physical geography. McArthur and Sachs using similar determinants show that both institutions and geographically related variables are strongly linked to income per capita (see their Table 1).

surrounding countries. They obtain a positive, but marginal significant, coefficient, which allows them to conclude that their findings provide some support for the spillover effects from neighboring countries proposed earlier by Chua (1993)[4]. In the same line, Ades and Chua (1997) find that the spillover effect can be negatively affected by political instability.

This issue has also been addressed by Ciccone (1997) who models and then estimates, by non-linear least squares, the degree of technological interdependence across countries within a data set of 98 countries for the period 1965-1985. Using the same variables that Mankiw, Romer and Weil used, he finds that productivity spreads out across neighboring countries, that is, there is a high level of technological interdependence among them. Moreno and Trehan (1997) carry out several tests to determine if location matters for growth. Using data for 93 countries for the period 1965-1989, they show that a country's growth rate is positively influenced by the growth rate of neighboring countries, result that is robust to conditioning on the set of variables used in Mankiw, Romer and Weil. Therefore, they find that there are substantial growth spillovers across countries. Finally, Conley and Ligon (2002) develop an empirical approach to measuring cross-country spillovers based on a decomposition of the spatial covariance function of growth rates into: i) the part that is due to a country's own observable characteristics, ii) the part that is attributable to each country's unobservable characteristics and iii) the part related to the covariance between a country's unobservable and its neighbors' observable characteristics. Employing Barro's 1991 data set, as a benchmark specification, and several measures of economic distance such as UPS shipping rates for large packages and airline fares between countries, which capture the cost of shipping physical or human capital between countries, and a geographic distance measure, they find strong evidence of spatial correlation between neighboring countries and also that spillovers explain a significant amount of long run growth rates' spatial covariation.

The present chapter extends previous studies by approaching spatial proximity as a determinant of a country's economic growth through spatial econometric techniques. Within the above studies Moreno and Trehan (1997) is the only one that uses this kind of technique in their estimations. However, we take a step further and make use of several tests and estimators employed in spatial econometrics to explore and evaluate spatial relationships across countries. First, we explore spatial dependence across countries carrying out some tests such as the *Global Moran Index*, *Moran's Index* in regression residuals, Lagrange Multiplier tests and *Moran Scatterplots*. Second, we use robust Lagrange Multiplier tests to evaluate the appropriate spatial model. Third, we take into account the endogeneity issue by estimating the growth model by means of instrumental variables. Finally, we update and extend the data set by incorporating infrastructure variables and some institutional variables such as government's credibility and commitment and bureaucracy quality.

Spatial econometrics has been widely used in studying convergence and growth in regional economics. For instance, Rey and Montouri (1999) examine the spatial dependence within the US regions in a growth model of unconditional convergence for the period 1929-1994. That study finds strong patterns of both global and local spatial autocorrelation, and shows that the magnitude of the spatial effects is significant and positively correlated with US regional income. Similarly, Magalhães et al (2000) apply spatial econometrics for the Brazilian regional convergence using state data for the sample 1970-1995. As in the US's

---

[4] See R. Barro and X. Sala i Martin (1995), page 442.

case, they find strong patterns of spatial correlation among Brazilian states. In particular, the results suggest that the unconditional convergence process seems to be more a regional feature rather than a global process. From a microeconomic perspective, Escobal and Torero (2000) develop a model of Peruvian households and province consumption growth over time and use spatial econometrics to verify the presence of persistent spatial concentration that comes from geography. The results suggest that what appears to be considerable geographic differences in consumption standards in Peru, can be explained when the spatial concentration of households with observable non-geographic characteristics is taken into account.

Research on European regions' economic growth analysis is increasingly using spatial econometrics. For instance, Fingleton (1999) analyses the determinants of the European region productivity growth using information for 178 regions. He finds significant cross-region externalities as a consequence of technological change spillovers that result from capital accumulation. Vayá et al (1998) estimate a growth model that includes externalities across regional economies using data for Spain and the European regions. In their model, the levels of technology of a region depend on the level of technology of its neighbors. For both cases, the authors find that the growth rates of a region are a positive function of the stock of capital of its neighbors. Then, besides the fact that cross-region externalities raise the steady state level, growth rates are affected by investment in the neighboring economies. García de la Vega and Herce (2000) have studied the relationship between trade and growth in the European Union and have found that the European integration process has promoted trade, particularly between close neighbors, and that trade has been the channel of diffusion of interdependent growth. Paci and Pigliaru (2001) have analyzed the role of technology heterogeneity and diffusion in GDP per worker convergence across 131 European regions for the 1978-97 period, the spatial pattern of regional heterogeneity in technology and the relevance of such pattern for the econometric analysis of the regional convergence in Europe. The results indicate that technology heterogeneity is important for convergence. Given a region's current technological gap, its capacity to profit from it in terms of growth depends not only on its individual effort, but also on the neighbors' performance. López-Bazo et al (1999) analyze the disparities and convergence on both GDP per worker and per capita in the European Union applying spatial association test. Similarly, Baumont et al (2001) investigate the European regional convergence process showing that spatial dependence matter in the estimation of the β-convergence on a sample of 138 regions on 11 European countries over the 1980-1995 period.

We investigate spatial dependence within a sample of 98 countries over three decades (1965-75, 1975-85, 1985-95), assuming that a country's growth rate is related to the growth rates of its nearby countries. Using spatial econometric techniques the present chapter provides some interesting empirical results. First, from the exploration analysis we find that spatial relationships across countries are indeed relevant, suggesting that a country's growth rate is related with that of its neighboring countries. Second, when we control for other variables included in the growth literature the performance of a country also depends on the growth rate of its surrounding countries, i.e. spatial dependence is a robust result. Third, we prove the existence of spatial error correlation. Consequently, the exclusion of spatial dependence will cause misspecification of the model. Fourth, the convergence rate from the spatial model is quite similar when compared to the OLS estimation, indicating that it appears not to be influenced by the omission of spatial dependence, i.e. convergence is a robust result.

In sum, ignoring the role of spatial relationship can underestimate spillover effects and externalities across economies.

The reminder of the chapter is organized as follows. Section 2 introduces the empirical specification. Section 3 discusses the data set. Section 4 explores cross-country spatial dependence. Section 5 presents the empirical results and section 6 concludes.

2. Empirical Specification

2.1. Spatial Effects Specification and Estimation

Spatial econometrics has not been extensively applied in studies on cross-country economic growth, partly because the neighboring effect has not been sufficiently addressed yet. This econometric approach includes in the estimating equation information on space or localization. Following, the first law of geography proposed by W. Tobler (1979): "*Everything is related to everything else, but near things are more related than distant things*" (page 379), it is clear that spatial dependence constitutes a feature with high applicability in economic growth.

Traditionally, each economy has been considered as an independent unit and the possible space-interactions among countries have been largely ignored (Rey and Montouri, 1999). According to Driscoll and Kraay (1995) the assumption of independent cross sectional units is inappropriate because countries are probably going to be exposed to common disturbances which will produce correlation among errors from different cross sectional units. Anselin (1988) states that spatial correlation can be understood as the lack of independence among observations in a cross sectional or panel data set. In particular, spillover effects constitute an important element in explaining growth among countries; therefore the geographical dimension must be studied. In addition, the fact that countries or regions are divided by artificial boundaries, which do not always correspond with the real spatial dimension of the spillover effects, can lead to a measurement error problem that need to be take into account (Magalhães et al, 2000).

Spatial correlation can be understood as the lack of independence among observations in a cross sectional or panel data set and it can occur when spatial dependence is fundamental to the model, known as spatial lag model, and when errors are spatially correlated, known as spatial error model[5]. In the first case a spatial lag of the dependent variable is included in the set of control variables. Thus, a country's growth rate will be associated to those rates in its nearby countries after controlling by other determinants. The formulation for a pooled data set is the following:

$$y_{it} = \alpha + \rho\, W y'_{it} + \beta x'_{it} + \varepsilon_{it} \quad \forall\, t=1,\ldots,T,\ \forall\, i=1,\ldots,n \qquad (1)$$

where:

$$\varepsilon_{it} \sim iid,\ N(0,\sigma^2)$$

[5] For an introduction to the spatial econometric methods see for instance L. Anselin (1988), and J. LeSage (1999).

i represents the geographical units, in this case a country.
α is a constant term.
y is the per capita income rate of growth.
x is the set of other control variables.
W is the spatial weighted matrix.
ρ is the coefficient of the "spatially lagged" dependent variable.

The W matrix represents a weight matrix associated with the autoregressive spatial process of the dependent variable. The specification of this matrix is *ad-hoc* since we do not estimate this matrix within the model. There is not a single procedure to select it. One way to specify such matrix correctly is by taking into account the theory behind the model. In our case we select the contiguity matrix and the second order contiguity matrix. The first one is a simple symmetric matrix that records 1 when country i and j share a common boundary and 0 otherwise. The second one represents a spatial lag of the contiguity matrix. That is, it introduces information of the neighbors' neighbors. This type of matrix is useful when we use pooled data and assume the presence of spatial diffusion process through time. Subsequently, the initial effects in a specific country can affect not only its neighboring countries, but through time also its neighbors' neighbors. More complex specifications of weight matrices can take into account such as a spatial weight matrix with geographical distance with or without a critical cut-off. Other specifications that include economic and social issues for example trade relationships, capital flows and migration across countries are more difficult to implement since the weights should be exogenous to the model. However, these types of weights can be chosen if their endogeneity is considered explicitly in the model specification. The inclusion of these types of matrices in the growth equation will be part of our future research agenda.

The second form of spatial dependence, spatial error, in a regression model concerns the residual. Spatial dependence could be present in the residuals when there are some omitted unobservable variables that can be spatially correlated. An example that illustrates this point could be the case of a river that is important in the economic activity of a particular country that not only goes through this country but also goes through the territory of its surrounding countries. Also, spatial error correlation could be the consequence of a shock that is common to some countries in a region. As Rey and Montouri (1999) state, a random shock in a country will not only affect the growth rate in that country but also the growth rates of other countries because of the presence of the spatial error dependence. The formulation for the spatial error model is given by:

$$y_{it} = \alpha + \beta x'_{it} + \varepsilon_{it} \; \forall \; t=1,\ldots,T, \; \forall \; i=1,\ldots,n \tag{2}$$

and the error exhibits the following spatial autoregressive process:

$$\varepsilon_{it} = \lambda W \varepsilon'_{it} + \mu_{it} \tag{3}$$

where: y_{it}, x_{it} and W are defined in the same way as before, and λ is the spatial error coefficient. Now, ε_{it} has no longer the usual diagonal variance matrix and consequently OLS estimates are not efficient. Joining equations (2) and (3), the spatial error model can be expressed as:

$$y_{it} = \alpha + \beta x'_{it} + (I - \lambda W)^{-1}\mu_{it} \tag{4}$$

where:

$\mu_{it} \sim iid,\ N(0,\sigma^2)$

2.2. A Standard Growth Model with Interdependence Across Countries

This section presents a simple growth model that includes interdependencc across countries throughout the productivity term. We assume the traditional Cobb-Douglas production function:

$$Y_{i,t} = K_{i,t}^{\alpha} N_{i,t}^{\phi} (Q_{i,t} L_{i,t})^{1-\alpha-\phi} \tag{5}$$

where:
Y_{it}: GDP of country i in time t.
K_{it}: includes both physical and human capital for country i in time t.
N_{it}: includes physical and social infrastructure for country i in time t.
L_{it}: labor of country i in time t.
Q_{it}: aggregate productivity term of country i in time t.
α, ϕ are positive parameters

Equation (5) expressed in per capita and logs terms yields:

$$\ln y_{i,t} = \alpha \ln k_{i,t} + \phi \ln n_{i,t} + (1-\alpha-\phi)\ln Q_{i,t} \tag{6}$$

and taking derivatives with respect to t:

$$\gamma_{y_{i,t}} = \alpha\gamma_{k_{i,t}} + \phi\gamma_{n_{i,t}} + (1-\alpha-\phi)\gamma_{Q_{i,t}} \tag{7}$$

where $\gamma_{y_{i,t}}$ is the growth rate of per capita GDP, $\gamma_{k_{i,t}}$ and $\gamma_{n_{i,t}}$ are the growth rate of the per capita production factors and $\gamma_{Q_{i,t}}$ is the productivity growth rate.

The dynamic equations for k and n are given by:

$$\gamma_{k_{it}} = s_{k_{i,t}} e^{(\alpha-1)\ln k_{it} + \phi \ln n_{it} + (1-\alpha-\phi)\ln Q_{it}} - (\ell + \delta) \tag{8}$$

$$\gamma_{n_{it}} = s_{n_{i,t}} e^{\alpha \ln k_{it} + (\phi-1)\ln n_{it} + (1-\alpha-\phi)\ln Q_{it}} - (\ell + \delta) \tag{8'}$$

where $\ell = \dot{L}/L$, δ is the depreciation rate,[6] and $s_{k_{it}}$ and $s_{n_{it}}$ are the shares of output allocated to accumulation of physical and human capital and physical and social infrastructure, respectively.

[6] For simplicity, the depreciation rates of k and n are assumed to be the same.

In order to express the above equations as a linear approximation in the neighborhood of the steady state we take a first order Taylor expansion of (8) and evaluate it in the steady state, in which the growth rate of y, k, n and s_k and s_n are assumed to be constant. Indicating the steady state value by the asterisk symbol (*), we have:

$$\gamma_{k_{it}} = (\alpha - 1)(\ell + \delta)(\ln k_{it} - \ln k^*) + \phi(\ell + \delta)(\ln n_{it} - \ln n^*) + (1 - \alpha - \phi)(\ell + \delta)(\ln Q_{it} - \ln Q^*) \tag{9}$$

$$\gamma_{n_{it}} = \alpha(\ell + \delta)(\ln k_{it} - \ln k^*) + (\phi - 1)(\ell + \delta)(\ln n_{it} - \ln n^*) + (1 - \alpha - \phi)(\ell + \delta)(\ln Q_{it} - \ln Q^*) \tag{9'}$$

and,

$$\ln k_{it} - \ln k^* = (\ln k_{i0} - \ln k^*)e^{\beta t} \tag{10}$$

$$\ln n_{it} - \ln n^* = (\ln n_{i0} - \ln n^*)e^{\beta t} \tag{10'}$$

$$\ln Q_{it} - \ln Q^* = (\ln Q_{i0} - \ln Q^*)e^{\beta t} \tag{10''}$$

$$\ln y_{it} - \ln y^* = (\ln y_{i0} - \ln y^*)e^{\beta t} \tag{10'''}$$

where $\beta = -(\ell + \delta)(1 - \alpha - \phi)$ is the speed of convergence. Re-writing (10''') we can obtain the equation:

$$\ln(y_{it} / y_{io}) = (1 - e^{\beta t}) \ln y^* - (1 - e^{\beta t}) \ln y_{i0} \tag{11}$$

and, $\ln y^* = \alpha \ln k^* + \phi \ln n^* + (1 - \alpha - \phi) \ln Q^*$, then

$$\ln y^* = \frac{\alpha}{1 - \alpha - \phi} \ln s_{k_{i,t}} + \frac{\phi}{1 - \alpha - \phi} \ln s_{n_{i,t}} - \frac{\alpha + \phi}{1 - \alpha - \phi} \ln(\ell + \delta) + (\alpha + \phi) \ln Q_{it} + (1 - \alpha - \phi) \ln Q^* \tag{12}$$

Substituting ln y* in (11) we obtain:

$$\ln(y_{it} / y_{i0}) = -(1 - e^{\beta t}) \ln y_{i0} + (1 - e^{\beta t})[\frac{\alpha}{1 - \alpha - \phi} \ln s_{k_{i,t}} + \frac{\phi}{1 - \alpha - \phi} \ln s_{n_{i,t}} - \frac{\alpha + \phi}{1 - \alpha - \phi} \ln(\ell + \delta) + (\alpha + \phi) \ln Q_{it} + (1 - \alpha - \phi) \ln Q^*] \tag{13}$$

Now, we assume that spatial relationships across countries can be modeled explicitly letting the aggregate production of each country (Q_{it}) be endogenous. We assume that this productivity depends on the economic performance of its neighbors as follows:

Let S be the set of the n countries considered and S_i be the set of country i neighboring countries such as $S_i \subset S$. Then,

$$\forall_i \in S; \qquad Q_{i,t} = A_t \left\{ \prod_{j \in S} \left({y_{j,t}} \big/ {Y_{j,0}} \right)^{w_{i,j}} \right\}^{\rho} \quad i \neq j \tag{14}$$

where: i and j denotes countries, A_t is the level of technology, which is assumed to be exogenous and constant across countries to simplify terms, ρ is the measure of the neighbor effect (ρ >0) and $w_{i,j}$ is an element of the weight matrix (W) discussed before, such that:

$w_{i,j} = 1$ if $j \in S_i$,

$w_{i,j} = 0$, otherwise

As a result, the level of productivity of country i will be influenced by an exogenous level of productivity and by the rate of growth of its neighbors. Substituting (14) in logs term in (13) we have that:

$$\begin{aligned}
&\ln(y_{i,t} / y_{i,0}) = -(1-e^{\beta t}) \ln y_{i0} + \\
&\quad (1-e^{\beta t})[\frac{\alpha}{1-\alpha-\phi} \ln s_{k_{i,t}} + \frac{\phi}{1-\alpha-\phi} \ln s_{n_{i,t}} - \frac{\alpha+\phi}{1-\alpha-\phi} \ln(\ell+\delta) + \\
&\quad (\alpha+\phi) \ln A_t + (\alpha+\phi)\rho(\sum_j w_{i,j} \ln(y_{jt} / y_{j0})) + \\
&\quad (1-\alpha-\phi) \ln A^* + (1-\alpha-\phi)\rho(\sum_j w_{i,j} \ln(y_{jt} / y_{j0})^*)]
\end{aligned} \tag{15}$$

Equation (15) gives the expression for the growth rate of per capita GDP as a function of the parameters of the model, the initial level of income and the rate of growth of the neighboring countries.[7]

3. Data

To estimate the growth equation we pool cross sectional units from 98 countries and time series information over three decades (1965-75, 1975-85 and1985-95). Altogether we have 273 complete observations, because some information is not available. The data sources and variable definitions are listed in the appendix as well as the list of countries considered.

The data set includes some of the traditional variables used in growth regressions. The macroeconomic variables included in the right-hand side are: i) the initial value of the per-capita GDP; the sign and size of this coefficient indicate the speed of adjustment of an economy's per capita income in reaching its own steady state values; ii) the investment-GDP ratio; higher values of this variable will lead to an increase in the economy's steady state levels and will encourage economic growth; iii) government's consumption ratio by turn has an inverse relationship with economic growth; one reason could be that government size is associated with inefficiency and corruption, as well as it implies a crowding out effect on private consumption which is more income elastic; iv) black market premium on the foreign exchange rate is an indicator of market distortions; and iv) terms of trade is an instrument to enhance export efficiency and it is a source of growth as it has been pointed out in the trade literature.

Regarding demographic variables, the estimated equation includes fertility rate and life expectancy at birth. The former has a negative impact on economic growth while life expectancy is anticipated to have a positive effect. Higher values of life expectancy could indicate good quality health, good nutrition and adequate work habits, among others.

Concerning stock variables, an adequate provision of infrastructure is an important factor that helps to explain economic growth. Esfahani and Ramírez (2003) show that the contribution of infrastructure services to GDP growth is significant and, in general, surpasses the costs of provision of those services. We include as a proxy for physical infrastructure the rate of growth of per capita telephone lines that prove to be very significant in their estimation. In addition, improvements in education imply human capital accumulation and augmented labor technical change. The schooling variable used in the estimation is the gross enrollment ratio for secondary education. We use this variable rather than others frequently used in the literature such as average number of years of secondary education achieved by the population of age 25 years and older because we have information for more countries. A common caveat is that we do not control for quality of education.

The institutional variables play a central role in economic growth. The chosen variables reflect, on one side, the political aspect of a country and, on the other, the quality of its institutions. A democracy index is a proxy for the first institutional feature. However, the effect of this variable on economic growth has been ambiguous in the empirical growth literature. For instance, Kormendi and Meguire (1985), Scully (1988), Pourgerami (1988) have found a positive relation between democracy and growth while Barro (1996), and Landau (1986) have found a negative correlation. Others such as Levine and Renelt (1992) and Alesina et al (1996) do not find any correlation. The second variable is an index related to government's credibility and commitment (*contract enforcement*). We expect a positive sign since this index reflects a country's institutional characteristics that make policy-makers fulfill the government's obligations and should produce appropriate incentives for investments.[8] The last variable considered is the bureaucratic quality. Higher quality implies favorable conditions to grow.

[7] The papers of M. L. García de la Vega and J. Herce (2000) and E. Vayá et al (1998) provide a good explanation of how spatial econometric techniques can be applied to a specification based on theoretical growth models, see page 16 and pages 9 to 11, respectively.

[8] See, H. Esfahani and M.T. Ramírez (2003).

4. Exploring Spatial Dependence Across Countries

An intuitive and useful way to start analyzing spatial dependence is by looking at Figure 1 that shows a map in which we classify countries in three groups according to their per capita income in 1995: high, middle and low income. Some spatial clusters are evident. First, high income countries are concentrated in Europe, North America and Australia while low income countries are mostly located in Sub-Saharan Africa and South Asia. Second, almost all countries are surrounded by countries with the same level of income. The main exceptions are North African and Middle Eastern countries, middle income countries which have poor neighbors, and Japan and Korea, rich countries, surrounded by middle income countries.

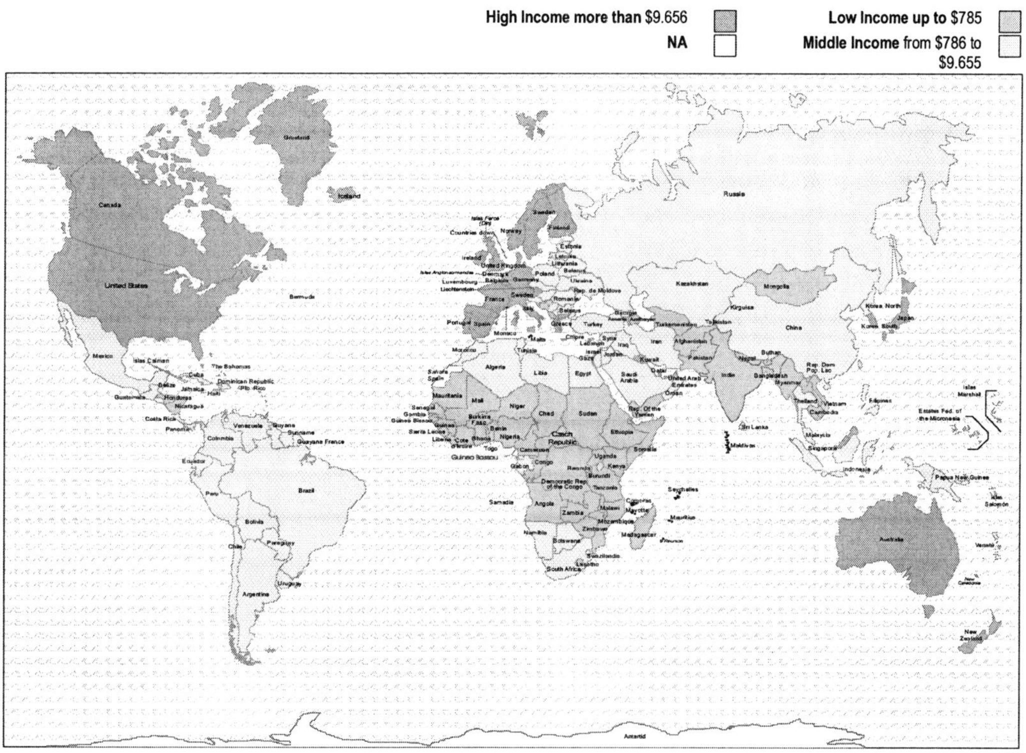

Figure 1: Per capita income in 1995
Source: The income information was taken form World Bank, World Development Report, 2000.

Given the evidence of income clustering provided by the map, the next step is to test whether there is spatial dependence across countries' economic growth[9]. We first carry out some tests, using the two types of weighting matrices mentioned above, to detect the presence of spatial autocorrelation. The first test is the Global Moran Index for the GDP per capita growth rate using information for the entire sample. This index allows us to estimate the

[9] The exploration analysis was carried out using the software SpaceStat, version 1.91 (L. Anselin, 2001).

effect of spatial proximity by computing an index of spatial autocorrelation that measures the interrelationship of economic growth across neighboring countries[10]. The index is defined as:

$$I = \frac{n\sum_{i,j}^{n} w_{i,j} z_i z_j}{\sum_i \sum_j w_{i,j} \sum_{i=1}^{n} z_i^2} \quad i \neq j \tag{16}$$

where: $z_i = x_i - \mu$ and $z_j = x_j - \mu$, are the observations on a variable (x) for country i and j, respectively, expressed as deviation from the mean (μ). In this case x is a country's GDP per capita growth rate, $w_{i,j}$ is an element in the spatial weights matrix defined above (W) and n is the sample size. If the *z-value* for the Moran's Index is positive and significant a positive spatial autocorrelation exists, then similar values of x are spatially clustered. Contrary, a negative and significant *z-value* indicates the presence of a negative spatial autocorrelation, i.e. no clustering.

The *z-value* of the Global Moran coefficient, reported in Table 1, is positive and highly significant then, the null hypothesis of non spatial dependence is rejected, regardless of the weight matrix that was used. This result clearly suggests the presence of a strong positive spatial autocorrelation meaning that GDP per capita growth rates across countries are clustered over the whole period under analysis. Thus, countries with high (low) GDP per capita growth rates are located near to other countries with high (low) GDP per capita growth rates.

The other tests are an extension of the Moran's Index to measure spatial autocorrelation in regression residuals, which concerns the spatial error case, and two Lagrange Multiplier (LM) tests for both spatial error and spatial lag dependence with their respective robust versions. These tests are based on the regression of GDP per capita growth rate on initial per capita GDP, investment-GDP ratio, government expenditure, black market foreign exchange premium, terms of trade, fertility rate, life expectancy at birth, telephones lines, secondary education, government commitment and credibility, bureaucracy quality and democracy score, i.e. the benchmark regression using the information of 98 countries over three decades presented in Table 2.

The results reported in Table 1 show that the Moran's Index from the regression residuals is highly significant which confirms the presence of spatial error autocorrelation. On the other hand, the LM tests are asymptotic and follow a χ^2 distribution with one degree of freedom. These tests test the null hypothesis of no spatial dependence against the alternative hypothesis of spatial dependence. As pointed out by Anselin and Florax (1995), the use of Lagrange Multiplier tests provides a good guide to decide which specification, between spatial error and spatial lag, is the most appropriate.[11] According to the χ^2 statistic from the Lagrange Multiplier tests, reported in Table 1, in all models, we can clearly reject the null hypothesis of non-spatial dependence, indicating the presence of spatial correlation arising from both the errors and the dependent variable.

[10] See L. Anselin et al (1995) for more details.

Table 1: Diagnostics for spatial dependence

Weights Matrix: Contiguity Matrix (row-standardized weights)[1/]			
Moran's Indexes **Ho: No spatial dependence**	**Moran Index**	**z-Value**	**Probability**
Global Moran's I	0.3701	6.7780	0.0000
Moran's I from regression residuals (error dependence)	0.1508	3.0725	0.0021
Lagrange Multiplier tests **Ho: No spatial dependence**	**Degree of Freedom**	**z-Value**	**Probability**
Lagrange Multiplier from regression residuals (error dependence)	1	7.4056	0.0065
Lagrange Multiplier from regression model (lag dependence)	1	13.9027	0.0002
Robust Lagrange Multiplier tests **Ho: No spatial dependence**	**Degree of Freedom**	**z-Value**	**Probability**
Robust Lagrange Multiplier from regression residuals spatial error test (robust to a spatial lag)	1	0.3626	0.5470
Robust Lagrange Multiplier from regression model spatial lag test (robust to the presence of spatial error dependence)	1	6.8597	0.0088

Weights Matrix: Second Order Contiguity Matrix (row-standardized weights)[1/]			
Moran's Indexes **Ho: No spatial dependence**	**Moran Index**	**z-Value**	**Probability**
Global Moran's I	0.3067	6.2995	0.0000
Moran's I from regression residuals (error dependence)	0.1362	3.0536	0.0022
Lagrange Multiplier tests **Ho: No spatial dependence**	**Degree of Freedom**	**z-Value**	**Probability**
Lagrange Multiplier from regression residuals (error dependence)	1	7.5293	0.0061
Lagrange Multiplier from regression model (lag dependence)	1	18.2213	0.0000
Robust Lagrange Multiplier tests **Ho: No spatial dependence**	**Degree of Freedom**	**z-Value**	**Probability**
Robust Lagrange Multiplier from regression residuals- spatial error test (robust to a spatial lag)	1	0.7276	0.3936
Robust Lagrange Multiplier from regression model- spatial lag test (robust to the presence of spatial error dependence)	1	11.4196	0.0007

[1/] row-standardized such that the elements in each row sum to 1.

Since the two LM tests are highly significant, it is difficult to conclude which is the most appropriate specification: the spatial error model or the spatial lag model. To deal with this issue we use two additional tests: a LM test for spatial error dependence that is robust to ignored spatial lag dependence and for spatial lag dependence that is robust to ignored spatial error dependence. The robust tests suggest that the spatial lag model could be the appropriate one since the robust Lagrange Multiplier for the spatial lag is highly significant while the robust Lagrange Multiplier for the spatial error is no longer significant.

To complete the diagnostics and to visualize the spatial clustering we depict some Moran scatterplots. To simplify the interpretation we present four graphs (Figure 2). The first one corresponds to the Moran scatterplot for GDP per capita growth rate for the average 1965-1995 period. The second is the scatterplot using information from the last decade (1985-

[11] Since these tests require normality, it is important to mention that normality is satisfied in all cases. We failed to reject the null hypothesis that residuals were normally distributed.

1995), the next is for the period 1975-1985 and the last graph employs information for the 1965-1975 decade.

Table 2: Per capita GDP growth equation OLS and 2SLS estimations

Estimation Method	OLS (1)	2SLS (2)
Number of observations	273	273
LIK	694.32	
R^2- adj.	0.4757	0.4915
Variables	Coefficient/Stdr. Dev (in parenthesis)	
Constant	0.0491 (0.0592)	0.0056 (0.0607)
Log of Initial GDP per capita	-0.0228 (0.0034)	-0.0234 (0.0036)
Log of Investment-GDP ratio	0.0094 (0.0027)	0.0053 (0.0031)
Log of Government Expenditures	-0.0119 (0.0036)	-0.0095 (0.0042)
Log of (1+ Black Market Foreign Exchange Premium)	-0.0053 (0.0023)	-0.0058 (0.0025)
Terms of Trade	0.1461 (0.0237)	0.1555 (0.0233)
Log of Fertility Rate	-0.0110 (0.0065)	-0.0114 (0.0065)
Log of Life Expectancy at Birth	0.0304 (0.0156)	0.0406 (0.0153)
Telephones Growth	0.1452 (0.0381)	0.1570 (0.0384)
Gross Enrollment ratio for Second. Education	0.0109 (0.0106)	0.0105 (0.0105)
Contract Enforcement	0.0032 (0.0009)	0.0035 (0.0009)
Bureaucracy Quality	0.0007 (0.0012)	0.0009 (0.0012)
Democracy Score	0.0005 (0.0005)	0.0005 (0.0005)

The Moran scatterplots display the spatial lag *Wx*, in the vertical axis, against *x*, in the horizontal axis, both standardized[12]. As we mentioned above, the *x* variable corresponds to the GDP per capita growth rate and *Wx* is the weighted average of the neighboring values. As Anselin (1995) states the Moran's I can be interpreted as the slope coefficient in a linear regression of *Wx* on *x* since the *x* are in deviations from the mean. This interpretation offers a way to observe the association between *x* and *Wx* in a bivariate scatterplot[13].

---

[12] Spatial weights matrix is row-standardized such that the elements in each row sum to 1.
[13] For details see L. Anselin (1995), pages 38-41.

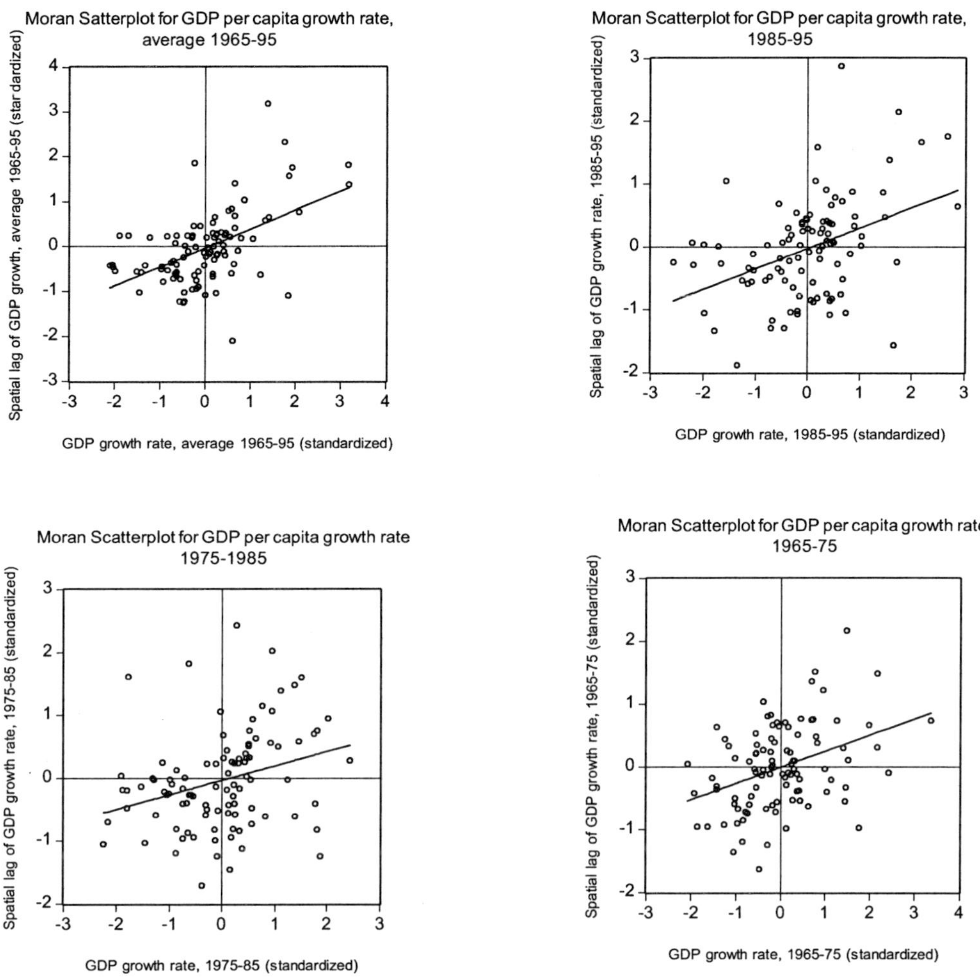

Figure 2: Moran scatterplots by decades

The four quadrants of the graphs identify the relationship between a country and its neighbors as follows: i) Quadrant I, located at the top on the right, a country with high economic growth surrounded by countries with high economic growth (HH), ii) Quadrant II, in the top left, a country with low economic growth bordered by high economic growth countries (LH), iii) Quadrant III, in the bottom left, a country with low economic growth surrounded by countries with low economic growth (LL), and Quadrant IV, in the bottom right, a country with high economic growth bordered by countries with low economic growth (HL). The same definition holds when x is the log of initial per capita GDP. The type of relationship in Quadrants I and III is the positive spatial autocorrelation indicating the association between similar values while the relationship in Quadrants II and IV is the negative spatial autocorrelation indicating the association between dissimilar values. If the information is dispersed in the four quadrants, there is not spatial autocorrelation.

Figure 2 indicates in all cases the presence of a positive spatial association among countries. This result suggests the existence of some kind of spatial clubs. To illustrate this result, in the first graph, who takes the average value between 1965 and 1995, we observe that the spatial clustering is evident. That is, the HH and LL types of clusters are predominant: 32 countries are in Quadrant I (HH) and 34 countries are located in Quadrant III (LL). The remaining countries are located in Quadrant II (14) and in Quadrant IV (18)[14].

The results presented in this section suggest the existence of a strong spatial dependence pattern in the sample under analysis. Then, it is necessary to include the spatial effects in the estimation of the growth equation. The presence of spatial correlation makes the OLS estimates inefficient. Ignoring spatial dependence can result in significant model misspecification. To assess this problem we apply the spatial econometrics approach.

5. Results

To compare the results from the spatial estimations to those obtained from the standard estimations we first present in Table 2 the results from the per capita GDP growth equation estimated by simple OLS and by 2SLS[15]. Given that some of the right hand side variables are endogenous the 2SLS estimation is more appropriate. The instruments include some of the original variables and lags of other variables such that the instrumental variables for an observation in each decade refer to the earlier decade.

In general, in both estimations, the coefficients are significant and show the expected sign, with the exception of democracy, education and bureaucracy quality. As we mentioned above, the role of democracy in economic growth estimations has been controversial, our results suggest a positive relationship but not a significant one. Regarding education, its coefficient is positive but insignificant[16]. The non-significance of education in empirical estimations of macro growth model is not an unusual result[17]. Krueger and Lindahl (2000) state that the fact that recent studies have found that increments in education attainment are not correlated to economic growth seems to be a spurious result coming from the high rate of measurement error in the cross-country education database.

The remaining results are similar to others obtained in the literature. The convergence rate is about 2% in the estimations. Per capita growth rate increases with investment rate, terms of trade, credibility and commitment to honor government's obligations (*contract enforcement*)[18], life expectancy and physical infrastructure. On the contrary, per capita GDP growth declines with market distortions, high fertility rates and government consumption.

Given the evidence of spatial interrelationship between countries provided by the previous section, the results from the OLS and 2SLS regression are biased since we are

---

[14] In Appendix 2, we present the classification of the spatial association by decades for all the countries in the sample with their respectively Moran I coefficient. The tables describe a country's classification through time.

[15] Heteroscedasticity and normality tests were carried out on all estimations, both OLS and spatial. In the case of heteroscedasticity the tests, Breusch and Pagan and adjusted Breusch and Pagan test, reject the null hypothesis of constant variance. On the other hand, the normality test, Kiefer and Salmon test, can not reject the null hypothesis of normality then, errors are normal. Since we find hetersocedasticity problems in all estimations, the standard errors were computed based on the adjusted White variance matrix, i.e. we perform a robust inference.

[16] We also use the average number of years of secondary education achieved by the population of age 25 years and older. Using this indicator of education does not change the results, i.e. its coefficient is not significant in the regressions.

[17] An interesting discussion of the role of education in economic growth and its lack of significance in empirical studies is presented in W. Easterly (2002), Chapter 4, p.p. 71-84.

[18] H. Esfahani and M.T. Ramirez (2003) found that contract enforcement is one of the main institutional variables that affect significant and positively both economic and infrastructure growth, see their Tables 2 and 4.

omitting a significant explanatory variable in the regression model. Also the estimations are no longer efficient, because the correlation between error terms is ignored.

Table 3: Per capita GDP growth equation: spatial LAG model estimations

Estimation Method	SPATIAL LAG- ML		SPATIAL LAG- IV (2SLS)	
W-Matrix	Contiguity (1)	2nd Order Contiguity (2)	Contiguity (3)	2nd Order Contiguity (4)
Number of observations	273	273	273	273
LIK	701.086	702.484		
R^2-adj	0.5304	0.5350	0.5212	0.5330
Variables	Coefficient/Stdr Dev (in parenthesis)			
Spatial Lag (ρ)	0.1934	0.2303	0.4111	0.2990
	(0.0519)	(0.0571)	(0.1018)	(0.0894)
Constant	0.0264	0.0191	-0.0219	-0.1738
	(0.0564)	(0.0562)	(0.0614)	(0.0606)
Log of Initial GDP per capita	-0.0217	-0.0228	-0.0198	-0.0237
	(0.0028)	(0.0027)	(0.0033)	(0.0032)
Log of Investment-GDP ratio	0.0083	0.0084	0.0050	0.0057
	(0.0024)	(0.0024)	(0.0030)	(0.0029)
Log of Government Expenditures	-0.0104	-0.0107	-0.0062	-0.0082
	(0.0032)	(0.0032)	(0.0040)	(0.0039)
Log of (1+ Black Market Foreign Exchange Premium)	-0.0053	-0.0058	-0.0059	-0.0063
	(0.0028)	(0.0028)	(0.0029)	(0.0029)
Terms of Trade	0.1295	0.1307	0.1149	0.1337
	(0.0197)	(0.0195)	(0.0223)	(0.0209)
Log of Fertility Rate	-0.0094	-0.0090	-0.0079	-0.0091
	(0.0055)	(0.0055)	(0.0058)	(0.0057)
Log of Life Expectancy at Birth	0.0336	0.0366	0.0416	0.0465
	(0.0143)	(0.0143)	(0.0154)	(0.0153)
Telephones Growth	0.1347	0.1336	0.1307	0.1367
	(0.0280)	(0.0278)	(0.0299)	(0.0293)
Gross Enrollment ratio for Second. Education	0.0095	0.0117	0.0063	0.0119
	(0.0100)	(0.0099)	(0.0106)	(0.0104)
Contract Enforcement	0.0026	0.0029	0.0021	0.0030
	(0.0011)	(0.0011)	(0.0011)	(0.0011)
Bureaucracy Quality	0.0009	0.0009	0.0011	0.0010
	(0.0012)	(0.0012)	(0.0013)	(0.0012)
Democracy Score	0.0004	0.0004	0.0004	0.0005
	(0.0004)	(0.0004)	(0.0004)	(0.0004)
Spatial Lag Dependence Test - Likelihood Ratio Test				
Value	13.5318	16.3286		
Probability	0.0002	0.0000		
Lagrange Multiplier Test on Spatial Error Dependence				
Value	0.7230	1.5945	4.3335	1.1069
Probability	0.3951	0.2067	0.0374	0.2928

Table 4: Per capita GDP growth equation: spatial error model estimations

Estimation Method	SPATIAL ERROR- ML		SPATIAL ERROR- 2SLS	
W-Matrix	Contiguity (1)	2nd Order Contiguity (2)	Contiguity (3)	2nd Order Contiguity (4)
Number of observations	273	273	273	273
LIK	698.92	700.55		
R^2	0.4946	0.4971	0.4343	0.4164
Variables	Coefficient/Stdr Dev (in parenthesis)			
Spatial Error (λ)	0.2193	0.2360	0.3076	0.3525
	(0.0618)	(0.0751)	(0.000)	(0.000)
Constant	0.0356	0.0289	-0.0017	-0.0069
	(0.0609)	(0.0591)	(0.026)	(0.0649)
Log of Initial GDP per capita	-0.0244	-0.0218	-0.0250	-0.0216
	(0.0029)	(0.0028)	(0.0036)	(0.0033)
Log of Investment-GDP ratio	0.0083	0.0086	0.0046	0.0063
	(0.0025)	(0.0024)	(0.0032)	(0.0029)
Log of Government Expenditures	-0.0126	-0.0102	-0.0109	-0.0057
	(0.0034)	(0.0033)	(0.0044)	(0.0042)
Log of (1+ Black Market Foreign Exchange Premium)	-0.0048	-0.0062	-0.0050	-0.0063
	(0.0028)	(0.0028)	(0.0029)	(0.0029)
Terms of Trade	0.1337	0.1324	0.1344	0.1307
	(0.0206)	(0.0199)	(0.0222)	(0.0213)
Log of Fertility Rate	-0.0139	-0.0113	-0.0152	-0.0124
	(0.0058)	(0.0057)	(0.0062)	(0.0062)
Log of Life Expectancy at Birth	0.0381	0.0346	0.0482	0.0445
	(0.0152)	(0.0149)	(0.0166)	(0.0163)
Telephones Growth	0.1339	0.1283	0.1381	0.1253
	(0.0282)	(0.0284)	(0.0298)	(0.0302)
Gross Enrollment ratio for Second. Education	0.0089	0.0077	0.0080	0.0040
	(0.0103)	(0.0103)	(0.0110)	(0.0113)
Contract Enforcement	0.0025	0.0032	0.0025	0.0032
	(0.0011)	(0.0011)	(0.0012)	(0.0011)
Bureaucracy Quality	0.0010	0.0007	0.0012	0.0009
	(0.0013)	(0.0012)	(0.0013)	(0.0013)
Democracy Score	0.0004	0.0003	0.0004	0.0003
	(0.0004)	(0.0004)	(0.0004)	(0.0004)
Spatial Error Dependence Test - Likelihood Ratio Test				
Value	9.1994	12.4542		
Probability	0.0024	0.0004		
Lagrange Multiplier Test on Spatial Lag Dependence				
Value	1.5835	4.8620		
Probability	0.2082	0.0274		
Test on Common Factor Hypothesis-Likelihood Ratio Test				
Value	37.6029	17.3323		
Probability	0.0002	0.1375		

Even though the exploration analysis suggests that the appropriate model might be the spatial lag we present in this section the results from both specification. Tables 3 and 4 summarize the results from the estimations of the growth equation taking into account the spatial lag model and the error spatial model, respectively[19]. For comparison purpose, besides the spatial effects, the estimations presented in these tables include the same set of control variables than those reported in Table 2. In the first case, we are considering that economic growth of each country is affected by the economic growth of its neighboring countries, and consequently it is influenced by its own geographical position, in the second case we assume that spatial dependence emerges from the error term.

The regressions were carried out including the contiguity W matrix and the second order contiguity matrix; the results from both specifications are quite similar. However, spatial effects are slightly higher when the second order contiguity matrix is taking into account. This matrix could be more relevant because it includes a broad spectrum of spatial correlations. For instance, contagious and trade relationship among a set of countries could be more explicit in this type of matrix. In addition, given that the dataset includes information for three decades for each country, the second order matrix has the advantage that it involves dynamic relationships among countries within a geographical region.

The estimation of the spatial lag model is performed by Maximum Likelihood (ML) and by Instrumental Variables (IV). According to Table 3, the parameter associated with the spatially lagged dependent variable, ρ, is highly significant.. Then, a country's economic growth is indeed affected by the performance of its neighbors. For instance, as it is implied by the value of ρ, from the first and second column of Table 3, an increase of 1 percent point in the weighted growth rate of countries neighboring country i, will produce an increase of 0.19 points in the growth rate of that country after controlling for the other determinants, in the case of the contiguity matrix, and of 0.23 points, in the case of the second order contiguity matrix. This effect is even larger in the IV estimations.

With respect to the other explanatory variables, the results regarding signs and significance are similar than those presented in Table 2, although there are some changes in the regression coefficients. The rate of convergence obtained by the spatial specifications (between 2.17% and 2.28% in ML and 1.98% and 2.37% in IV) is quite similar that the one found in the original specification (2.28% in OLS and 2.34% in 2SLS), which suggests that the rate of convergence is a robust result.

The log likelihood (LIK) and the R^2 indicate that the fit of the model improves considerably when the spatial lag is included in the model. The LIK increases from 694 for the OLS to 701 for the spatial lag, and the adjusted R^2 from 0.475 to 0.530, respectively. The LM test on spatial error dependence indicates that the spatial lag model is the appropriate one since no spatial dependence remains in the residuals, except for the model estimated in column 3.

The estimation of the spatial error model is also carried out by Maximum Likelihood (ML) and by 2SLS (Table 4). The spatial error parameter (λ) is highly significant in all cases confirming the results of the exploration section. Relative to OLS estimates, the spatial error model has a better fit, as its LIK is 698.9 compared with 694 for OLS. However, this fit is inferior to that of the spatial lag model. There are some changes in the coefficients compared to the results of the standard model, but the results regarding signs and significance are

---

[19] The results were obtained using the spatial econometric software *SpaceStat*, version 1.91 (Anselin, 2001).

similar. Concerning the rate of convergence, it is very similar than those obtained by the spatial lag model and by the standard model. Finally, the results from the common factor hypothesis test, using the contiguity matrix, indicate that the spatial error model is inappropriate as it was suggested in the exploration analysis.

From the convergence point of view, the results suggest that the rate of convergence is robust to changes in the model specification. This fact indicates that the exclusion of spatial dependence in the traditional growth regressions does not affect considerably this rate. This result is the same than the reported in other studies such as Moreno and Trehan (1997), Rey and Montouri (1999), Magalhães et al (2000) and Vayá et al (1998), who find a slightly lower rate of convergence estimated under the presence of spatial relationships. Baumont et al (2001) under the spatial error model find a convergence speed for the European regions of 1.2%, higher than the unconditional β convergence speed of 0.85% estimated by OLS. However, in spite of the slightly improvement in the convergence speed once the spatial effects are controlled for, the convergence process in the European regions remains weak.

In short, the spatial coefficients, ρ and λ, are positive and statistically significant in both models. This result combined with the spatial correlation tests, reiterates the relevance of taking into account spatial relationships across countries in economic growth models. The results indicate that economic growth is indeed explained by geographical factors.

6. Conclusions

The role of a country's geographic location is an empirical issue that has been taken into consideration in the growth literature just only recently. This chapter uses spatial econometrics to estimate a standard growth model that includes cross-country interdependence, in which a country's economic growth depends on the growth rate of its neighbors throughout the productivity term. Based on a sample of 98 countries over three decades (1965-75, 1975-85, 1985-95) and using several tests to explore and evaluate spatial dependence the chapter finds some interesting results. First, spatial relationships across countries are quite relevant. A country economic growth is affected by the performance of its neighbors and by its own relative geographical position. This result suggests that the spillover effects among countries are important for growth. Taking into account spatial correlations we correct for the exclusion of spatially dependent explanatory variables. Our results indicate that spatial interrelation across countries cannot be ignored in the analysis of economic growth. Ignoring such relationships can result in significant model misspecification or omitted variables problem.

Second, the convergence rate from the spatial model is quite similar when compared to the OLS estimation. Then, this rate appears not to be influenced by the omission of the spatial autocorrelation, suggesting that the speed of convergence of 2% is a robust result.

For future research it might be interesting to use spatial econometrics to explore income level determinants across countries and the study of integration and economic performance. In addition, it might be interesting to address the robustness of our findings when more complex specifications of the weighting matrix are considered; alternative specifications would explicitly incorporate economic issues such as trade relationships, capital movements, distance weighted by income and migration across countries.

ACKNOWLEDGEMENTS

We are indebted to J. Bonet, A. M. Iregui, M. Misas, J. Otero, C. Pombo, A. Saavedra and F. Sanchez for helpful comments on earlier drafts of this chapter. The views expressed are those of the authors and not of the Central Bank of Colombia or of its Board of Directors and not of the Inter-American Development Bank. The usual disclaimer applies to any remaining errors or omissions.

APPENDIX 1

The data for per capita GDP, investment rate, government consumption, education, black market premium on foreign exchange and terms of trade were obtain from Barro and Lee (1994), *Penn World Tables 5.6 dataset*, "World Development Indicators (WDI) CD-ROM" from the *World Bank*, and "World Currency Year Book", 1996 (published by Currency Data & Intelligence, Brooklyn, NY). Infrastructure came from *International Telecommunication Union Publications* (several years) and WDI CD-ROM. Life expectancy and fertility rate were taken also from the "World Development Indicators (WDI) CD-ROM" from the *World Bank*. For democracy, the data base of Jaggers and Gurr's *Polity III* (1996) was used; this index is a grade obtained from the average of eight indexes that classify the process of election of the policy makers of a country and the restrictions imposed over them. Commitment and credibility (*contract enforcement*) came from the *International Country Risk Guide (ICRG)* data file (1995); this index is based on survey information and shows the country's institutional characteristics that motivate its leaders to respect the duties of the government (the higher the value of the variable, the higher the level of commitment). Finally, for the bureaucratic quality the ICRG and the *Business Environmental Risk Intelligence* (taken from Knack and Keefer, 1995) datafiles were used; this variable is based on survey information and indicates autonomy from political pressures and decision and control to rule without drastic policy changes or disruptions in the services brought by the government.

Summary Statistics of Variables Included in Estimation, 98 Countries

Variable	Mean	Std. Dev.	Minimum	Maximum
Growth rate of GDP per capita	0.0164	0.0262	–0.0548	0.1112
Log of initial GDP per capita	7.7630	1.0236	5.6699	9.7153
Growth rate of per-capita telephones	0.0525	0.0433	–0.0805	0.2244
Gross enrollment ratio for second. education	0.3908	0.2898	0.0100	1.0000
Log of investment as percentage of GDP	–1.9976	0.6972	–4.3135	–0.9826
Terms of trade change	0.0061	0.0615	–0.0832	0.3214
Democracy score	4.2111	4.3929	0.0000	10.0000
Bureaucracy quality	3.2712	1.7071	0.5000	8.5000
Contract enforcement	5.9393	1.9797	1.0000	10.0000
Log(1+ exch. rate black market premium)	0.2340	0.4440	0.0000	4.8454
Log of government expenditure	-1.7690	0.4016	-2.7704	-0.7022
Log of fertility rate	1.4419	0.5082	0.2546	2.0794
Log of life expectancy at birth	4.0621	0.2001	3.5860	4.3477

APPENDIX 1B

Countries included in the estimations and data availability

Country	**Data Availability**		
	1965-1975	1975-1985	1985-1995
1. Algeria	Complete data	Complete data	Black Market Premium not available
2. Argentina	Complete data	Complete data	Complete data
3. Australia	Complete data	Complete data	Complete data
4. Austria	Complete data	Complete data	Complete data
5. Bangladesh	Growth rates of telephones per capita and democracy not available	Complete data	Complete data
6. Belgium	Complete data	Complete data	Complete data
7. Bolivia	Complete data	Complete data	Complete data
8. Botswana	Complete data	Complete data	Complete data
9. Brazil	Complete data	Complete data	Complete data
10. Burkina-Faso	Education not available	Education not available	Education not available
11. Burundi	Education, commitment and bureaucracy not available.	Education, commitment and bureaucracy not available.	Education, commitment and bureaucracy not available.
12. Cameroon	Complete data	Complete data	Complete data
13. Canada	Complete data	Complete data	Complete data
14. Chad	Education, commitment and bureaucracy not available.	Education, commitment and bureaucracy not available.	Education, commitment and bureaucracy not available.
15. Chile	Complete data	Complete data	Complete data
16. Colombia	Complete data	Complete data	Complete data
17. Congo	Complete data	Complete data	Complete data
18. Costa Rica	Complete data	Complete data	Complete data
19. Cote d'Ivoire	Complete data	Complete data	Complete data
20. Cyprus	Complete data	Complete data	Complete data
21. Denmark	Complete data	Complete data	Complete data
22. Dominican Rep.	Complete data	Complete data	Complete data
23. Ecuador	Complete data	Complete data	Complete data
24. Egypt	Complete data	Complete data	Complete data
25. El Salvador	Complete data	Complete data	Complete data
26. Ethiopia	Complete data	Complete data	Complete data
27. Finland	Complete data	Complete data	Complete data
28. France	Complete data	Complete data	Complete data
29. Germany	Complete data	Complete data	Complete data

Countries included in the estimations and data availability (Continued)

Country	**Data Availability**		
	1965-1975	1975-1985	1985-1995
30. Gabon	Education not available	Education not available	Education not available
31. Gambia	Education, commitment and bureaucracy not available.	Education, commitment and bureaucracy not available.	Education, commitment and bureaucracy not available.
32. Ghana	Complete data	Black Market Premium not available	Complete data
33. Greece	Complete data	Complete data	Complete data
34. Guatemala	Complete data	Complete data	Complete data
35. Guinea	Education not available	Education not available	Education not available
36. Haiti	Complete data	Complete data	Complete data
37. Honduras	Complete data	Complete data	Complete data
38. Iceland	Black Market Premium, commitment and bureaucracy not available	Black Market Premium, commitment and education not available	Black Market Premium, commitment and bureaucracy not available
39. India	Complete data	Complete data	Complete data
40. Indonesia	Complete data	Complete data	Complete data
41. Iran, I.R. of	Complete data	Complete data	Complete data
42. Iraq	Complete data	Complete data	Black Market premium, not available
43. Ireland	Complete data	Complete data	Complete data
44. Israel	Complete data	Complete data	Complete data
45. Italy	Complete data	Complete data	Complete data
46. Jamaica	Complete data	Complete data	Complete data
47. Japan	Complete data	Complete data	Complete data
48. Jordan	Complete data	Complete data	Complete data
49. Kenya	Complete data	Complete data	Complete data
50. Korea	Complete data	Complete data	Complete data
51. Lesotho	Commitment and bureaucracy not available	Commitment and bureaucracy not available	Terms of Trade, commitment and bureaucracy not available
52. Madagascar	Complete data	Complete data	Complete data
53. Malawi	Complete data	Complete data	Complete data
54. Malaysia	Complete data	Complete data	Complete data
55. Mali	Complete data	Complete data	Complete data
56. Malta	Complete data	Complete data	Complete data

Countries included in the estimations and data availability (Continued)

Country	Data Availability		
	1965-1975	1975-1985	1985-1995
57. Mauritania	Education , commitment and bureaucracy not available	Education , commitment and bureaucracy not available	Education , commitment and bureaucracy not available
58. Mauritius	Black Market Premium, commitment and bureaucracy not available	Black Market Premium, commitment and bureaucracy not available	Black Market Premium, commitment and bureaucracy not available
59. Mexico	Complete data	Complete data	Complete data
60. Mozambique	Complete data	Democracy not available	Black Market Premium not available
61. Morocco	Complete data	Complete data	Complete data
62. Nepal	Complete data	Complete data	Complete data
63. Netherlands	Complete data	Complete data	Complete data
64. New Zealand	Complete data	Complete data	Complete data
65. Nicaragua	Complete data	Complete data	Complete data
66. Niger	Complete data	Complete data	Complete data
67. Nigeria	Complete data	Complete data	Black Market Premium not available
68. Norway	Complete data	Complete data	Complete data
69. Pakistan	Complete data	Complete data	Complete data
70. Panama	Complete data	Complete data	Black Market Premium not available
71. Paraguay	Complete data	Complete data	Complete data
72. Peru	Complete data	Complete data	Black Market Premium not available
73. Philippines	Complete data	Complete data	Complete data
74. Portugal	Complete data	Complete data	Complete data
75. Rwanda	Education not available	Complete data	Complete data
76. Senegal	Complete data	Complete data	Complete data
77. Singapore	Terms of trade change not available	Complete data	Complete data
78. Somalia	Education not available	Education not available	Education not available
79. South Africa	Complete data	Complete data	Complete data
80. Spain	Complete data	Complete data	Complete data
81. Sri Lanka	Complete data	Complete data	Complete data
82. Sweden	Complete data	Complete data	Complete data
83. Switzerland	Complete data	Complete data	Complete data
84. Syria	Complete data	Complete data	Black Market premium not available

Countries included in the estimations and data availability (Continued)

Country	Data Availability		
	1965-1975	1975-1985	1985-1995
85. Tanzania	Complete data	Complete data	Complete data
86. Thailand	Complete data	Complete data	Complete data
87. Togo	Complete data	Complete data	Complete data
88. Trinidad & Tobago	Black Market Premium not available	Complete data	Complete data
89. Tunisia	Complete data	Complete data	Complete data
90. Turkey	Complete data	Complete data	Complete data
91. Uganda	Complete data	Complete data	Complete data
92. United Kingdom	Complete data	Complete data	Complete data
93. United States	Complete data	Complete data	Complete data
94. Uruguay	Complete data	Complete data	Complete data
95. Venezuela	Complete data	Complete data	Complete data
96. Zaire	Democracy not available	Complete data	Complete data
97. Zambia	Complete data	Complete data	Complete data
98. Zimbabwe	Complete data	Complete data	Complete data

APPENDIX 2

Classification of Spatial Association using GDP per capita growth rate, Average 1965-95 (standardized)

High-High : Positive spatial association	**Low-Low: Positive spatial association**
Austria, Belgium, Canada, Cyprus, Denmark, Egypt, France, Germany, Greece, Iceland, India, Indonesia, Ireland, Israel, Italy, Japan, Korea, Malaysia, Malta, Morocco, Nepal, Netherlands, Norway, Panama, Portugal, Singapore, Spain, Sri Lanka, Thailand, Tunisia, United Kingdom, United States.	Algeria, Bolivia, Burkina-Faso, Burundi, Cameroon, Chad, Costa Rica, Cote d'Ivoire, El Salvador, Ethiopia, Gambia, Ghana, Guatemala, Guinea, Honduras, Iran, Kenya, Madagascar, Malawi, Mali, Mauritania, Mozambique, Nicaragua, Niger, Rwanda, Senegal, Somalia, Tanzania, Togo, Trinidad & Tobago, Uganda, Zaire, Zambia, Zimbabwe.
High-Low: Negative spatial association	**Low-High: Negative spatial association**
Australia, Botswana, Brazil, Chile, Colombia, Congo, Dominican Rep, Ecuador, Finland, Jordan, Lesotho, Mauritius, Mexico, Nigeria, Pakistan, Paraguay, Syria, Turkey.	Argentina, Bangladesh, Gabon, Haiti, Iraq, Jamaica, New Zealand, Peru, Philippines, South Africa, Sweden, Switzerland, Uruguay, Venezuela.
Moran I: 0.4118 Z-value: 4.6516 Probability: 0.0000	

Note: High, more than 1.6% GDP per capita growth, Low, less than 1.6% GDP per capita growth.

Classification of Spatial Association using GDP per capita growth rate, 1985-95 (standardized)

High-High : Positive spatial association	Low-Low: Positive spatial association
Australia, Austria, Bangladesh, Belgium, Canada, Costa Rica, Cyprus, Denmark, France, Germany, Greece, India, Indonesia, Ireland, Italy, Jamaica, Japan, Korea, Malaysia, Malta, Nepal, Netherlands, New Zealand, Norway, Pakistan, Philippines, Portugal, Singapore, Spain, Sri Lanka, Thailand, United Kingdom.	Algeria, Botswana, Burkina-Faso, Burundi, Cameroon, Chad, Congo, Dominican Rep, Gabon, Gambia, Guatemala, Honduras, Iran, Iraq, Jordan, Malawi, Mali, Mauritania, Morocco, Niger, Nigeria, Paraguay, Rwanda, Senegal, Togo, Trinidad & Tobago, Venezuela, Zaire, Zambia, Zimbabwe.
High-Low: Negative spatial association	**Low-High: Negative spatial association**
Chile, Colombia, El Salvador, Finland, Ghana, Guinea, Israel, Lesotho, Mauritius, Mozambique, Somalia, Syria, Tanzania, Tunisia, Turkey, Uganda, United States, Uruguay.	Argentina, Bolivia, Brazil, Cote d'Ivoire, Ecuador, Egypt, Ethiopia, Haiti, Iceland, Kenya, Madagascar, Mexico, Nicaragua, Panama, Peru, South Africa, Sweden, Switzerland.
Moran I: 0.3242 Z-value: 3.6005 Probability:0.0003	

Note: High, more than 1% GDP per capita growth, Low, less than 1% GDP per capita growth.

Classification of Spatial Association using GDP per capita growth rate, 1975-85 (standardized)

High-High : Positive spatial association	Low-Low: Positive spatial association
Algeria, Austria, Bangladesh, Belgium, Canada, Cyprus, Denmark, Egypt, Finland, France, Germany, Greece, Iceland, India, Indonesia, Ireland, Italy, Japan, Korea, Malaysia, Malta, Morocco, Nepal, Netherlands, Norway, Philippines, Singapore, Sri Lanka, Sweden, Switzerland, Syria, Thailand, Tunisia, United Kingdom, United States.	Argentina, Bolivia, Cote d'Ivoire, Costa Rica, Dominican, Ecuador, El Salvador, Ethiopia, Gambia, Ghana, Guinea, Haiti, Honduras, Iran, Jamaica, Kenya, Madagascar, Malawi, Mozambique, Nicaragua, Niger, Nigeria, Senegal, Somalia, South Africa, Tanzania, Togo, Turkey, Uruguay, Zaire, Zambia, Zimbabwe.
High-Low: Negative spatial association	**Low-High: Negative spatial association**
Australia, Botswana, Brazil, Burkina-Faso, Burundi, Cameroon, Chile, Colombia, Congo, Jordan, Lesotho, Mali, Mauritius, Mexico, Pakistan, Panama, Paraguay, Portugal, Rwanda, Trinidad & Tobago.	Chad, Gabon, Guatemala, Israel, Iraq, Mauritania, New Zealand, Peru, Philippines, Spain, Uganda, Venezuela.
Moran I: 0.2307 Z-value: 2.5940 Probability: 0.0095	

Note: High, more than 1% GDP per capita growth, Low, less than 1% GDP per capita growth.

Classification of Spatial Association using GDP per capita growth rate, 1965-75 (standardized)

High-High : Positive spatial association	Low-Low: Positive spatial association
Colombia, Congo, France, Gabon, Iceland, Indonesia, Israel, Italy, Jamaica, Japan, Korea, Lesotho, Malaysia, Panama, Philippines, Portugal, Singapore, South Africa, Spain, Syria, Thailand, Tunisia, Turkey, Zimbabwe.	Argentina, Australia, Bangladesh, Burkina-Faso, Burundi, Chile, Cote d'Ivoire, Denmark, El Salvador, Ethiopia, Gambia, Ghana, Guatemala, Guinea, Honduras, India, Madagascar, Malawi, Mali, Mauritania, Mauritius, Mozambique, Nepal, New Zealand, Nicaragua, Niger, Senegal, Somalia, Sri Lanka, Trinidad & Tobago.
High-Low: Negative spatial association	**Low-High: Negative spatial association**
Algeria, Austria, Belgium, Bolivia, Botswana, Brazil, Canada, Costa Rica, Dominican, Ecuador, Finland, Greece, Iran, Ireland, Kenya, Mexico, Netherlands, Nigeria, Norway, Rwanda, Tanzania.	Cameroon, Chad, Cyprus, Egypt, Germany, Haiti, Iraq, Jordan, Morocco, Pakistan, Paraguay, Peru, Philippines, Sweden, Switzerland, Togo, Uganda, United Kingdom, United States, Uruguay, Venezuela, Zaire, Zambia.
Moran I: 0.2562 Z-value: 2.8687 Probability: 0.0041	

Note: High, more than 1% GDP per capita growth, Low, less than 1% GDP per capita growth.

REFERENCES

Acemoglu Daron, S. Johnson and J. A. Robinson. 2000. "The Colonial Origins of Comparative Development: An Empirical Investigation," *NBER, Working Paper* No. 7771.

Ades Alberto F. and H.B. Chua 1997. "Thy neighbour's curse: regional instability and economic growth", *Journal of Economic Growth*, 2 p.p. 279-304.

Alesina Alberto and R. Perotti. 1996. "Income distribution, political instability and investment," *European Economic Review*, vol. 80, pp. 1203-1228.

Anselin Luc. 1988. *Spatial Econometrics: Methods and Models*, Dordrecht Kluwer Academic Publishers.

Anselin Luc. 1995. *SpaceStat version 1.80 User's Guide*, manuscript University of Illinois at Urbana-Champaign.

Anselin Luc. 2001. *SpaceStat, a Software package for the Analysis of Spatial Data*, version 1.91. TerraSerr, Inc.

Anselin Luc and R. Florax. 1995. *New Directions in Spatial Econometrics*, Springer Verlag Berlin.

Barro Robert and J-W. Lee. 1994. "Data Set for a Panel of 138 Countries," manuscript.

Barro Robert and X. Sala-i-Martin. 1995. *Economic Growth*, New York: Mac-Graw Hill Inc.

Barro Robert. 1996. "Democracy and Growth," *Journal of Economic Growth*, Vol.1, No. 1, p.p. 1-27

Baumont Catherine, C. Ertur and J. Le Gallo. 2001. "The European Regional Convergence Process, 1980-1995: do Spatial Regimes and Spatial Dependence matter? Working paper, LATEC UMR-CNRS 5118, University of Burgundy.

Calvo Sara and C. M. Reinhart. 1996. "Capital Flows to Latin America: Is There Evidence of Contagion Effects," *Private Capital Flows to Emerging Markets.*

Canning David. 1998. "A Database of World Infrastructure Stocks, 1950-1995,"*World Bank Economic Review*, Vol. 12, pp. 529-547.

Ciccone Antonio. 1997. "Externalities and Interdependent Growth: Theory and Evidence," Manuscript, University of California at Berkeley and Univeritat Pompeu Fabra. Download from Social Science Electronic Publishing, Social Science Research Network.

Chua Hak B. 1993. *Regional Spillovers and Economic Growth*, Ph.D. dissertation, Harvard University (cited in Barro and Sala i Martin, 1995).

Conley Timothy and E. Ligon. 2002. "Economic Distance and Cross-Country Spillovers", *Journal of Economic Growth*, 7 pp. 157-187.

Currency Data & Intelligence. 1996. *World Currency Year Book*, Brooklyn, NY.

Driscoll John and A. Kraay. 1995. "Spatial Correlation in Panel Data" Brown University, Department of Economics, working paper 95/34. Download from Social Science Electronic Publishing, Social Science Research Network.

Easterly William. 2002. *The Elusive Quest for Growth: Economists' Adventures and Misadventures in the Tropics*, the MIT Press, Cambridge, Massachusetts.

Escobal Javier and M. Torero. 2000. "Does Geography Explain Differences in Economic Growth in Peru?", Inter-American Development Bank, Research Network Working Paper # R-404.

Esfahani Hadi S. and M. T. Ramírez. 2003. "Institutions, Infrastructure, and Economic Growth," *Journal of Development Economics, Vol. 70 Issue 2*. pp. 443-477.

Fingleton Bernard. 1999. "Regional Economic Growth and Convergence: Insights from a Spatial Econometric Perspective", manuscript University of Cambridge.

García de la Vega María Luz and J. Herce. 2000. "Integration and Growth in the EU: The role of trade", Documento de Trabajo 2000-20, FEDEA, download from Social Science Electronic Publishing, Social Science Research Network.

Gallup John L, J.D. Sachs and A.D. Mellinger. 1999. "Geography and Economic Development", *International Regional Science Review*, 22 (2), pp. 179-232.

Hall Robert and C.I. Jones. 1999. "Why do some countries produce so much more output per worker than others?," *Quarterly Journal of Economics*, Vol. 114, pp. 83-116

Heston Alan and R. Summers. 1995. *Penn World Tables Mark 5.6 dataset*, University of Pennsilvania.

International Telecommunication Union Publications, *Telecommunication Indicators*, several years.

Jaggers Keith and T. R. Gurr. 1996. Polity III: Regime Type and Political Authority, 1800-1994, Computer file. Boulder, CO: Keith Jaggers/College Park, MD: Ted Robert Gurr, producers. Ann Arbor, MI: Inter-university Consortium for Political and Social Research, distributor.

Knack Stephen and P. Keefer. 1995. "Institutions and Economic Performance: Cross-Country Tests Using Alternative Institutional Measures," *Economics and Politics*, 7.3, pp. 207-227.

Kormendi Roger C. and P. Meguire. 1985. "Macroeconomic Determinants of Growth: Cross-Country Evidence," *Journal of Monetary Economics,* Vol. 16, pp. 141-163.

Krueger Alan and M. Lindahl. 2000. "Education for Growth: Why and for Whom?", Working Paper # 429, Industrial Relations Section, Princeton University.

Landau Daniel. 1986. "Government and Economic Growth in the LDCs: An Empirical Study for 1960-1980," *Economic Development and Cultural Change,* Vol. 35, pp. 35-76.

LeSage James P. 1999. "The Theory and Practice of Spatial Econometrics," Department of Economics, University of Toledo.

Levine Ross and D. Renelt. 1992. "A Sensitivity Analysis of Cross-Country Growth Regressions," *American Economic Review,* Vol. 82, pp. 942-963.

López-Bazo Enrique, E. Vayá. A.J. Mora and J. Suriñach. 1999. "Regional Economic Dynamics and Convergence in the European Union", *Annals of Regional Science*, 33 (3), pp. 343-70.

McArthur John W. and J. D. Sachs. 2001. "Institutions and Geography: Comment on Acemoglu, Johnson and Robinson (2000)", *NBER Working Paper* No. 8114.

Magalhães André, G. Hewings and C. R. Azzoni. 2000. "Spatial Dependence and Regional Convergence in Brazil", *Regional Economics Applications Laboratory*, REAL 00-T-11. University of Illinois at Urbana-Champaign.

Moreno Ramon and B. Trehan. 1997. "Location and the Growth of Nations", *Journal of Economic Growth*, 2 pp. 399-418.

Paci Raffaele and F. Pigliaru. 2001. "Technological diffusion, spatial spillovers and regional convergence in Europe", Nota di Lavoro 36-2001, Fondazione Eni Enrico Mattei, Download from Social Science Electronic Publishing, Social Science Research Network.

Political Risk Services, Inc. 1995. International Country Risk Guide Data, 1982-95, Computer file, Syracuse, NY: Compiled by IRIS Center, University of Maryland, College Park, MD.

Pourgerami Abbas. 1988. "The Political Economy of Development: A Cross-National Causality Test of Development-Democracy-Growth Hypothesis," *Public Choice,* Vol.58 (2), pp. 123-141.

Rey Sergio J. 1.999. "Spatial Empirics for Economic Growth and Convergence," manuscript, San Diego State University.

Rey Sergio J. and B. D. Montouri. 1999. "US Regional Income Convergence: A Spatial Econometric Perspective," *Regional Studies,* Vol.33 (2), pp. 143-156.

Sachs Jeffrey D. and A.M. Warner. 1995. "Natural Resources Abundance and Economic Growth", *NBER Working Paper* No. 5398.

Sachs Jeffrey D. 2001. "Tropical Underdevelopment", *NBER Working Paper* No. 8119.

Scully Gerald W. 1988. "The Institutional Framework and Economic Development." *Journal of Political Economy,* Vol. 96 (3), pp. 652-662.

Tobler W. 1979. "Cellular Geography," *Philosophy in Geography*, pp. 379-386, Dordrecht: Reidel.

Vayá Esther, E. López-Bazo, R. Moreno and J. Suriñach. 1998. "Growth and Externalities across economies. An empirical analysis using spatial econometrics", working paper, Department of Econometrics, Statistics and Spanish Economy, University of Barcelona.

World Bank. 1990, 1994 and 2000. World Development Report, Washington D.C

World Bank. *World Development Indicators* (*WDI*), CD-ROM.

In: Economic Growth Issues
Editor: L. A. Finley, pp. 53-71
ISBN 1-59454-555-3

Chapter 3

ESCAPING LOCK-IN IN AN ENDOGENOUS GROWTH MODEL WITH TWO COMPETING TECHNOLOGIES[1]

Reyer Gerlagh[2] and Marjan W. Hofkes
IVM, Institute for Environmental Studies, Vrije Universiteit,
Amsterdam, The Netherlands

ABSTRACT

In this paper we develop a simple endogenous growth model with two competing production technologies and productivity spillover effects between firms that use the same technology. Investments are directed to the technology with highest current and future returns. Since current investments increase future returns through spillovers, the economy will usually lock in, specializing in one of the two technologies. In the case that the economy has selected a highly pollutant technology, sustainable growth requires a transition towards the clean technology. We analyze the scope for (environmental) policies that induce such a transition.

Keywords: Endogenous growth, Lock-in, Transition, Convergent expectations

INTRODUCTION

Many are concerned that a continuously growing world economy is at odds with the inherently limited supply of natural resources as well as with the solution of environmental problems caused by increasing levels of various emissions. Matching exponential output

---

1 The authors want to thank Sjak Smulders for his useful comments on an earlier version of this paper, especially for contributing to Figure 1. Also Cees Withagen is acknowledged for his useful remarks. We are also grateful to others that have helped us with constructive comments. All remaining errors are ours. The authors acknowledge financial support by the Netherlands Organisation for Scientific Research (NWO) under contract number 05.39.101 and 016.005.040 and thank FEEM for publishing a previous version of the paper as a report, *Note di Lavoro 12.2002*.
2 Correspondence: Reyer Gerlagh, IVM/VU, De Boelelaan 1115, 1081 HV Amsterdam, the Netherlands, tel. +31 - 20 - 44 49502, fax. +31 - 20 - 44 49553, email. gerlagh@ivm.vu.nl.

growth with limited resource inputs and limited absorption capacities of ecosystems will require production to become less dependent upon the use of natural resources and less polluting per unit of output. This makes it clear why the direction of technological change, towards 'clean' or resource extensive technologies, is an essential parameter determining the feasibility of sustainable development. Searching the literature for a model to study the issue, we find two classes of models looking into the sources of technological progress, the neo-classical endogenous growth models, and the so-called evolutionary growth models.

Neo-classical growth theory has its roots in the 1950s when Solow (1956) and Swan (1956) developed their theoretical framework for understanding world-wide growth of output. In the Solow-Swan model, however, technological progress is exogenous; long-run growth comes like 'manna from heaven'.[3] The model offers no clue as to the sources of economic growth and the bias of technological change in the long run. In the 1980s, the growth model was further developed leading to the so-called new or endogenous growth theory emerging in the early 1990s (e.g. Romer, 1990, Rebelo, 1991).[4] This new growth theory explicitly describes two sources of technological change, non-intentional learning and intentional research and development. An important contribution of new growth theory is that it enables the study of policies that enhance or direct learning and research, and it enables the analysis of welfare implications of different directions and levels of economic growth.

In the late 1990s, the new growth theory was linked to the issue of sustainable development. In several articles, implications of environmental policies on economic growth were studied. Also, the more fundamental question was raised whether sustained economic growth is compatible with the conservation of the environment (Bovenberg and Smulders 1995, Smulders 1995, and Hofkes 1996). The conclusion emerged that sustainable development and economic growth can go together if there is a steady flow of technological innovations that increase the efficiency of resource use (Aghion and Howitt 1998, Ch. 5). Yet, the typical endogenous growth model has an important omission. It does not make a distinction between 'clean' and 'dirty' technologies, while this distinction is believed to be the key to the understanding of sustainable economic development. The concerns about climate change are a case in point. There is increasing support for the idea that, if substantial carbon dioxide emission reductions are to be achieved, a technological transition away from hydrocarbon based energy sources towards non-carbon energy sources will be needed. However, the common endogenous growth models with natural resources treat sustainable development as a uniform decrease of the environmental intensity of production, without distinguishing 'clean' from 'dirty' production technologies.

At the same time, the focus on technological diversity is one of the major elements in the class of evolutionary models (e.g. Nelson and Winter, 1982), which has its roots in the Schumpetarian tradition. Evolutionary models typically describe a diverse set of technologies,[5] a diversification mechanism broadening the set, such as the arrival of random innovations, and a selection mechanism for the reproduction of specific technologies. Jointly, the continuous diversification and selection mechanisms cause a drift in the characteristics of

---

3 The Solow-Swan model can explain the stylised facts of growth as listed by Kaldor (1961), but it has been heavily criticised for its prediction of convergence between rich and poor countries. There is now a broad literature on absolute and conditional convergence; we leave the subject aside, however.

4 See [Jones and Manuelli 1997] for an overview of endogenous growth models.

5 This technological variety may be embodied in firms, sectors or countries. For example, in (Nelson and Winter, 1982), the set consists of firms that possess different capabilities, procedures, and decision rules.

the current technology set. Those technologies that are most successful given the economic environment, the institutions, and policy regulations, are the fittest and will be reproduced.

Within the context of evolutionary models, technological regimes, technological transitions, and technological lock-ins play a central role (see e.g. Dosi, 1982, Nelson and Winter, 1982, Arthur, 1989). Following Street and Miles (1996), a technological regime refers to "the whole complex of scientific knowledge, engineering practices, process technologies, infrastructure, product characteristics, skills and procedures which make up the totality of a technology." In the context of this paper, where we abstract from a detailed analysis of most of these elements, we will use the term technology cluster instead of the term technological regime. Many spillover effects exist between technologies within the same cluster, resulting in increasing returns to scale. Between technology clusters, fewer spillover effects exist. Once a specific cluster has gained a relative advantage over competing technology clusters (that is a cluster of technologies that can be used to produce a substitute good), the scale effects will enhance its dominance. The economy will specialize in technologies typical of that cluster, instead of following a uniform growth path over all technologies within different clusters. This phenomenon of specialisation in a cluster is known as a lock-in.

For many environmental problems, the solution may require a technological transition away from a technological regime that is emission intensive or heavily rests upon the exploitation of specific natural resources, towards technological regimes that are less emission intensive or less dependent on resource exploitation. In this paper, we study policies that can unlock the economy from an emission or resource intensive technology cluster, and that set in motion a transition towards a cluster of environmentally more friendly technologies.

We develop an endogenous growth model based on the Romer (1986) *AK* model in which investments in the capital stock increase labor productivity. We extend the basic one-sector model, and describe two competing sectors, representing clusters of technologies that have strong internal spillover effects. The problem of lock-in is described as the existence of multiple locally stable equilibria. A technological transition corresponds to the selection of a locally stable equilibrium different from the present one. This paper studies the mechanisms of, and policy initiatives necessary to set in motion, such a transition.[6,7]

In the literature, there are two opposing streams considering history and expectations, respectively, as the factors that determine the selection of one specific equilibrium, out of a set of multiple locally stable equilibria (see Krugman, 1991). The first stream, which believes that the historical path of development is of critical importance, is represented both in the mainstream economic literature (e.g. Ethier, 1982, Krugman, 1981, 1987) and in the evolutionary economics literature (Arthur, 1986). The second stream holds the view that expected economic development is the key determinant of choice of equilibrium (e.g. Chen

[6] Tahvonen and Salo (2001) also describe an endogenous growth economy with a transition from non-fossil-fuel energy technologies to fossil-fuel energy technologies, and backwards. Different from our analysis, in their paper, the transition is set in motion by the different characteristics of both energy technologies, that is the increasing costs of the non-fossil-fuel technology, and the depletion of fossil fuels, respectively. In Tahvonen and Salo there is no ambiguity in the selection of the inter-temporal equilibrium.

[7] The recent literature also suggests that niche markets can be essential for the locking out of an economy, securing a minimal market size for infant technologies (Cowan and Hulten, 1996, Islas, 1997). In this paper, we abstract from this phenomenon.

and Shimomura 1998). In this view, self-fulfilling prophecies play an important role, and accordingly, a major responsibility of the public agency is to create convergent expectations as to the future direction of economic development. In our model, both history and expectations play a role.

As regards the interplay between present policies, history, and expectations, our paper fits into a broader literature on environmental policies and the selection of socially preferred equilibrium out of a multiple set of possible equilibria. Recent papers such as Mäler (2000) and Kremer and Morcom (2000) study policies that would move an economic and environmental system locked in an inferior steady state to an environmentally superior steady state. Similar to these two papers, in our paper, we study the scope for government intervention that aims at the selection of an environmentally preferred dynamic equilibrium. In another way, abstracting from the environmental concerns, our analysis is also related to the endogenous growth literature that studies multiple balanced growth paths. Recent examples of endogenous growth models that contain multiple equilibria include Chen and Shimomura (1998) and Zhang (1998). In Chen and Shimomura (1998), only self-fulfilling expectations matter in selecting the equilibrium. There is no path dependency. Zhang (1998) asks for public intervention to ensure the economy selects the preferred equilibrium. In his model, like in ours, history and expectations play an important role.

The paper is organized as follows. In section 2 the set-up of our basic model, without an environmental externality, will be discussed. In section 3, we will analyze equilibrium path solutions of this basic model. In section 4, we study the consequences of an environmental constraint for economic growth and analyze the scope for environmental policies. Section 5 concludes.

Model Set up

We consider a so-called AK model with endogenous growth in the tradition of the Romer (1986) model.[8] Our model adds to the literature in that we consider two sectors for production of the single man-made good, instead of one, studying the effects of the non-convexity in the production set on optimal investments, the selection of one sector for specialization, and the possibility for a transition when environmental constraints lock the economy in an inferior steady state.

An infinitely-lived consumer maximizes inter-temporal welfare, as given by:

$$\max\ w = \int_0^\infty e^{-\rho t} U(C_t - \nu R_t)\,\mathrm{d}t, \tag{1}$$

where C_t is the consumption of a single consumer good in period t, and R_t is resource use (or pollution), which adds negatively to the utility function. For convenience, we assumed that the resource externality can linearly be expressed in consumer good units.

The production side of the economy is described by two sectors. Each sector, i=1,2, represents a different cluster of technologies that is available for the production of the consumer good. Both technologies are characterized by a Cobb-Douglas production function:

[8] A good reading of the model can be found in Barro and Sala-i-Martin [1995, Ch. 4]

$$Y_i = \eta_i K_i^{\alpha} (H_i L_i)^{1-\alpha}, \tag{2}$$

where η_i is a constant overall productivity coefficient, K_i is the capital stock, H_i is the human knowledge productivity factor, and L_i denotes the employed labor force. Resource use is linked to the output of sector 1, $R=Y_1$.[9] Thus, the model distinguishes a clean and a dirty sector. In other aspects, both sectors are treated symmetrically.

The capital stock depreciates with rate δ, while gross investments I_i are added to the stock:

$$\dot{K}_i = I_i - \delta K_i. \tag{3}$$

Capital has a spill over to labor productivity. Part of this spillover, ζ, is sector-specific, and the remainder is non-sector-specific:

$$H_i = \zeta K_i + (1-\zeta)(K_1+K_2), \tag{4}$$

for $0<\zeta<1$. If in both sectors the capital stock increases by factor 2, then in both sectors labor productivity increases by the same factor (4), and in both sectors output increases by factor 2 (2). Thus, the overall production frontier of the economy has constant returns to scale in the capital stock as in the Romer (1986) growth model, thereby permitting a sustained growth path.

Consumption plus investments are constrained by gross production:

$$C + I_1 + I_2 = Y_1 + Y_2. \tag{5}$$

Finally, labor supply, $\overline{L}$, which is assumed to be constant and inelastic, matches labor demand:

$$L_1 + L_2 = \overline{L}. \tag{6}$$

Without loss of generality, we assume that labor units are chosen such that $\overline{L}=1$. We can thus describe the labor allocation by the variable $l_1=L_1$, which denotes the share of labor used in the first sector.

Optimal Paths

The Hamiltonian for the welfare maximization program reads:

[9] In fact we assume that the production function in sector 1 has a Leontief specification with respect to resource use.

$$\begin{aligned} \boldsymbol{H} = \; & U(C-\nu R) - \chi(C + I_1 + I_2 - Y_1 - Y_2) \\ & -p_1(Y_1 - \eta_1 K_1^{\alpha}(H_1 L_1)^{1-\alpha}) - p_2(Y_2 - \eta_2 K_2^{\alpha}(H_2 L_2)^{1-\alpha}) \\ & -\psi_1(\delta K_1 - I_1) - \psi_2(\delta K_2 - I_2) \\ & -\lambda_1(H_1 - K_1 - (1-\zeta)K_2) - \lambda_2(H_2 - K_2 - (1-\zeta)K_1) \\ & -w(L_1 + L_1 - \bar{L}) \\ & +\mu_1 I_1 + \mu_2 I_2 - \tau(Y_1 - R) \end{aligned} \tag{7}$$

where χ is the price for the consumer good, or the shadow price of the commodity balance (5), we have p_i the shadow price for the production identity (2), ψ_i is the co-state variable (or shadow price) for the state variables K_i, (3), λ_i is the shadow prices for the variable H_i (4), w is the wage or shadow price for the labour constraint (6), and we add the Lagrangean terms $\mu_1 I_1$ and $\mu_2 I_2$ to account for the non-negative investments constraints, $I_i \geq 0$, which can be binding along an optimal path. The resource shadow price is denoted by τ. It follows immediately from the first order conditions for R and C that $\tau = \nu U'(.) = \nu\chi$. In the next section, we will study implications of resource use on the optimal path. First, in this section, we will abstract from the resource externalities and study dynamics and the lock-in phenomenon for the simplified case with $\tau = \nu = 0$. Alternatively, we may consider this situation as representing an economy before environmental awareness has risen.

The first order conditions for Y_1 and Y_2 ($\partial \boldsymbol{H}/\partial Y_i = 0$) set the prices for both output goods equal to marginal utility:

$$p_1 = p_2 = \chi = U'(C). \tag{8}$$

Labor is allocated so as to maximize its productivity, and its distribution over both sectors immediately adjusts to the current capital and human knowledge stock distribution. Labor productivity (the wage) is denoted by w. Now, for both sectors the wage should equal marginal labor productivity in the specific sector, w_i, given by:

$$w_i = (1-\alpha)\chi\eta_i K_i^{\alpha} H_i^{1-\alpha} L_i^{-\alpha}, \tag{9}$$

for $i=1,2$, and along an optimal path, we have $w=w_1=w_2$. For given capital stock K_i and human knowledge H_i, the labor market equilibrium is found by setting $w_1 = w_2$, which gives:

$$l_1 = \frac{\eta_1^{1/\alpha} K_1 H_1^{(1-\alpha)/\alpha}}{\eta_1^{1/\alpha} K_1 H_1^{(1-\alpha)/\alpha} + \eta_2^{1/\alpha} K_2 H_2^{(1-\alpha)/\alpha}} = 1/(1 + \frac{\eta_2^{1/\alpha} K_2 H_2^{(1-\alpha)/\alpha}}{\eta_1^{1/\alpha} K_1 H_1^{(1-\alpha)/\alpha}}). \tag{10}$$

The equation shows that a higher capital stock K_i, which in turn implies a higher human knowledge productivity factor H_i, increases the labor share l_i employed in sector i (keeping the capital stock in the other sector constant). We notice that the labor allocation is homogeneous of degree zero in K, since H_i is also linearly homogeneous in the vector K. That is, l_1 only depends on the relative shares of capital in both sectors. For convenience, we define the level of the capital stock in the first sector as a share of the total capital stock,

$$k_1 \equiv K_1/(K_1+K_2). \tag{11}$$

Now, (10) can be written in reduced form as

$$l_1 = F(k_1; \alpha, \zeta, \eta_1, \eta_2), \tag{12}$$

for continuous $F(.):(0,1)\rightarrow(0,1)$. Notice that $F(0;.)=0$ and $F(1;.)=1$; if all capital is allocated to the first sector, then all labor is allocated to the first sector as well, and if all capital is allocated to the second sector, then labor is allocated thereto as well.

After investments, there is no capital mobility between the two sectors. Capital formation follows from past and present investment decisions. First order conditions for investments I_i give the equality $\psi_i+\mu_i=\chi$, which says that the capital stock prices ψ_i equals unity unless investments are zero: $\psi_i\leq\chi$ with equality if $I_i>0$. Using the complementarity sign, $\perp$, we write:

$$\psi_i \leq \chi \quad \perp \quad I_i \geq 0. \tag{13}$$

for $i=1,2$. In less technical terms, the inequality states that investments take place only when the aggregated and discounted future returns on capital, reflected in the price of capital, ψ_i,

$$\psi_i(t) = \int_t^{\infty} e^{-(\delta+\rho)(s-t)} q_i(s)\,\mathrm{d}s\,, \tag{14}$$

are sufficient to balance the costs of investments, i.e. $\psi_i=\chi$, where q_i is the immediate capital return for sector i. Equation (14) is a rewriting of the standard dynamic equation for the stock price dynamics, based on the derivative of the Hamiltonian for the capital stock K_i,:

$$\dot{\psi}_i = \rho\psi_i - \partial \boldsymbol{H} / \partial K_i = (\rho+\delta)\psi_i - q_i\,. \tag{15}$$

The value of the immediate capital returns q_i is given by:

$$q_i = \alpha\eta_i\chi K_i^{\alpha-1}(H_iL_i)^{1-\alpha} + \lambda_i + (1-\zeta)\lambda_{-i}\,, \tag{16}$$

where we use subscript "$-i$" when referring to the other sector. After substitution of

$$\lambda_i = (1-\alpha)\eta_i\chi K_i^{\alpha} H_i^{-\alpha} L_i^{1-\alpha}\,, \tag{17}$$

which follows from the first order condition for the labor productivity stock H_i, we arrive at

$$\begin{aligned} q_i &= \alpha\eta_i\chi K_i^{\alpha-1}(H_iL_i)^{1-\alpha} + (1-\alpha)\eta_i\chi K_i^{\alpha} H_i^{-\alpha} L_i^{1-\alpha} + \\ &\quad + (1-\zeta)(1-\alpha)\eta_{-i}\chi K_{-i}^{\alpha} H_{-i}^{-\alpha} L_{-i}^{1-\alpha} \end{aligned}\,. \tag{18}$$

On the right hand side, we find the direct contribution of capital to production as in (2), the indirect contribution through the increase in human knowledge in the own sector, H_i, as represented in (4), and the indirect contribution through the increase in human knowledge in the other sector H_{-i}. Similar to the labor allocation l_1, the returns on capital q_i are homogeneous of degree zero in the total capital stock; q_i is a function of the relative capital stock, which we can write in reduced form as

$$q_1 = G(k_1;\alpha,\zeta,\eta_1,\eta_2)\text{, and } q_2 = G(1-k_1;\alpha,\zeta,\eta_2,\eta_1), \tag{19}$$

for continuous $G(.):(0,1)\rightarrow(0,\infty)$. For the capital stock share converging to zero, $k_1\rightarrow 0$, we have:

$$G(0;\alpha,\zeta,\eta_1,\eta_2) = \alpha\eta_1^{1/\alpha}\eta_2^{(\alpha-1)/\alpha}(1-\zeta)^{(1-\alpha)/\alpha} + (1-\zeta)(1-\alpha)\eta_2 . \tag{20}$$

And for $k_1\rightarrow 1$, we have:

$$G(1;\alpha,\zeta,\eta_1,\eta_2) = \eta_1 . \tag{21}$$

A graphical representation of the possible capital returns q_1 and q_2 as a function of k_1 is given in

Figure 1. This figure assumes that immediate capital returns increase with the capital shares; q_1 is upwards sloping and q_2 is downwards sloping. Numerical calculations for various parameter values shows that indeed, the curves most-often look as presented here. For some parameter values, the immediate return to capital q_1 does not increase monotonically in k_1, but the ratio between q_1 and q_2 is monotonically increasing, which is the important feature used in the arguments below. We also note that, for substantial productivity differences between the two sectors $\eta_1 << \eta_2$, it is possible that one sector is dominant over the other and the figure qualitatively changes, e.g. $q_1 < q_2$ for all capital shares k_1. Here, we will assume sufficient comparability between the two sectors and spill over effects within each sector such that there is a non-trivial capital share k_1 for which $q_1 = q_2$, denoted by point A in the figure, and $q_1 > q_2$ for larger k_1 and $q_1 < q_2$ for smaller k_1.

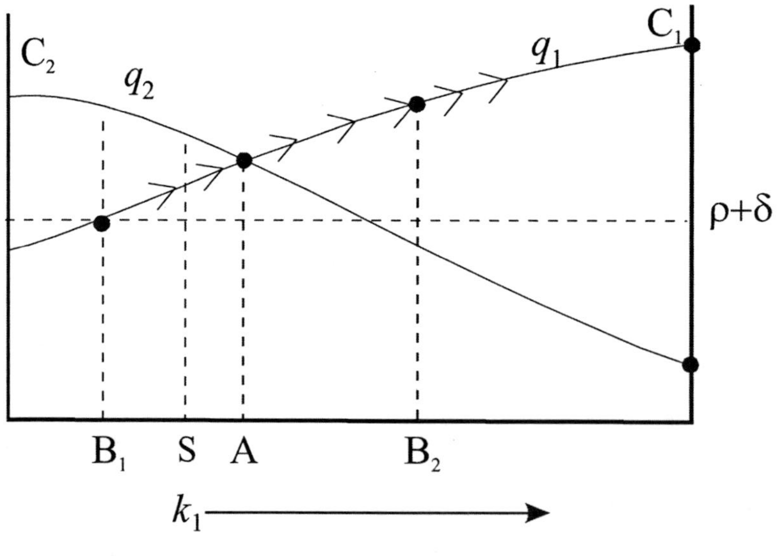

Figure 1. Returns on capital as a function of the capital share k_1

To ensure that a sustained growth path is feasible and optimal, we assume that for all possible initial values of k_1, one of the two sectors has capital returns exceeding the capital depreciation rate δ plus the pure time preference ρ:

$$\min_{k_1}(\max\{G(k_1;\alpha,\zeta,\eta_1,\eta_2),G(1-k_1;\alpha,\zeta,\eta_2,\eta_1)\})>\rho+\delta \tag{22}$$

Under this assumption, there is always one sector for which capital returns can support sustained economic growth, and investments are always positive in at least one sector.

Investments will take place in the sector with the highest present and future returns, captured in the capital price ψ_i (14). The full dynamic analysis of investments is somewhat complicated, and as a starting point, we assume that the initial state of the economy is such that, at $t=0$, capital returns in the first sector are equal to capital returns in the second sector, $q_1(0)=q_2(0)$, for the optimal labor share l_1 given by (10). That is, the economy starts at point A in

Figure 1. Furthermore, we assume that the economy selects the first sector to invest in, $I_1>0$, $I_2=0$, and we ask ourselves whether this selection is consistent with an optimal path. Capital in both sectors depreciates, but only in the first sector the depreciation is counterbalanced by investments, so that the capital stock and the human productivity factor of the first sector increase relative to the levels in the second sector, and consequently, the capital productivity in the first sector relative to the capital productivity in the second sector increases, $q_1>q_2$. Once the economy selects the first sector for investments, the returns to capital in the first sector exceed the returns to capital in the second sector, and since for all future periods we have $q_1>q_2$, for the current decision, $\psi_1>\psi_2$ so that the selection becomes self-enforcing. Investments in the second sector remain zero, and the economy specializes fully in the first sector. A lock-in occurs. In

Figure 1, the initial situation for $t=0$ is represented by point A, the arrows towards point C show the increase in the relative capital stock k_1 as the economy specializes. The economy converges to the steady state C_1 with $k_1=1$, $l_1=1$, $r=\eta_1-\delta$, $g=(\eta_1-\rho-\delta)/\gamma$, $\psi_1=1$, and $\psi_2<1$, where g is the common growth rate for output, investments, and consumption. Growth is positive, $g>0$, because of assumption (22). Similarly, the economy can converge to the steady state C_2 with $k_1=0$, $l_1=0$, $r=\eta_2-\delta$, $g=(\eta_2-\rho-\delta)/\gamma$, $\psi_1<1$, and $\psi_2=1$.

In short, if $q_1(0)=q_2(0)$, then the choice to invest only in the first sector is consistent with the first order optimality conditions. Obviously, if the economy were initially, at period $t=0$, in another state to the right of A in

Figure 1, with $q_1(0)>q_2(0)$, the same investments decisions could be rationalized and the economy would still converge to a full specialization in the first sector.

However, though this may not be obvious, even if initial capital returns in the first sector are below capital returns in the first sector, $q_1(0)<q_2(0)$, a path can exist that satisfies the first order conditions for optimality and in which the economy selects the first sector for specialization. More precisely, there is an interval of initial states $k_1\in(B_1,B_2)$ such that for any initial state within this interval, there exists both a path with full specialization in the first and a path with full specialization in the second sector, both paths being consistent with the first order optimality conditions. Krugman (1991) refers to this interval as the 'overlap'.[10] This

[10] There is no simple analytical formula that determines the levels of B_1 and B_2.

finding, of two different paths that select different steady states to which they converge, is a well-known phenomenon in the literature. An early analysis is by Skiba (1978), who analyzed optimal investments under a convex-concave production function, and proved the existence of two stable steady states and one unstable steady state in-between. In our economy, we have a similar situation, as A represents an unstable steady state (balanced growth path), while C_1 and C_2 represent two stable steady states (balanced growth paths). The unstable balanced growth path A is straightforwardly constructed by taking the relative capital stocks for which $q=q_1(0)=q_2(0)$, and choosing investments as

$$I_i = ((q-\rho)/\gamma + (1-1/\gamma)\delta)K_i. \tag{23}$$

The resulting path has growth rate $g=(q-\rho-\delta)/\gamma>0$ (22). For any initial capital state near the unstable steady state, Skiba showed that two paths exist that satisfy the first order conditions, converging to either one of the two stable steady states. Moreover, he made clear that there is a unique initial state S (known as the Skiba point) near the unstable steady state A that marks the boundary between optimal paths converging to one and to the other stable steady state. Regarding the stability and optimality properties, the situation in our economy is not different. From a welfare point of view, there is a level S for the relative capital stock k_1 to the right of which it is optimal to specialize in the first sector, and to the left of which it is optimal to specialize in the second sector. In the recent growth literature, Benhabib and Perli (1994), Chen and Shimomura (1998), and Ladrón-de-Guevara *et al.* (1999) discuss similar dynamic patterns in relation to the existence of multiple equilibrium paths.

Yet, in our economy, the precise analysis of dynamics is somewhat more complex than suggested above, since we have two state variables K_1 and K_2, and two associated co-state variables ψ_1 and ψ_2. To study in more detail the selection mechanisms in our economy, we will construct a phase diagram in state-co-state space (K_1,K_2,ψ_1,ψ_2). A complete phase diagram for the state-co-state would require an analysis in four dimensions. Fortunately, the analysis of the four-dimensional state-co-state space (K_1,K_2,ψ_1,ψ_2) can be reduced to the two-dimensional state-co-state space (k_1,φ), since, as we have seen above, the labor allocation and capital returns only depend on the relative capital share k_1, and either one of the two capital prices ψ_1 and ψ_2 has value χ, so that

$$\varphi \equiv (\chi+\psi_1-\psi_2)/2\chi \tag{24}$$

defines a one-to-one mapping of the feasible equilibrium values for $(\psi_1,\psi_2)\in[0,\chi]^2$ on $\varphi\in[0,1]$. The following figure pictures the mapping.

The value $\varphi=0$ stands for the situation in which $\psi_1=0$ and $\psi_2=\chi$, only capital for the second sector has a positive value. If $0<\varphi<1/2$, then $0<\psi_1<\chi$ and $\psi_2=\chi$; the capital stock in the first sector has a positive value, but its value is so low that no investments take place, $I_1=0$ (13). The value $\varphi=1/2$ stands for the situation in which $\psi_1=\psi_2=\chi$. It is possible that both sectors have positive investments levels $I_1>0$ and $I_2>0$. If $1/2<\varphi<1$, then $\psi_1=\chi$ and $0<\psi_2<\chi$; the capital stock in the second sector has a positive value, but its value is so low that no investments take place, $I_2=0$ (13). Finally, $\varphi=1$ stands for the situation in which $\psi_1=\chi$ and $\psi_2=0$, only capital for the first sector has a positive value.

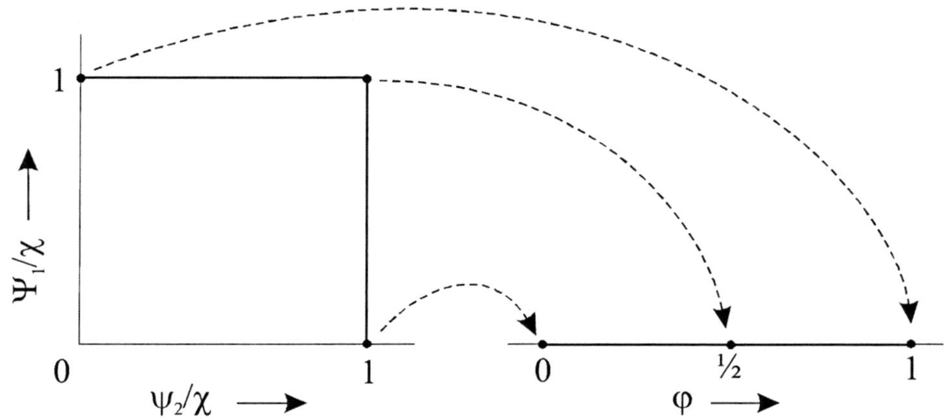

Figure 2. Mapping of $(\psi_1, \psi_2) \in [0, \chi]^2$ on $\varphi \in [0,1]$ as in (24).

Now, we are in the position to study the dynamics in (k_1,φ) space (Figure 3). We follow the common procedure; we first consider the dynamics of k_1, and then we consider the dynamics of φ in (k_1,φ)-space.

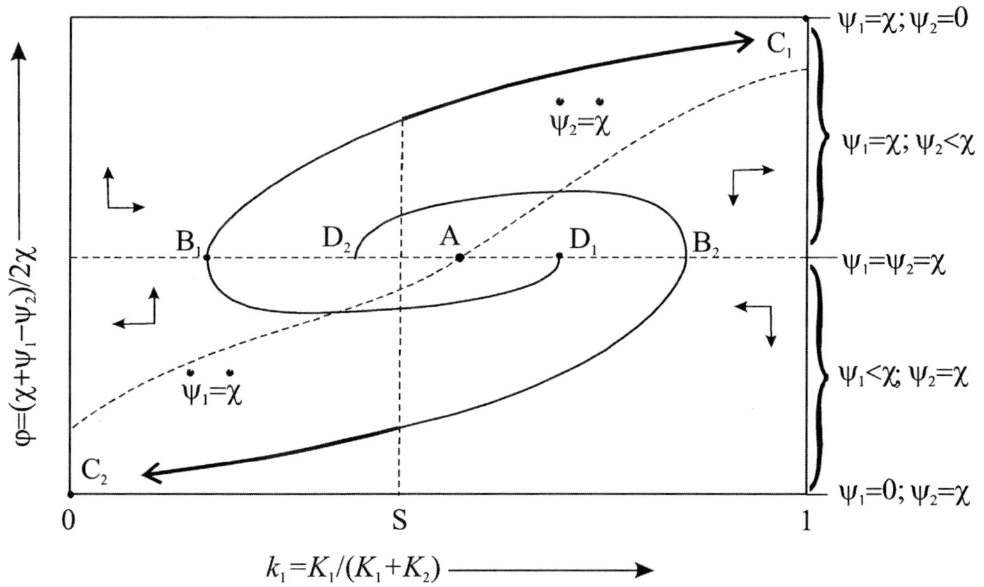

Figure 3. Phase diagram for the capital stock and capital prices

For $0 \le \varphi < 1/2$, we have $0 \le \psi_1 < \chi$ and $\psi_2 = \chi$, and in turn $I_1 = 0$ and $I_2 > 0$ (13). Since both capital stocks have the same depreciation rate δ, investments in the second sector ensure that the share of the second capital stock in the total capital stock will increase, $\dot{k}_1 < 0$. In analogy, for $1/2 < \varphi \le 1$, we have $\psi_1 = 1$ and $0 \le \psi_2 < 1$, and in turn $I_1 > 0$ and $I_2 = 0$ (13), and the share of the first capital stock in the total capital stock will increase, $\dot{k}_1 > 0$. Thus, below the line $\varphi = 1/2$, or $\psi_1 = \psi_2 = \chi$, paths are directed to the left, and above the line, paths are directed to the right:

$$\psi_1 < 1; \psi_2 = 1 \Rightarrow \dot{k}_1 < 0, \text{ and } \psi_1 = 1; \psi_2 < 1 \Rightarrow \dot{k}_1 > 0. \quad (25)$$

The direction of movement for φ is determined by the relative returns on capital q_i when comparing both sectors. For $0 \le \varphi < ½$, ($0 \le \psi_1 < \chi$, $\psi_2 = \chi$) we can immediately deduce $\dot{\psi}_2 = \dot{\chi}$ and thereby, $\dot{\varphi} = 0$ is equivalent to $\dot{\psi}_1 = \psi_1 \dot{\chi} / \chi$. For notational convenience, we define the interest rate as common, $r = \rho - \dot{\chi} / \chi$. Substituting of ψ_i's dynamics in (15), we get

$$q_1 = (r + \delta)\psi_1, \text{ and} \quad (26)$$

$$q_2 = (r + \delta)\psi_2 = (r + \delta)\chi, \quad (27)$$

which, in turn, gives

$$\dot{\varphi} = 0; \varphi \le ½ \Leftrightarrow \psi_1 = \chi\, q_1/q_2; \psi_2 = \chi, \quad (28)$$

where we can rewrite the right-hand-side in terms of φ as follows: $\varphi = (q_1/2q_2)$. Equivalently, we have

$$\dot{\varphi} = 0; ½ \le \varphi \Leftrightarrow \psi_1 = \chi; \psi_2 = \chi\, q_2/q_1. \quad (29)$$

or in terms of φ: $\varphi = 1 - (q_2/2q_1)$. Now, on the basis of the capital returns drawn in Figure 1, we can draw the line $\dot{\varphi} = 0$ in Figure 3 as a function of the capital share in the first sector k_1. The line runs from just above the left-lower corner upwards to the point A, where $q_1 = q_2$, $\psi_1 = \psi_2 = \chi$, and $\varphi = ½$, further upwards to just below the right upper corner.

The dynamics in state-co-state of paths satisfying the first order conditions are drawn in the figure. When a path satisfying the first order conditions crosses the line $\dot{\varphi} = 0$, its motion is horizontal, and when it crosses the line $\varphi = ½$, its motion is vertical, though the latter feature is not obvious. We have to exclude the possibility of a more complicated behavior when the line hits the horizontal line $\varphi = ½$. That is, we have non-singular time interval for which $\psi_1 = \psi_2 = \chi$, $I_1 > 0$, $I_2 > 0$. From equation (15), we have

$$\psi_1 = \psi_2 = \chi \Rightarrow \dot{\psi}_1 - \dot{\psi}_2 = q_2 - q_1. \quad (30)$$

Thus, when $\varphi = ½$, we can only have an interval of positive investments in both sectors when $\dot{\varphi} = 0$, and this requires that the immediate returns in both sectors, q_i, are equal. Such is only the case at point A. Indeed, immediately above equation (23), we constructed a steady state at point A. In all other cases, the path crosses the line $\varphi = ½$.

At first instance, it may seem that the phase diagram does not exclude paths that hit the right or left axis, $k_1 = 0$ or $k_1 = 1$, before moving to the corner. We can argue, however, that such paths do not exist. If the economy fully specializes in, say, the second sector, and no investments take place in the first sector, then the capital stock level in the first sector will decrease exponentially due to depreciation, but will remain positive. This rules out paths that touch the boundaries $k_1 = 0$ or $k_1 = 1$, before converging to the corner. Similarly, we can exclude paths that hit the lower and upper boundaries set by $\varphi = 0$ and $\varphi = 1$. Unless the capital stock in sector i is zero, its value will be strictly positive, and no path will hit the top or floor of the diagram. Accordingly, optimal paths in the lower part of the diagram (below $\dot{\varphi} = 0$ and below $\varphi = ½$), must converge to the left-lower corner or leave the area by crossing the line $\dot{\varphi} = 0$. Similarly, optimal paths in the upper part of the diagram (above $\dot{\varphi} = 0$ and above $\varphi = ½$) must converge to the right-upper corner or leave the area by crossing the line $\dot{\varphi} = 0$.[11]

To conclude this section, we comment on the policies required to ensure the decentralized economy selects an optimal path. If, within each sector, the firms are small, they will neglect the spillover effects of their investments on the productivity in other firms, and investments in the competitive equilibrium will fall short of the social optimum. It is therefore necessary for the social planner to have instruments available such as subsidies that internalize the investment spillovers. Similar to the one-sector AK-model, in our economy, the social planner needs to ensure that the level of investments match their social optimum. In the model with two sectors, however, the social planner also needs to guide the economy with respect to the distribution of investments over both sectors, that is, the social planner has to determine the direction of economic growth and it has to ensure that the individual firms select the proper sector (technology) to invest in.

For all initial states between B_1 and B_2, there are two paths that satisfy the first order optimality conditions, one converging to C_1, and the other converging to C_2, respectively. For given initial state, the market is indeterminate as to the direction of economic growth. Yet the Skiba point S marks a unique state to the left of which it is optimal to select the second sector, and to the right of which it is optimal to select the first sector for specialisation. The social planner has to ensure that the economy selects the proper path for its development (Bold in

Figure 3). As Krugman (1991) has pointed out, when an ambiguity persists for the path the economy will follow, the planner should create convergent expectations around aggregate investments in specific technologies. The social planner has to communicate that she will support the preferred investment path, and that, if necessary, she will take measures to lock out the other possible future investment path (similar to the policy in Kremer and Morcom 2000). Now we are ready to continue with the second step of our analysis, i.e. to introduce, next to the investment externality and the 'choice of technology' externality, a third, environmental, externality in our model.

Environmental Constraints and a Transition Policy

After the extensive analysis of the general dynamics, we are now in the position to study in a relatively straightforward manner the model's behavior under environmental constraints. Environmental concerns may arise if the economy has specialized in a sector (technology) that turns out to be highly polluting or relatively resource intensive. We can think of the fossil fuel technologies that are associated with greenhouse gas emissions. So-called backstop technologies with zero emissions may provide an alternative energy supply, but these alternative technologies have lower immediate capital returns and will need substantial initial investments to become competitive. While a technology transition may be beneficial from an

[11] We also notice that the phase diagram does not rule out spiral paths around the unstable steady state A that converge to a limit cycle. However, these paths are not relevant, since a cycling between the two sectors will cause welfare losses as it does not fully profit from the increasing returns to scale. The optimal path must select immediately one sector for specialisation.

environmental point of view, in an economic sense, the past selection of the fossil-fuel technologies can be irreversible; the economy is locked in.

In our model, let us assume that the economy has specialized in the first sector and has reached the balanced growth path C_1. Growth has continued for some time, but at some time, detrimental effects of resource use, necessary for the production in the first sector, become significant. We can think of resources becoming scarce, manifested through increasing resource extraction costs, or, alternatively, we can think of resource use causing pollution that decreases the amenity values of the environment. Furthermore, we assume that the second sector provides an alternative 'green' growth path, in the sense that resource use will pose no significant limit to its expansion. This linkage is captured through the identity $R=Y_1$. Thus, if the economy succeeds in making a successful transition, the economy could continue on an undisturbed sustained growth path.

While the economy grows and maintains its selection of the first sector, the environmental externality will receive a (Pigouvian) shadow price, internalized through a tax τ levied on the output of the first sector. It follows immediately from the first order conditions for R and C that $\tau=\nu U'(.)=\nu\chi>0$. Taking the first order conditions for Y_1, we find that the net output price for goods produced in the first sector is reduced by factor $(1-\tau)$. In turn, labor productivity and capital returns in the first sector decrease and net capital investments decrease.

The question addressed in this section is: which policy is required to set in motion the transition towards the 'clean' sector (technology). We take as a starting point the situation where the environmental externality is fully internalized. We can distinguish three possibilities. First, immediate capital returns in the second sector exceed immediate capital returns in the first sector, and a transition begins without the need for any further policy (Figure 4). Second, it is possible that the immediate capital returns in the first sector decrease, but still exceed the capital returns in the second sector for the actual situation, $q_1>q_2$, which is at the right side of

Figure 5. Nonetheless, a transition becomes attainable, as there are two paths possible, one staying in the current steady state with $\psi_1>\psi_2$, the other moving to the clean sector with $\psi_1<\psi_2$, though this change in selection of the steady state needs additional policy measures to be set in motion. The third possibility is that, though the capital productivity in the second sector improves relative to the capital productivity in the first sector, this does not warrant a transition. We now elaborate on the first two cases.

Given output taxes τ for the first sector, returns to labor decrease by factor $(1-\tau)$ and the labor distribution (10) changes into:

$$l_1 = 1/(1+\frac{\eta_2^{1/\alpha}K_2H_2^{(1-\alpha)/\alpha}}{(1-\tau)^{1/\alpha}\eta_1^{1/\alpha}K_1H_1^{(1-\alpha)/\alpha}}). \qquad (31)$$

Similarly, the capital returns for the capital stock in the first sector q_1 decrease by factor $(1-\tau)$ inasmuch as the direct and indirect contribution to the output of the first sector is concerned (18):

$$\begin{aligned} q_i = (1-\tau)\alpha\eta_i K_i^{\alpha-1}(H_iL_i)^{1-\alpha} + ((1-\tau)1-\alpha)\eta_i K_i^{\alpha}H_i^{-\alpha}L_i^{1-\alpha} \\ + (1-\zeta)(1-\alpha)\eta_{-i}K_{-i}^{\alpha}H_{-i}^{-\alpha}L_{-i}^{1-\alpha}. \end{aligned} \qquad (32)$$

We notice that since the Pigouvian tax decreases capital returns in the first sector, which is dominant, it also decreases the growth rate of the economy. In reduced form, we may write

$$q_1 = \tilde{G}(k_1;\alpha,\zeta,\eta_1,\eta_2,\tau,0)\text{, and } q_2 = \tilde{G}(1-k_1;\alpha,\zeta,\eta_2,\eta_1,0,\tau), \tag{33}$$

where we added tax parameters for both sectors to the function $G(.)$. Under full specialization, $k_1=1$, the capital returns become

$$q_1 = \tilde{G}(1;\alpha,\zeta,\eta_1,\eta_2,\tau,0) = (1-\tau)\eta_1\text{, and} \tag{34}$$

$$\begin{aligned} q_2 &= \tilde{G}(0;\alpha,\zeta,\eta_2,\eta_1,0,\tau) = \\ &= \alpha\eta_2^{1/\alpha}\eta_1^{(1-\alpha)/\alpha}(1-\zeta)^{(1-\alpha)/\alpha} + (1-\tau)(1-\zeta)(1-\alpha)\eta_1 \end{aligned}. \tag{35}$$

While the output tax for the first sector decreases the returns on labor and capital within this sector, it relatively raises the returns on labor and capital in the second sector. When the Pigouvian tax increases from zero to a positive value, the unstable steady state A in

Figure 1 for which $q_1=q_2$, the Skiba point S, and the transition points B_1 and B_2 shift to the right. If taxes are such that the immediate capital returns in the first sector drop below the immediate returns in the second sector, $q_1<q_2$, for all k_1. The total returns to investments will then also satisfy $\psi_1<\psi_2$ and it becomes optimal for every single firm to shift investments to the second sector, and the transition takes off. (Figure 4). In this case, it suffices for the social planner to levy the Pigouvian tax τ, since it ensures that the optimal path, which defines a transition, is the only path consistent with the first order conditions.

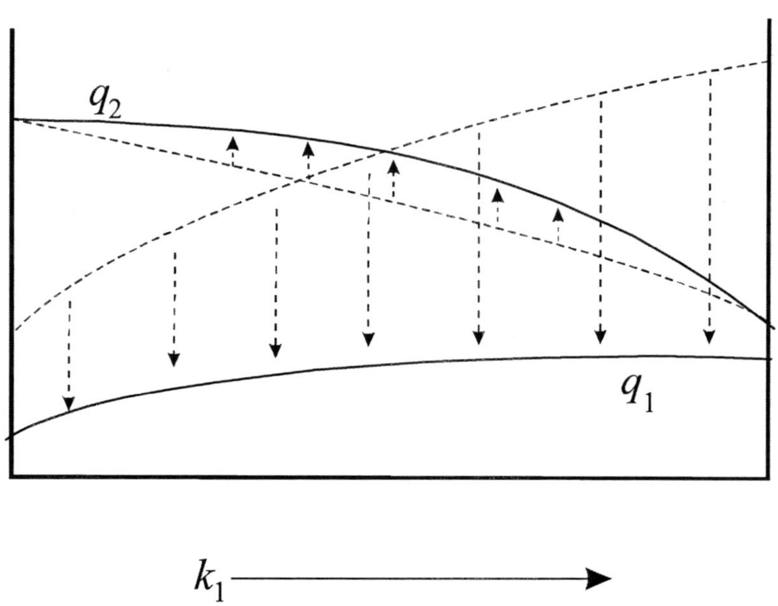

Figure 4. Immediate capital returns lowered by a resource tax τ; induced transition
In the second case, the Pigouvian tax is insufficient to raise the returns to capital in the second sector above the returns in the first sector (

Figure 5), given the historic full specialization in the first sector. Yet, a transition towards the second sector may be optimal when taking into account future capital returns. In the actual situation, which is at the right side of

Figure 5, $q_1>q_2$. Nonetheless, a transition becomes attainable, as there are two paths possible, one staying with the 'dirty' sector, and for this path, $\psi_1(0)>\psi_2(0)$, the other moving to the clean sector supported by $\psi_1(0)<\psi_2(0)$. Under these circumstances, the social planner has to lock out the first sector and to guide the economy to ensure that it selects the second sector for investments. If the planner does not develop an explicit transition policy, for every individual firm, continued investments in the first sector are still consistent with profit maximization. Though a transition is also consistent with the first order conditions, its initiation requires that the individual agents believe it will take place. Public intervention is required to initiate the transition, for example by eliminating the current balanced growth path, as in Kremer and Morcom (2000). An effective policy would be if the planner announces a future environmental levy above the Pigouvian level in case the transition does not take place. The announcement will force all individual firms to move their investments to the second sector, forming a coherent strategy. Notably, the threat of increased environmental levies need not be implemented, as the mere announcement suffices to enforce the transition to be set in motion. Finally, it should be noted that in this case a pure environmental policy, which fully internalizes the environmental externality, does not suffice to reach the welfare optimum. In fact we are back in the basic model where next to an internalization of the investment externality the government has to guide the economy to select the optimal technology.

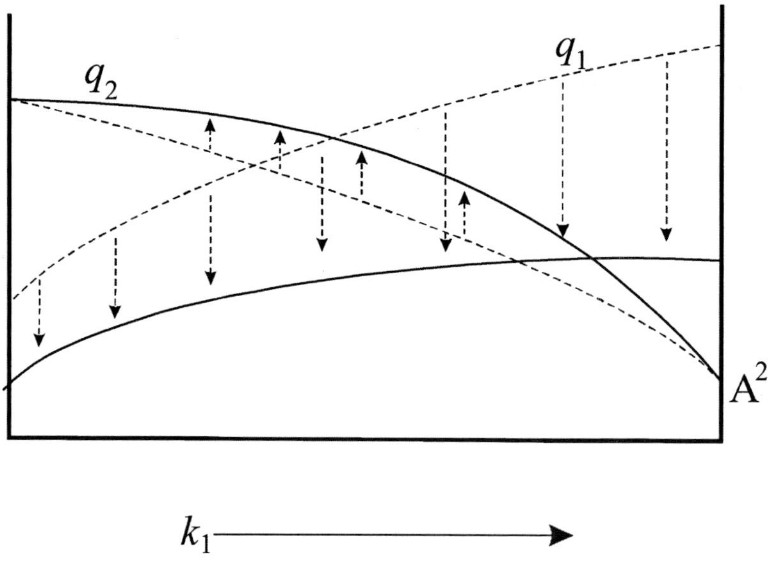

Figure 5. Immediate capital returns lowered by a resource tax τ; no induced transition

For small environmental externalities, we end up in the third case, in which the resource externality is insufficient to justify a transition towards the alternative technology. The net present value of the transition costs exceeds the net present value of environmental damages, and there is no need for the government to guide the economy starting a transition. Still the intervention of the government is needed to internalize the capital spill-overs as well as the environmental externalities as such.

CONCLUSION

In this paper we have constructed a model that combines elements of endogenous growth theory with the concept of lock-in that has its roots in the evolutionary economics literature. We described an endogenous growth model with two sectors (technologies) that both have strong internal spillovers. In this economy, there exist multiple growth paths satisfying the first order conditions. More specifically, the economy can choose to specialize in either one of the two sectors. Current investments determine the relative growth of both sectors, and thereby the selection of the growth path, and in turn, current investments are determined by the immediate and expected capital returns in both sectors. Since future capital returns are positively related to present investments, there is a positive feedback, and the selection of one or another sector (technology) for investments is ambiguous, but once the selection is made, it is self-enhancing.

Both history and expectations play a role in the selection of equilibrium. In the case that immediate capital productivity does not differ too much between the two sectors, the economy can specialize in either of the sectors. It is quite possible that the economy specializes in the sector that has the lowest immediate capital returns. To ensure the selection of the socially optimal path, the social planner has to create coherent expectations about the direction of economic growth, as already pointed out by Krugman (1991).

If the economy has specialized in a sector that rests heavily on resource use, or that causes environmental pollution, this may constrain future growth if there is a limited resource supply or a limited pollution absorption capacity. If immediate capital returns do not differ too much between the 'clean' and 'dirty' sector, the announcement of environmental policies supporting a transition to the 'clean' sector suffices to set in motion the transition, without the need for actual environmental regulations to take place. In the case of a substantial advantage of the 'dirty' sector, in terms of immediate capital returns, a transition may need the support of environmental levies or subsidies. In all cases there is a role for the government to ensure the internalization of the investment spill-overs as well as of the environmental externalities.

The implication of our analysis for environmental policy is twofold. First, it makes clear that the impact of environmental levies and subsidies on economic production is not restricted to marginal changes in production inputs and outputs. Environmental regulations may bring about the development of specific technologies that cause a substantial shift in the production input-output matrix. Second, the analysis stresses the importance of a clear and reliable policy regarding the future direction of economic growth. The government can guide technology dynamics by demonstrating that continued pollution would be responded to by stringent environmental policies. The certainty of a 'green' future stimulates individuals to search for technological innovation in this direction, thereby reducing the need for actual stringent environmental regulations. When applied to the issue of climate change, it follows that a clear policy statement on future emission reductions will lessen the need for high-level carbon dioxide taxes needed to bring these reductions about.

REFERENCES

Aghion P. and P. Howitt, 1998, *Endogenous growth theory* (MIT Press, Cambridge, Massachusetts).

Arthur,W.B. 1989, Competing Technologies, Increasing Returns, and Lock-in by Historical Events., *The Economic Journal* 99, 116-131.

Askenazy,P. and C.Le Van. 1999, A Model of Optimal Growth Strategy, *Journal of Economic Theory* 85, 24-51.

Atkinson,A.B. and J.E.Stiglitz. 1969, A New View of Technological Change, *The Economic Journal* 79, 573-578.

Barro R.J. and X. Sala-i-Martin, 1995, *Economic growth*, MIT Press, Cambridge, Massachusetts.

Benhabib J. and R. Perli, 1994, Uniqueness and indeterminacy: on the dynamics of endogenous growth, *Journal of Economic Theory* 63, 113-142.

Bovenberg A.L. and S.A. Smulders, 1995, Environmental quality and pollution-augmenting technological change in a two-sector endogenous growth model, *Journal of Public Economics* 57, 369-391.

Chakravorty U., J. Roumasset, and K. Tse, 1997, Endogenous substitution among energy resources and global warming, *Journal of Political Economy* 105, 1201-1234.

Chen,B.L. and K.Shimomura. 1998, Self-fulfilling Expectations and Economic Growth: a model of technology adoption and industrialization, *International Economic Review* 39, 151-170.

Ciccone,A. and K.Matsuyama. 1999, Efficiency and Equilibrium with Dynamic Increasing Aggregate Returns Due to Demand Complementarities, *Econometrica* 67, 499-525.

Cowan,R. and S.Hulten. 1996, Esacaping Lock-In: The Case of the Electric Vehicle, *Technological Forecasting and Social change* 53, 61-79.

Dosi G., 1982, Technological Paradigms and Technological Trajectories, *Research Policy* 11, 147-162.

Ethier, W., 1982, Decreasing Costs in International Trade and Frank Graham' Argument for Protection, *Econometrica*, 50, 1243 – 1268.

Freeman,C. 1994, The Economics of Technical Change, Cambridge *Journal of Economics* 18, 463-514.

Greiner A. and W. Semmler, 1996, Multiple steady states, indeterminacy, and cycles in a basic model of endogenous growth, *Journal of Economics* 63, 79-99.

Hofkes M.W., 1996, Modelling sustainable development: an economy-ecology integrated model, *Economic Modelling* 13, 333-353.

Islas,J. 1997, Getting round the lock-in in electricity generating systems: the example of the gas turbine, *Research Policy* 26, 49-66.

Jones L.E. and R.E. Manuelli, 1997, Endogenous growth theory: An introduction, *Journal of Economic Dynamics and Control* 21, 1-22.

Kaldor, N., 1961, Capital Accumulation and Economic Growth, in: Lutz & Hague (eds.), *The Theory of Capital*, St. Martin's Press New York, 177 – 222.

Kremer,M. and C.Morcom. 2000, Elephants, *American Economic Review* 90, 212-234.

Krugman, P., 1981, Trade, Accumulation and Uneven Development, *Journal of Development Economics*, 8, 149 – 161.

Krugman, P., 1987, The Narrow Moving Band, the Dutch Disease, and the Competitive Consequences of Mrs. Thatcher: Notes on Trade in the Presence of Dynamic Economies of Scale, *Journal of Development Economics,* 27, 41 – 55.

Krugman,P., 1991, History versus Expectations, *Quarterly Journal of Economics* 106, 651-667.

Ladrón-de-Guevara,A., S.Ortigueira, and M.S.Santos. 1999, A Two-Sector Model of Endogenous Growth with Leisure, *Review of Economic Studies* 66, 609-631.

Mäler,K.-G., 2000, Development, Ecological Resources and Their Management: a study of complex dynamic systems, *European Economic Review* 44, 645-665.

Nelson, R.R. and Winter, S.: *An Evolutionary Theory of Economic Change.* Harvard University Press, Cambridge, MA, 1982.

Rebelo,S. 1991, Long-Run Policy Analysis and Long-Run Growth, *Journal of Political Economy* 99, 500-521.

Romer,P.M. 1990, Endogenous Technological Change, *Journal of Political Economy* 98, S71-S102.

Romer P., 1986, Increasing returns and long-run growth, *Journal of Political Economy*, 94, 1002-1037.

Skiba A.K., 1978, Optimal growth with a convex-concave production function, *Econometrica* **46**: 527-539.

Smulders S.A., 1995, Entropy, environment, and endogenous economic growth, *International tax and public finance* 2, 319-340.

Solow,R.M. 1956, A Contribution to the Theory of Economic Growth, *Quarterly Journal of Economics* 70, 65-94.

Street,P. and I.Miles, 1996, Transition to Alternative Energy Supply Technologies: the case of windpower, *Energy Policy* 24, 413-425.

Swan, T.W., 1956, Economic growth and capital accumulation, *Economic Record*, 32: 334-361.

Tahvonen O. and S.Salo, 2001. Economic growth and transitions between renewable and nonrenewable energy resources, *European Economic Review* **45**: 1379-1398.

Unruh,G.C. 2000, Understanding carbon lock-in, *Energy Policy* 28, 817-830.

Wright,G. 1997, Towards a more Historical Approach to Technological Change, *The Economic Journal* 107, 1560-1566.

Zhang,J. 1998, Global Behaviour of a System with Imperfect Private-Public Substitutability, *Journal of Public Economics* 67, 437-454.

Zhang,J. 2000, Public Services, Increasing Returns, and Equilibrium Dynamics, *Journal of Economic Dynamics and Control* 24, 227-246.

In: Economic Growth Issues
Editor: L. A. Finley, pp. 73-104
ISBN 1-59454-555-3

Chapter 4

A MODEL OF STATE INFRASTRUCTURE WITH DECENTRALIZED PUBLIC AGENTS: THEORY AND EVIDENCE

Raul A. Barreto[1, 2]
Department of Economics, University of Adelaide, Adelaide,
South Australia, 5005, Australia

ABSTRACT

The imperative of the state, irrespective of its organization, is to provide law and order, contract enforcement, and property rights. The government provides the foundation for markets to function and for society to prosper. A common thread in any government is that, for a given society, the state holds a monopoly over most of its services. Although the state may choose not to exploit this market power, the public agents that represent the state within the aggregate production process, necessarily will.

The following paper presents a macroeconomic framework that explicitly considers the local monopoly power of public agents. In the context of a representative agent model, I consider a private sector production function versus a public sector production function in which both sectors compete over labor and capital. Estimates are made of the productivity of private versus public capital, of private versus public labor, and of public infrastructure within the private sector production function. The theoretical implications of decentralized public agents are then analyzed within an endogenous growth framework.

The results suggest that the elasticity of public infrastructure is significantly lower than previous estimates. They also confirm that the elasticity of private infrastructure is country specific. The theoretical results suggest that decentralization of public agents which, intuitively is greater in less developed countries than industrialized ones, is associated with steeper growth paths that lead to lower steady state capital labor ratios

---

[1] The author is grateful to Patricia Sourdin for research assistance, the University of Adelaide, School of Economics for invaluable discussion, and The Australian Research Council for financial support.
[2] Tel: +61-8-8303-5757. Fax: +61-8-8223-1460. e-mail: raul.barreto@adelaide.edu.au

and per capita consumption levels. This implies that shocks to less developed countries have more dramatic effects but shorter life spans than shocks to industrialized countries, or more simply, business cycles in developing countries are shorter but more volatile.
"Sure there are dishonest men in local government. But there are dishonest men in national government too." - Richard M. Nixon [1913-1994]

Keywords: Decentralization, Infrastructure, Aggregate productivity, Growth

INTRODUCTION

The imperative of the state, irrespective of its organization, is to provide law and order, contract enforcement, and property rights. All of the goods and services provided by government, from alleviation of market failures to the enforcement of standards, fall into these three broads categories. The government provides the foundation for markets to function and for society to prosper. Hence, irrespective of type, whether monarchy, dictatorship, communism, or democracy, the role of the state, at its most fundamental level, is essentially the same. A common thread in any government is that, for a given society, the state holds a monopoly over its services. The fact that there is no competition in the provision of most state services breeds its own type of inefficiency that in most societies is typically accepted, if not actually expected, by the private sector. The following paper considers the broad implications of the state's monopoly over its services on growth and productivity.

Although the government is generally the sole provider of its services, it does not behave like a traditional monopolist. The goods and services provided by the public sector are various and not always clearly defined. Furthermore, the ability of the government to centrally coordinate its services breaks down as one moves from mandate to actual provision.

The central theme in this paper is that the government actually provides its services through a network of decentralized self-seeking agents. Government employees, i.e. public agents, each have a degree of power over some aspect of what the state provides. As a result, the provision of public services at the most basic level, is carried out by individuals who find themselves in positions of power and, bowing to incentives, consequently maximize their respective welfare functions.

An important distinction is between publicly produced goods and pure public goods.[3] I assume that pure public goods are a subset of publicly produced goods. Non-rival and non-exclusive goods production falls into the state's categorical role of property rights delimitation. In fact, many publicly produced services such as law and order as well as contract enforcement, are to a large degree quite rival and exclusive. Even infrastructure, such as transportation and communication, is not really a pure public goods due to being subject to user fees. Therefore, the Samuelson [1954] condition over optimal provision of pure public goods is limited to a subset and does not adequately describe the state's broader control over law and order, property rights, and contract enforcement.

There are numerous examples within society of public services that are provided by welfare maximizing decentralized agents as described above. One may enter the department of motor vehicles to find ten workers each behind their respective windows yet only one

[3] Throughout the paper, I use a rather loose definition of public goods. By public goods, I really mean publicly provided goods, services, and infrastructure.

window is actually open. Or consider the police officer who exercises his prerogative to stop speeders whenever he is so inclined. And when he does actually stop the speeder, he may or may not issue a ticket depending upon his mood, his predispositions, and or the speeder's attributes. In other words, that police officer actually dispenses law and order as he sees fit, not necessarily as the legal code prescribes. Lastly, consider the judiciary system in any economy. A judge is supposed to be impartial but they not always are. Furthermore, the degree of sophistication required to invoke the judiciary system coupled with a high opportunity cost to individual firms and or individuals can limit access to elites. In most cases, public services are dispensed by agents, which are paid competitive wages, yet may also realize additional benefits to public employment. These benefits, I argue, are significant and stem from the market power of the state that is ultimately exercised by its agents.

There is a rich literature on decentralization of governance, most often referred to as "fiscal federalism." In general, the concern is the manner in which public goods are disseminated across society and the efficiency aspects of authority in the hands of local government versus central government. Most authors analyze fiscal federalism as an alternative mechanism to provide efficient provision of public goods and the preservation of market incentives.[4] A review of the issues with particular regard to developing countries appears in Bardham [2002].

The contribution of this paper, distinct from previous work, is my regard for the representative government agent, who exists irrespective of structural organization of the state, in the context of a generalized macroeconomic model. I liken the representative public agent to a local monopolist who is able to exploit her market power due to a lack of proper accountability. Her incentives exist irrespective of the degree of fiscal federalism within her society. Although several authors have explored aspects of accountability and fiscal federalism,[5] none have considered the more general macroeconomic implications of decentralization of public authority amongst the agents of the government.

The implications of the principal agent problem that stems from decentralized control over government services by agents are great. Policy makers, especially those in developing countries, are keenly aware their importance. The impact of decentralization on development is most readily apparent in large developing countries such as Brazil, India, Indonesia, and China. In such places, neither the central nor the local government is capable of exercising the optimal degree of control over its representatives. Public agents may act unilaterally or could be subject to capture by elites, as suggested by Bardhan and Mooherjee [2001]. Although specific reasons for this lack of control vary from country to country, some generalizations may be made. Government agents expect to personally profit from their positions in the public sector. It is one of the main incentives to seek public employment. Furthermore, the general population may expect a certain degree of dishonesty or corruption of public servants. In many places, there exist long and rich histories of public sector corruption. Its existence is treated as a fact of life that all must be resigned to endure.[6]

---

[4] For example, see Qian and Weingast [1997]. Fiscal federalism in the United States is considered in the four papers that comprise the "Symposium on Fiscal Federalism" which appears in the JEL, Autumn 1997.

[5] Most notably Seabright [1996] discusses political accountability in a theoretical model with central and locally elected officials competing over control rights. Other papers addressing different dimensions of this principal-agent problem include Besley and Case [1995], Beasley and Coate [1999] and Tommasi and Weinschelbaum [1999].

[6] For example, in the Middle East, payment of *Baksheesh* is part of the expected protocol when dealing with a public official. Similarly in Paraguay, where cronyism and corruption were institutionalised during a 35

Every single element that makes up the macroeconomy, irrespective of its role, may be classified as either a public or a private asset. This important accounting fact allows us to classify each and every good or service available to society by its state of nature. Furthermore, the accounting constraint that governs both labor and capital justifies the explicit consideration of an aggregate private sector production function versus an aggregate public sector production function.

The difference in market organization between the public and private sectors combined with the binding accounting constraint over all resources are of the utmost importance to understanding the equilibrium price and quantity of labor, capital, public goods and private goods. The overwhelming majority of research on the role of public infrastructure within an aggregate production function framework assumes that public capital is an unpaid input to production. Most authors assume that public capital is trivially produced from tax revenue. This wholly inadequate convention conveniently sidesteps the issue of a public sector production function as well as any issues relating to the resource accounting constraint while maintaining the real cost, in taxes, of public goods and services. Furthermore, the trivializing assumption that $G = \tau Y$ does not account for the significant labor and capital inputs in public sector production.

This paper presents an alternative methodology to modeling the state's role as the producer of public infrastructure within the context of an aggregate production function that explicitly considers the government's natural monopoly as well as the general equilibrium constraint on resources. The basic framework is well documented in both the theoretical and applied literatures on public capital. One of the simplest treatments of public goods from growth theory is Barro [1990].[7] Papers that estimate the return to public infrastructure within an aggregate production function generally follow Aschauer [1989,1990].[8] A common assumption adopted to capture non-exclusivity, which is shared by all of the theoretical models that underlie this research, is that public capital is an unpaid input within the production process. In other words, the cost function faced by firms resembles the following, $Y(K,L,G) = P_G G + wL + rK = wL + rK$ where $P_G = 0$ and all public services, *G*, are paid for by tax revenues. This framework fails to account for either the inherent difference in market structure between the public sector and the private sector or the public-private accounting constraint over resources.

I consider an aggregate production function where public infrastructure is a productive input along with private capital and labor. Although subsidized by tax revenues, public goods must still be explicitly paid for via user fees,[9] such that the demand for public goods is

---

dictatorship, private citizens expect to pay speed money, known there as *coima*, for anything from phone service to passports. Examples in the literature that document this phenomenon include Geddes and Neto [1992], Barreto [1996], and Crook and Manor [1998].

7 Other papers that explicitly consider infrastructure in the context of an endogenous growth model include Barreto [2000], Dasgupta [1999], Turnofsky [1996], and Futagami, Morita, & Shibata [1995].

8 Other notable papers that estimate the positive impact of public capital include Morrison and Schwartz [1996], Nadiri and Mamuneas [1994], Berndt and Hansson [1992], Lynde and Richmond [1992], and Munnell [1990]. However, papers that find a negligible impact of public capital include Holtz-Eakin [1994], Garcia-Mila and McGuire [1992], and Hulten and Schwab [1984, 1991].

9 User fees for public services are described analytically by Samuelson [1954]. More recent examples include Barreto [2000] in the context of an endogenous growth model with corruption and Bardhan and Mookherjee [2001] in the context of fiscal federalism within developing countries.

downward sloping.[10] But unlike capital and labor, which by assumption, are provided competitively, government services are sold at an endogenously determined premium. The premium is a function of the tax rate, the opportunity cost to the public agent, which in this case is the competitive wage, and the marginal product of public infrastructure.

Previous econometric studies generally regress output on total capital, total labor, and total government to yield a higher than expected estimates of public infrastructure productivity. By not explicitly considering the accounting constraint, the relative size of government is smaller and its estimated productivity is consequently higher.[11]

The paper is organized as follows. Section 2 describes the theoretical framework that describes the allocation of labor and capital across the public and private sectors. The resulting allocations determine the price and quantity of provision of public goods. Section 3 estimates the productivity of capital, labor, and public infrastructure within the context of the allocative framework. The results, exclusive to OECD countries, suggest the relatively high productivity of public labor and of private capital. Section 4 considers the model in the purely theoretical context of endogenous growth. The decentralized agent model predicts that the steady state effective capital-labor ratio is much greater than traditional growth models that account for a public sector might predict. Section 5 presents some concluding remarks.

THE MODEL

I consider an aggregate production function model where the state is an intermediate factor of production which not only requires real resources but is also administered by self-seeking, albeit decentralized, public agents. The representative firm pays user fees in addition to income taxes to the government in return for service. The user fee, i.e. the price of government services, has a limit of zero as the tax rate approaches its optimum. In other words, a society with perfect information could set taxes exactly right such that the user fee for public goods is truly zero[12] and consequently the model collapses to the more traditional treatment of public goods within the private production process. In practice therefore, the second best outcome implies the user fees for public goods must be positive.

As long as user fees are positive, the representative private agent faces a downward sloping demand for public goods. The demand for a service is unaffected by the good's nature in terms of its non-rivalry. On the other hand, the quantity demanded certainly changes in reaction to the supply of the good, which of course is a function of the good's nature and the tax rate. Previous work in the corruption literature that assumes a downward sloping demand for public goods includes Schliefer and Vishny [1990], Barreto [2000], and Bardhan and Mookherjee [2001].

[10] Dasgupta [1999] considers non-rival infrastructure inputs that are also purchased by the private sector. Similar to the approach taken here, the price of infrastructure is determined by equating the supply by the government to the demand by the private sector.

[11] Estimates vary widely from very high to low to insignificant. Aschauer [1989, 1990] estimates values for β from .38 to .56. Subsequent literature pushed this estimate down to something closer to .30. The lowest estimate belong to Eberts [1990], who found β to be .03.

[12] This is the market solution to the principal agent problem between agents. As P_G approaches zero, so do the monopoly rents available to the public agent.

In a perfect world, the selfless government employs labor and capital at their competitive rates as well as collects taxes in order to provide society with its services as efficiently as possible. Optimal provision of any normal good, such as G, from the theoretical point of view, is equivalent to the perfectly competitive equilibrium. We may therefore consider a government that employs resources to produce an intermediate good where deviation from the perfect competition benchmark represents allocative inefficiency.

Irrespective of whether one believes in the validity of the aggregate production function, it has several unequivocally useful applications.[13] Modern macroeconomic growth theory, on the other hand, is largely based the use of aggregate production functions that are conceptually derived from microeconomic foundations. Theoretical research that follows Ramsey [1928], Cass [1965], Koopmans [1965] and later Lucas [1988], implicitly adopts Samuelson's [1962] view that the aggregate production function is a useful parable to illustrate important facets about the production process and the consequent growth of output per capita. I adopt this latter view. Although I estimate the model given its aggregate production function framework, I make no claim about the models validity for estimation purposes.[14]

I consider the two sectors, public and private, separately. Given the non-trivial accounting constraint, the two sectors compete over both labor and capital. The inherent difference in market structures between sectors justifies the explicit consideration of the equilibrium wage and rental rate as the result of competition between the two separate aggregate production processes. Therefore, the model may be expressed generally as follows.

$$Y = F\left(K_Y, L_Y, G\right) \text{ and } G = H\left(K_G, L_G, \tau\right)$$

subject to

$$\overline{K} = K_Y + K_G \text{ and } \overline{L} = L_Y + L_G$$

Suppose that the public production function, which requires both capital and labor, produces public infrastructure. The private production function, which requires capital, labor, and public infrastructure, produces consumable goods on which all agents within society, public and private, ultimately depend. The privately employed representative laborer is paid his marginal product according to the demand from the competitive representative firm and the opportunity cost of private versus public employment. Perfect mobility of resources guarantee the representative public agent is also paid her marginal product, which must equal the private sector wage.

The government is a monopoly whose services are centrally mandated while decentrally administered by its agents. The relationship between the government and its agent is governed by the assumption that the public agent can neither directly affect the marginal product of the public good or service, i.e. its price, nor the marginal product of her work effort, i.e. her

[13] Criticisms of the APF generally follow Fisher [1965, 1969, 1971, 1983] who developed a set of theoretical conditions that are so rigid that successful aggregation, as implied by the APF framework, is all but impossible. Fisher's criticism, if taken to heart, completely discounts the use of the aggregate production function in order to estimate the productivity of infrastructure. See Felipe [2001].

wage. Instead the user fee for public goods is determined by the endogenous allocation of labor and capital across the public and private sectors. The second best resource allocation is a proxy for the less than optimal effort exerted by public agents.

Suppose the private sector produces all of society's consumable output through a production function that is homogeneous of degree one in capital (K_Y), labor (L_Y), and infrastructure (G).

$$Y = F\left(K_Y, L_Y, G\right) = AK_Y^{\alpha} G^{\beta} L_Y^{1-\alpha-\beta} \tag{2.1}$$

The central government collects taxes proportional to final production and hands over the revenue to its agents who produce and then sell the public good to the private sector. The public sector production function is defined as follows.[15]

$$G = H\left(\tau, K_G, L_G\right) = \tilde{G}\left(K_G, L_G\right) + \frac{\tau Y}{P_G} = AK_G^{\gamma} L_G^{1-\gamma} + \frac{\tau Y}{P_G} = \frac{\beta}{\beta - \tau} AK_G^{\gamma} L_G^{1-\gamma} \tag{2.2}$$

Both sectors are subject to the accounting constraints, $\overline{K} = K_Y + K_G$ and $\overline{L} = L_Y + L_G$ respectively. The central government would prefer its agents work such that G is provided as efficiently as possible. Thus the competitive and therefore optimal price of G is determined by $\Psi = P_G G - wL_G - rK_G = 0$. Competitively produced G is the optimum and thereby serves as a benchmark. The optimal tax rate in the above framework is simply $\tau^* = \beta$ where $\lim_{\tau \to \beta} P_G = 0$. In the perfect world benchmark, the elasticity of infrastructure is exactly known, taxes are set optimally, and government services, provided at the competitive equilibrium, are consumed at zero cost.

In an imperfect world, the elasticity of public infrastructure is not exactly known such that $\tau < \beta$.[16] Furthermore, if the decentralized public agents accept the value of public capital as well as the wage rate as given, competitive resource markets insure that their opportunity costs equal the private sector rental rate of capital and wage respectively. Therefore, the decentralized public agent maximizes her welfare function given competitive resource markets. The superscript bar over the variable denotes the public agent's inability to directly affect its value.

---

[14] The econometric exercise found herein compares the results from this specification to those of the traditional aggregate production function estimations that generally follow Aschauer [1989, 1990].

[15] Taxes lower the marginal cost of government such that $\lim_{\tau \to \beta} P_G = 0$. Furthermore, at the optimal tax rate of $\tau^* = \beta$ the government is perfectly efficient as $\lim_{\tau \to \beta} G = \tau Y$ and the model collapses to the more typical framework where public capital is an unpaid input.

[16] It is important to note that the optimal tax rate of $\tau^* = \beta$ insures that government services are consumed at zero cost. This is because $\lim_{\tau \to \beta} P_G = 0$ is independent of how close government production can approximate the competitive equilibrium. This corner solution strictly limits consideration of the tax rate to $0 \leq \tau < \beta$.

$$\begin{aligned}\Psi &= P_G G - w(1-\tau)L_G - r(1-\tau)K_G \geq 0 \\ &= \left[MPL_G - MPL_Y(1-\tau)\right]L_G + \left[MPK_G - MPK_Y(1-\tau)\right]K_G \geq 0\end{aligned} \tag{2.3}$$

$$\begin{aligned}\frac{\partial \Psi}{\partial L_G} &= \overline{P}_G \frac{\partial G}{\partial L_G} - \overline{w}(1-\tau) = \frac{\partial Y}{\partial L_Y}(1-\tau) \\ &= MPL_G - \overline{MPL_Y}(1-\tau) = \overline{MPL_Y}(1-\tau)\end{aligned} \tag{2.4}$$

$$\begin{aligned}\frac{\partial \Psi}{\partial K_G} &= \overline{P}_G \frac{\partial G}{\partial K_G} - \overline{r}(1-\tau) = \frac{\partial Y}{\partial K_Y}(1-\tau) \\ &= MPK_G - \overline{MPK_Y}(1-\tau) = \overline{MPK_Y}(1-\tau)\end{aligned} \tag{2.5}$$

Notice that the competitive private wage rate, w, is the marginal labor cost to the public agent. The marginal benefit of working in the public sector is the competitive wage plus the premium available to the public agent. Therefore, resources allocation is determined by marginal benefit equalizing marginal cost. The allocation rules governing labor and capital may be defined as follows.[17]

$$L_G{}^* = \frac{\beta(1-\gamma)}{2(1-\alpha-\beta)(1-\tau)+\beta(1-\gamma)} \cdot L \tag{2.6}$$

$$L_Y{}^* = \frac{2(1-\alpha-\beta)(1-\tau)}{2(1-\alpha-\beta)(1-\tau)+\beta(1-\gamma)} \cdot L \tag{0.7}$$

$$K_G{}^* = \frac{\beta\gamma}{2\alpha(1-\tau)+\beta\gamma} \cdot K \tag{2.8}$$

$$K_Y{}^* = \frac{2\alpha(1-\tau)}{2\alpha(1-\tau)+\beta\gamma} \cdot K \tag{0.9}$$

It is important to note that equations (2.6) through (0.9) are indeed socially sub-optimal allocation algorithms. One way for the social planner to overcome the principle agent problem is to provide public services as if they were competitive. Therefore, the benchmark rules for optimal resource allocation are defined as follows.

$$L_G{}^{PC} = \frac{\beta(1-\gamma)}{(1-\alpha-\beta)(1-\tau)+\beta(1-\gamma)} \cdot L \tag{2.10}$$

---

[17] See Appendix 1 for the derivation.

$$L_Y^{PC} = \frac{(1-\alpha-\beta)(1-\tau)}{(1-\alpha-\beta)(1-\tau)+\beta(1-\gamma)} \cdot L \tag{0.11}$$

$$K_G^{PC} = \frac{\beta\gamma}{\alpha(1-\tau)+\beta\gamma} \cdot K \tag{2.12}$$

$$K_Y^{PC} = \frac{\alpha(1-\tau)}{\alpha(1-\tau)+\beta\gamma} \cdot K \tag{0.13}$$

The only difference between the allocation algorithms is the constant, *2*, that appears in (2.6) through (0.9) but is absent in (2.10) through (0.13). Therefore, it is possible to analyze resource allocation more generally as follows: $\frac{L_G}{L} = z_L(\alpha,\beta,\gamma,\tau,\phi)$ and $\frac{K_G}{K} = z_K(\alpha,\beta,\gamma,\tau,\phi)$ where $\phi \geq 1$ determines the degree of allocative inefficiency due to decentralization.[18]

I contend that (2.6) through (0.9) represent second best equilibrium allocations resulting from local welfare maximization by decentralized public agents while (2.10) through (0.13) represent the first best socially optimum allocations. Figure 1 illustrates the two benchmark equilibria. Although L^* is the second best equilibrium allocation of labor given decentralized agents and L^{pc} is the equilibrium allocation of labor given the competitive optimum, that is not to say that other resource allocations may not be considered. In fact, one could analyze the implications of any resource allocation of L_Y versus L_G. For example, perfect information as well as complete impunity of public agents might leads to an allocation of L^m. The problem with L^m is that the public agent effectively gets a larger slice of a smaller pie. Relative to her private sector counterpart, the public agent may be wealthier, but she would still have been better off in absolute terms at L^*. Irrespective of whether the reader believes that L^* is indeed an equilibrium, it is nonetheless clear that L^{pc} is the best that society can hope to achieve and consequently any movement away from L^{pc} is sub-optimal.

There are three important observations regarding how the model can and should be practically applied. First, the model predicts rates of resource usage as a function of the production elasticities and the tax rate. Along these lines, the model also predicts that optimal resource usage is defined by (2.10) through (0.13) versus second best equilibrium resource usage which is defined by (2.6) through (0.9). Therefore, for any reasonable set of values for α, β, γ and τ, it is always the case that $z_L^* < z_L^{pc}$ and $z_K^* < z_K^{pc}$. Thus the further the economy is from optimal allocation, the lower is the relative resource usage by government.[19]

---

[18] Any resource allocation may be represented by changing this constant in which a $\phi = 1$ yields the competitive equilibrium and a $\phi = 2$ yields the decentralized public agent equilibrium. In Figure 1, any value $\phi > 1$ is equivalent to movement to the left of L^{pc} and any value $0 < \phi < 1$ is equivalent to movement right of L^{pc}.

[19] I only consider allocations to the left of L^{PC}, but the model is not limited thus.

The implications of this observation are relatively straightforward. One might hypothesize that industrialized countries are closer to L^{pc} than developing ones and movement away from L^{pc} represents the prevalence of public inefficiency through corruption. This view that corruption stems from the monopolistic exploitation of public services is discussed in Schliffer and Vishny [1990]. But one must take care when making a comparison of this type because the results, $z_L^{LDC} < z_L^{IND}$ and $z_K^{LDC} < z_K^{IND}$ as reflecting greater corruption in the LDC, only holds strictly when α, β, γ and τ are equivalent across the two countries in question.

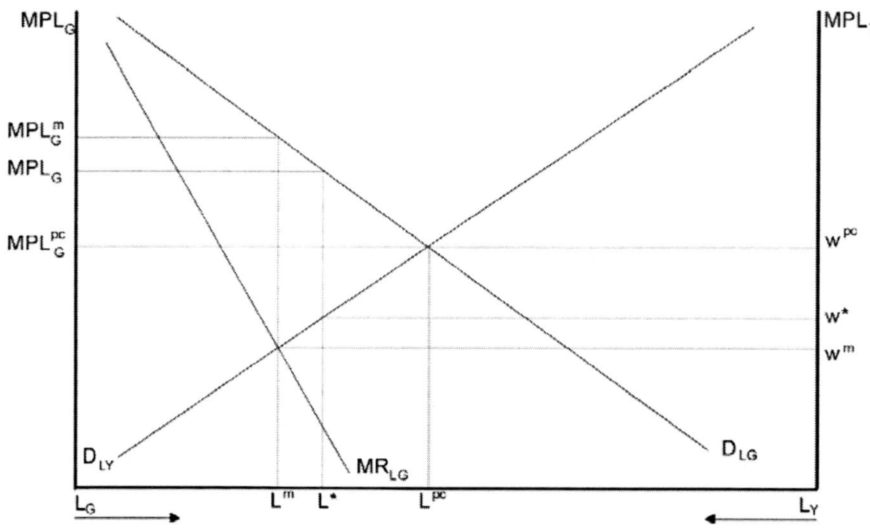

Figure 1

The second observation pertains to the coefficient values. They may, and in fact are quite likely to be, different across countries. For the theoretical model to be consistent with the stylized fact that the average government of a developing country employs relatively more of society's labor and relatively less of society's capital than the average government of an industrialized economy, barring differences in tax rate across countries, at least one of the three elasticities, α, β or γ, must differ between representative countries.

Consider the simplest scenario first. Assume that the production elasticities of public versus private capital, α and β, and the degree of allocative inefficiency, ϕ, are the same across countries, but the elasticity on capital in the public production function, γ, is different. If the productivity of public capital is greater in industrialized countries than in LDC's, the implication is that infrastructure development in industrialized countries is more capital intensive than in LDC's. In terms of the model, $\gamma^{IND} > \gamma^{LDC}$, given $\alpha^{IND} = \alpha^{LDC}$, $\beta^{IND} = \beta^{LDC}$ and $\phi^{IND} = \phi^{LDC}$, insures that both inequalities, $z_K^{IND} > z_K^{LDC}$ and $z_L^{IND} < z_L^{LDC}$, hold.

Alternatively, the output elasticities, α and or β, may also differ across countries. If we assume the elasticity on public capital, β, is constant and that $\alpha^{IND} < \alpha^{LDC}$, then homogeneity requires that $\left(1-\alpha^{IND}-\beta\right) > \left(1-\alpha^{LDC}-\beta\right)$. This implies that private capital in industrialized countries is less productive than private capital in developing countries.[20] If β actually decreases with development as the endogenous and traditional growth theories suggest, and $\alpha^{IND} < \alpha^{LDC}$, then the inequalities, $z_K^{IND} > z_K^{LDC}$ and $z_L^{IND} < z_L^{LDC}$, hold so long as the elasticity of capital in the public sector production function is restricted by $\gamma^{IND} > \gamma^{LDC}$. In other words, while the relative return on private capital is relatively lower in industrialized countries than in developing ones, the relative return on public capital is greater in industrialized economies than in developing ones. Intuitively, this suggests that factories are relatively more productive in developing countries while labor is relatively more productive in industrialized ones. Simultaneously, a courthouse is relatively more effective in industrialized countries while a police officer is relatively more effective in developing ones.

The final observation pertains to the tax rate, τ. If α, β, γ, and ϕ are equal across countries, then differing tax rates across countries yields $z_L^{low\ \tau} < z_L^{high\ \tau}$ and $z_K^{low\ \tau} < z_K^{high\ \tau}$. Moreover, the further the tax rate is below the optimal rate, the higher is the effective price of public capital. Since the effective tax rate in LDC's is generally less than the effective tax rate in industrialized countries,[21] the model predicts that LDC's will suffer less growth effects due to taxation but at the cost of lower welfare and greater income inequality.

Table 1 presents the relative resources usage rates and the average tax rates for a selection of countries. Given the three observations from above, several testable hypotheses may be drawn from the data. First, compare the USA to the UK where we observe that $z_L^{USA} < z_L^{UK}$ and $z_K^{USA} > z_K^{UK}$. Recall that if α, β, γ, and ϕ are equal across these two countries and the only difference is average tax rates, then both the public labor and the public capital usage rates should be lower in the UK. Since they are not, then one or all of the coefficients must be different between the two countries. Second, comparing the USA to France, we observe that $z_L^{USA} < z_L^{France}$ and $z_K^{USA} < z_K^{France}$. If the difference in the average tax rate between these two countries accounts for observed resource usage, then it should be that all of the other coefficients are the equal. Third, comparing the USA to Australia [or Canada], we observe that $z_L^{USA} < z_L^{Australia}$ and $z_K^{USA} < z_K^{Australia}$. Although the observed inequalities are consistent with the USA's lower tax rate, the difference is so marginal that it would seem unlikely to be the root of the difference in labor usage. Fourth, compare the USA to Japan where we observe $z_L^{USA} > z_L^{Japan}$ and $z_K^{USA} < z_K^{Japan}$. Since Japan has a lower average tax rate than the USA, unless the coefficients are different, both usage rates should be lower in the USA. Fifth, compare the USA to Portugal [or Italy]. Although the usage rates are almost equal, what if the government of Portugal is less efficient

[20] Nourzad [2000] found no difference in the marginal productivity of public capital between industrialized and developing countries but found that the marginal productivity of private capital to be relatively higher in developing economies.

[21] Average tax rate in European countries is strictly greater than 30% versus the average tax rate in Mexico and Turkey are 17% and 15% respectively. [so. World Bank Indicators, 1994]

than that of the USA due to corruption? If so, then one or all of the coefficients must differ for the usage ratios to be equal. These hypotheses are the subject of the next section.

Table 1

	USA	CANADA	AUSTRALIA	MEXICO	JAPAN	KOREA
Ky/K	0.88	0.85	0.86	0.82	0.82	0.86
Kg/K	0.12	0.15	0.14	0.18	0.18	0.14
Ly/L	0.84	0.80	0.76	0.86	0.94	0.90
Lg/L	0.16	0.20	0.24	0.14	0.06	0.10
Avg. tax rate	0.22	0.26	0.24	0.17	0.13	0.19

	FRANCE	ITALY	PORTUGAL	UK	GREECE	TURKEY
Ky/K	0.86	0.90	0.88	0.92	0.76	0.73
Kg/K	0.14	0.10	0.12	0.08	0.24	0.27
Ly/L	0.78	0.85	0.88	0.81	0.82	0.92
Lg/L	0.22	0.15	0.12	0.19	0.18	0.08
Avg. tax rate	0.48	0.39	0.35	0.47	0.40	0.16

Ky/K = average across time of [gross fixed capital formation by total industries]/[gross fixed capital formation] & Kg/K = average across time of [gross fixed capital formation by producers of govt services]/[gross fixed capital formation]. [so. *OECD National Accounts*, Vol II, Country Table 3, Items 46, 47 & 50, various years]. {* Data for Mexico and Turkey, [so. 2002, OECD, *Quarterly National Accounts*, country Table 5a]

Ly/L = average across time of [employment of persons by total industries]/[total employment of persons] & Lg/L = average across time of [government employment as percent of total employment]*, [so. 1996, OECD, *Historical Statistics, 1960-1994*, Table 2.15]. {* Data for Mexico = average across time of [employment of persons by producers of govt services]/[total employment of persons], [so. 1997, OECD, *Services, Statistics on value added and employment,* Country Table II]. Data for Korea and Greece = average across time [employment in public administration + defence + education + health + social work]/[total employment], [so. 2001, OECD, *Services, Statistics on value added and employment,* Country Table II]. Data for Turkey = share of public employment to total employment [1985-1999], [so. 2001, OECD Public Management Service].}

Avg. tax rate = average across time of [total tax revenue]/[output by total industries]. [so. for tax data from World Bank Indicators, 1994, and for output data from OECD National Accounts, Vol II, Table 12, Items 46, various years]

EMPIRICAL ESTIMATES OF THE COEFFICIENTS WITHIN THE MODEL

The following econometric exercise estimates the values of the coefficients, α, β and γ, for a panel of 16 OECD countries. I estimate the three coefficients using the dynamic equivalents to equations (2.1) and (2.2). This is convenient because it is not only theoretically justifiable, but also removes any unit roots in the data. I estimate the following four equations.

$$\frac{\dot{Y}}{Y}=\alpha\frac{\dot{K}_Y}{K_Y}+\beta\frac{\dot{G}}{G}+\left(1-\alpha-\beta\right)\frac{\dot{L}_Y}{L_Y} \tag{0.14}$$

$$\frac{\dot{G}}{G}=\gamma\frac{\dot{K}_G}{K_G}+\left(1-\gamma\right)\frac{\dot{L}_G}{L_G} \tag{0.15}$$

$$\frac{\dot{Y}}{Y}=\alpha\frac{\dot{K}_Y}{K_Y}+\beta\gamma\frac{\dot{K}_G}{K_G}+\beta\left(1-\gamma\right)\frac{\dot{L}_G}{L_G}+\left(1-\alpha-\beta\right)\frac{\dot{L}_Y}{L_Y} \tag{0.16}$$

$$\frac{\Delta GDP}{GDP}=\alpha\frac{\dot{K}}{K}+\beta\frac{\dot{G}}{G}+(1-\alpha-\beta)\frac{\dot{L}}{L} \tag{0.17}$$

Equation (0.16) is the simply equation (0.14) with the growth rate of G, equation (0.15), imbedded into it. Equation (0.17) is estimated for comparison purposes. It represents the more typical experiment, following Aschauer [1989], to estimate the elasticity of output with respect to public infrastructure versus private capital. The relationship between the data used to estimate this last equation and those used in the previous three estimations may be summarized by the following accounting constraints, $GDP=Y+G$, $L=L_G+L_Y$, and $K=K_G+K_Y$.

It is preferable to estimate the levels growth of K_G, K_Y, G, and Y than their per capita equivalents for three reasons. First, the theoretical values of the coefficients from the equations defined in levels are identical to those values from the equations in intensive form. Second, modern econometric software allows one to easily impose restrictions, such as constant returns to scale, on the coefficient estimates. Third, it is easier to estimate equation (0.16) in levels. In theory, the growth rates of public and private labor are equal, but in practice they are not. Therefore, the per capita version of equation (0.16) would need to also contain a term for the difference in the rates of growth of L_Y and L_G. Again, given the ability to easily restrict coefficients, estimation of per capita data is unnecessary and, in this case, cumbersome.

The data is an annual panel of 16 countries from 1970 until 1996.[22] The data is from the OECD, who conveniently separates output, fixed capital formation, and employment into the two categories, total industries and producers of government services.[23] Unfortunately, data on the stocks of public and private capital do not exist in a comparable series across countries. This problem has been addressed in many previous studies. The closest paper to this one in terms of data is Ford and Poret [1991], who use essentially the same OECD data that I do.

The econometric methodology employed is similar to the panel study by Nourzad [2000]. Table 2 presents the results of the five benchmark estimations, (0.14) through (0.17) plus one additional, i.e. equation (0.14) with a fitted value from equation (0.15).[24] They are specified as classical linear regression models [CLRM] with no control for country or period specific effects. Table 3 presents the results of the five equations specified as one way fixed effects models with controls for country specific effects [FE-country] and period specific effects [FE-period].[25] The capital and labor usage ratios reported in the previous section suggest likely differences in coefficients values across countries. In light of this, I interact the coefficient

22 The panel is not exactly balanced. Canadian data is from 1970-93. Danish data is from 1970-95. German [west] data is from 1970-92. Luxemburg's data is from 1970-91. Dutch data is from 1970-93. Portuguese data is from 1977-93. Swedish data is from 1970-94. British data is from 1971-95. Using a smaller balanced panel of 15 countries from 1971-95 does not significantly change any of the results.

23 The data source is various years of the OECD, *National Accounts, Detailed Tables, Volume II.* The relevant tables are 4, 12 and 15.

24 This effectively makes public infrastructure endogenous in the private production function and thereby allows some feedback from equation (0.15) to equation (0.14). See Flores de Frutos and Pereira [1993] for additional discussion.

25 The corresponding random effect model specification of the five equations in Tables 2 and 3 were also tested. Based on Hausman's specification test, in all cases, the random effect models may be rejected at high levels of significance in favour of the corresponding fixed effect formulations. A two way fixed effects model with controls for country as well as periods was also estimated. The results suggest that in the presence of period effects, country

estimates of α, β and γ for the entire panel with the country dummies. Table 4 reports the results of the five equations when the coefficient estimates are allowed to vary across countries.

Table 2

Equation	(3.1)	(3.2)	(3.3)	(3.4)	(3.1) w/ fitted G from (3.2)
Regression Type	[CLRM]	[CLRM]	[CLRM]	[CLRM]	[CLRM]
Dep. Var.	ΔY/Y	ΔG/G	ΔY/Y	ΔGDP/GDP	ΔY/Y
constant	**0.0432**	**0.0554**	**0.0545**	**0.0365**	**0.0431**
	(0.0059)	(0.0030)	(0.0028)	(0.0051)	(0.0048)
alpha	**0.1666**		**0.1895**	0.0302	**0.1882**
	(0.0278)		(0.0279)	(0.0316)	(0.0280)
beta	**0.2182**		**0.2032**	**0.2839**	**0.2024**
	(0.0691)		(0.0551)	(0.0612)	(0.0525)
gamma		**0.2227**	0.1923		
		(0.0720)	(0.1071)		
Akaike Info. Crit.	-3.8983	-3.0282	-3.8460	-3.7626	-3.8443
Adj. R Sq.	0.2983	0.0305	0.2577	0.3156	0.2594
SEE	0.0343	0.0531	0.0353	0.0367	0.0353

Numbers in parentheses are White corrected standard errors. Numbers in bold typeface indicate significance with confidence of 95% or greater.

Table 3

Equation	(3.1)		(3.2)		(3.3)		(3.4)		(3.1) w/ fitted G from (3.2)*	
Regression Type	[FE-country]	[FE-period]	[FE-country]	[FE-period]	[FE-country]	[FE-period]	[FE-country]	[FE-period]	[FE-country]	[FE-period]
Dep. Var.	ΔY/Y	ΔY/Y	ΔG/G	ΔG/G	ΔY/Y	ΔY/Y	ΔGDP/GDP	ΔGDP/GDP	ΔY/Y	ΔY/Y
alpha	**0.1657**	**0.1224**			**0.1883**	**0.1277**	**0.1878**	**0.1480**	**0.1417**	**0.1187**
	(0.0285)	(0.0283)			(0.0286)	(0.0302)	(0.0329)	(0.0324)	(0.0299)	(0.0300)
beta	**0.2162**	0.1132			**0.2007**	**0.1184**	**0.2868**	**0.1979**	**0.3743**	0.2061
	(0.0705)	(0.0726)			(0.0597)	(0.0376)	(0.0623)	(0.0775)	(0.0544)	(0.3136)
gamma			**0.2159**	**0.0690**	0.1800	0.0679				
			(0.0738)	(0.0337)	(0.1130)	(0.1714)				
Akaike Info. Crit.	-3.8265	-4.0075	-2.9728	-3.3596	-3.7738	-4.0012	-3.6892	-3.7867	-3.8771	-3.9781
Adj. R Sq.	0.2740	0.4240	0.0133	0.3459	0.2329	0.4064	0.2908	0.3721	0.3098	0.3911
SEE	0.0349	0.0316	0.0536	0.0436	0.0359	0.0316	0.0374	0.0352	0.0340	0.0320
16 Countries [chi Sq]	4.2756		9.0659		4.7287		5.4106		13.8845	
26 Years [chi Sq]		**132.1326**		**324.0836**		**224.3183**		**118.7764**		**112.6317**

Numbers in parentheses are White corrected standard errors. Numbers in bold typeface indicate significance with confidence of 95% or greater.
These two estimations use the fitted value for G from equation [3.2]:[FE-period].

---

effects are not jointly significant. In the presence of country effects, period effects are still jointly significant, but less so that the one way fixed effects model with controls for period.

The results from all of the experiments suggest that only the productivity of private capital differs across countries. The best estimates of those differences result from estimation of equation (3.3):[FE-period + FE-alpha] on table 4. Furthermore, the productivity of government represented by β, which is statistically the same across OECD countries, is significant and equal to anywhere from .11 to as high as .37. In general though, the data suggest that business cycles are indeed important and the coefficient on G is closer to the lower estimate. This is in sharp contrast to the most of the literature that follows Ashauer [1989], which finds much higher elasticities of output with respect to public infrastructure. It is interesting to note that the highest estimate for β results from estimation of equation (3.4) on Table 2. Recall that this equation represents the more typical experiment to estimate the productivity of public infrastructure. The estimates of γ suggest that the relative productivity of public capital also does not vary across OECD countries and is equal to something between .06 and .22. Unfortunately, this is by no means a strong result.

Table 4

Equation	(3.1)		(3.2)	(3.3)			(3.4)		(3.1) w/ fitted G from (3.2)*	
Regression Type	[FE-period + FE-alpha]	[FE-period + FE-beta]	[FE-period + FE-gamma]	[FE-period + FE-alpha]	[FE-period + FE-beta]	[FE-period + FE-gamma]	[FE-period + FE-alpha]	[FE-period + FE-beta]	[FE-period + FE-alpha]	[FE-period + FE-beta]
Dep. Var.	ΔY/Y	ΔY/Y	ΔG/G	ΔY/Y	ΔY/Y	ΔY/Y	ΔGDP/GDP	ΔGDP/GDP	ΔY/Y	ΔY/Y
alpha	0.1517	**0.1159**		**0.1437**	**0.1355**	**0.1289**	**0.2064**	**0.1401**	0.1310	**0.1128**
	(0.1122)	(0.0321)		(0.0522)	(0.0335)	(0.0332)	(0.1022)	(0.0351)	(0.1174)	(0.0316)
beta	0.0960	**0.1154**		**0.1260**	**0.1074**	**0.1090**	**0.2013**	**0.2114**	0.1684	**0.1128**
	(0.0912)	(0.0576)		(0.0418)	(0.0231)	(0.0495)	(0.0844)	(0.0668)	(0.3461)	(0.0316)
gamma			0.2301	0.0606	-0.2100	-0.2593				
			(0.1684)	(0.1743)	(0.1892)	(0.5863)				
*F.E. on coef. rel. to USA***	*alpha*	*beta*	*gamma*	*alpha*	*beta*	*gamma*	*alpha*	*beta*	*alpha*	*beta*
AUT	-0.0367	0.0644	0.4876	0.0383	-0.1600	0.1980	-0.0580	0.1118	-0.0303	-0.0138
	(0.1109)	(0.1231)	(0.3168)	(0.1163)	(0.2968)	(1.2677)	(0.1058)	(0.1116)	(0.1191)	(0.0862)
BEL	0.0262	0.0464	-0.1354	0.0407	-0.0375	0.1733	-0.0213	0.0493	0.0520	0.0418
	(0.1157)	(0.0692)	(0.1922)	(0.0578)	(0.1299)	(0.8482)	(0.1110)	(0.0667)	(0.1215)	(0.0966)
CAN	0.0750	-0.2072	-0.4642	0.0942	-0.2840	1.5149	0.0523	-0.1632	0.0759	-0.0248
	(0.1192)	(0.1174)	(0.3828)	(0.0702)	(0.3244)	(1.4273)	(0.1086)	(0.1041)	(0.1301)	(0.0659)
DNK	-0.0807	-0.0209	-0.1081	-0.0800	-0.0762	0.1796	-0.1397	-0.0270	-0.0656	0.0216
	(0.1087)	(0.0464)	(0.1771)	(0.0554)	(0.0612)	(0.5953)	(0.1000)	(0.0545)	(0.1181)	(0.0641)
FIN	0.0192	0.0202	-0.1127	0.0326	0.0769	-0.0526	-0.0445	0.0105	0.0366	0.0949
	(0.1170)	(0.0564)	(0.1733)	(0.0615)	(0.1820)	(0.8989)	(0.1081)	(0.0541)	(0.1222)	(0.0694)
FRA	0.0247	0.0120	-0.3089	0.0450	0.0639	0.2048	-0.0256	-0.0027	0.0547	0.0705
	(0.1191)	(0.0369)	(0.2238)	(0.0606)	(0.0504)	(0.6047)	(0.1079)	(0.0423)	(0.1240)	(0.0625)
GRW	0.0310	0.0530	-0.1047	0.0448	0.1081	0.4390	0.0040	0.0615	0.0468	0.0916
	(0.1252)	(0.0510)	(0.1665)	(0.0745)	(0.1486)	(0.8380)	(0.1195)	(0.0522)	(0.1322)	(0.0719)
ITA	-0.1092	-0.0285	-0.0985	-0.0965	-0.0082	0.0988	-0.1488	-0.0143	-0.0915	0.0450
	(0.1109)	(0.0522)	(0.1772)	(0.0490)	(0.1646)	(0.7323)	(0.1017)	(0.0590)	(0.1176)	(0.0902)
JAP	0.0949	0.0479	-0.0291	**0.1257**	-0.4790	1.1721	0.0554	0.0499	0.1162	0.1018
	(0.1129)	(0.0562)	(0.1710)	(0.0560)	(0.3365)	(0.9741)	(0.1043)	(0.0552)	(0.1189)	(0.0676)
LUX	-0.1019	-0.0696	-0.0567	-0.0797	0.5671	-0.8561	-0.0357	-0.0134	-0.0802	-0.0597
	(0.1366)	(0.1679)	(0.1763)	(0.0914)	(0.5018)	(1.1774)	(0.1740)	(0.2404)	(0.1409)	(0.2023)
NLD	-0.0866	0.0068	-0.2341	-0.0858	0.0168	0.2125	-0.0738	0.0493	-0.1094	-0.0141
	(0.1253)	(0.0882)	(0.1855)	(0.0799)	(0.1532)	(0.8343)	(0.1223)	(0.0869)	(0.1336)	(0.0745)
NOR	-0.0646	0.1142	0.1357	-0.0495	-0.1529	0.9218	-0.0908	0.1158	-0.0405	0.0981
	(0.1296)	(0.1005)	(0.2576)	(0.0832)	(0.1049)	(1.0244)	(0.1202)	(0.0975)	(0.1342)	(0.1320)
POR	0.0314	0.0556	-0.1255	0.0343	-0.0607	0.6167	-0.0399	0.0226	0.0670	**0.1619**
	(0.1250)	(0.0504)	(0.1809)	(0.0615)	(0.0898)	(0.8276)	(0.1132)	(0.0615)	(0.1212)	(0.0804)
SWE	-0.0992	-0.0527	-0.1510	-0.0922	-0.1582	0.1586	-0.1609	-0.0412	-0.0776	0.0026
	(0.1225)	(0.0743)	(0.1772)	(0.0722)	(0.1324)	(0.8779)	(0.1147)	(0.0731)	(0.1282)	(0.0812)
GBR	0.0652	-0.0189	-0.1915	0.0787	0.0481	0.2603	0.0049	-0.0110	0.0796	0.0353
	(0.1716)	(0.0838)	(0.1726)	(0.1343)	(0.1167)	(0.5972)	(0.1499)	(0.0732)	(0.1787)	(0.0933)
16 Countries [chi Sq]	**38.4624**	11.2940	18.7737	**46.3232**	9.0580	5.0314	**39.5032**	11.7772	**47.8395**	11.3069
Akaike Info. Crit.	-3.9654	-3.9702	-3.3437	-3.9758	-3.9721	-3.9643	-3.7375	-3.7391	-3.9497	-3.9225
Adj. R Sq.	0.4045	0.4073	0.3583	0.4120	0.4098	0.4052	0.3631	0.3641	0.3951	0.3784
SEE	0.0316	0.0315	0.0432	0.0314	0.0315	0.0316	0.0354	0.0354	0.0319	0.0323
26 Years [chi Sq]	**102.6835**	**137.6130**	**143.2692**	**177.4288**	**203.2585**	**189.2812**	**97.2618**	**125.1998**	**104.9775**	**115.5420**

Numbers in parentheses are White corrected standard errors. Numbers in bold typeface indicate significance with confidence of 95% or greater.

* These two estimations use the fitted value for G from equation [3.2]:[FE-period].

** Coefficient estimates are relative to the coefficient estimate for the USA [i.e. from equation [3.1]:[FE-period + FE-alpha], α_{AUT}=.1150=.1517-.0367].

Using the estimates from table 4, we may now address the hypotheses of the previous section. As the empirical results suggest, I assume that β and γ are constant across countries while α varies. We observe that $z_L^{USA} < z_L^{UK}$ and $z_K^{USA} > z_K^{UK}$. The tax effect can explain the labor inequality but not the observed capital inequality. Using the estimates from equation (3.3):[FE-period + FE-alpha], the elasticity of private capital in the USA is .14 versus that of the UK is .22. This is exactly what we should expect to find.

The second observation is that $z_L^{USA} < z_L^{France}$ and $z_K^{USA} < z_K^{France}$. Since the tax rate of the US is lower than that of France, we would have expected that the value of α to be very close to that of the USA. In fact, it seems that α_{FRA}=.19, which is above the US estimate. Since the difference in private capital productivity between France and the USA is smaller that that between the UK and the USA, it is still quite possible that the theory is consistent with the empirical evidence.

The third observation is that $z_L^{USA} < z_L^{Australia}$ and $z_K^{USA} < z_K^{Australia}$. The estimates of α suggest that α_{AUT}=.18, which is again higher than in the USA. Since the tax rate difference is so small, the higher productivity of private capital in Australia is to be expected.

The fourth observation is that $z_L^{USA} > z_L^{Japan}$ and $z_K^{USA} < z_K^{Japan}$. Given the tax rate differential alone, we would expect both usage rates to be lower in Japan. The estimate of private sector productivity in Japan is α_{JAP}=.27, which is much higher than the US estimate. In this case, the theory fails somewhat since the higher private capital productivity in Japan should raise public labor usage and lower public capital usage.

The final observation considers the usage rates between the USA and Portugal which are almost equal. The higher tax rate in Portugal, ceteris paribus, drives the expected usage rates of both public capital and public labor up. The observed productivity of private capital in Portugal, which is α_{POR}=.18, reinforces higher public labor usage but implies lower public capital usage. The only possible offsetting factor that might explain the observed similarity in the public labor usage rate is if Portuguese government is less efficient due to corruption than that of the US, i.e. $\phi^{POR} > \phi^{USA}$. It is interesting to note that of the OECD countries sampled, the average bureaucratic efficiency is 8.90.[26] Only in Italy (BI_{ITA}=6.33) and in Portugal (BI_{POR}=5.58) are the indices lower than in France (BI_{FRA}=8.25). In other words, if greater of autonomy of public agents leads to more corruption, and if that is indeed what is captured by these bureaucratic efficiency indices, then again, the theory is quite consistent with the evidence.

In summary, the data, for the most part, support the explicit specification of the private aggregate production function versus the public aggregate production function. Given further study with other data, the next step is to explicitly consider developing countries versus industrialized ones. I leave that to the future.

---

[26] Business International [BI] corruption indicator average 1980-1993, collected by Mauro [1995]: 10 [lowest corruption], 0 [highest corruption]

THEORETICAL IMPLICATIONS OF THE MODEL

The theoretical implications of the model are far reaching. Almost any endogenous growth model that is based on an aggregate production function framework, albeit with microeconomic foundations, can be easily altered to reflect a productive government with real resources costs. By doing so, one can compare the original work which reflects a trivially produced public sector where $G = \tau Y$ to a more robust version that includes a decentralized public sector as a departure from the utopian optimum. Although there is a wealth of literature to choose from, some well known papers on endogenous growth that readily lend themselves to this analysis include Lucas [1988], Barro [1990], Romer [1986, 1990], and Aghion and Howitt [1992].

The paper by Lucas [1988] is arguably a synthesis of the research pioneered by Ramsey [1928], Cass [1965], and Koopmans [1965] and the model attributed to Solow [1956] and Swan [1956]. Lucas describes the basic endogenous growth model where output is a function of technology augmented labor and capital. The rate of return on investment and the consequent saving are independent of the growth rate which is described by the Euler equation, *growth_rate=IES·[MPK-discount_rate]-tech_growth_rate*, where *IES* is the intertemporal elasticity of substitution.

In an extension to this line of research, Barro [1990] introduces government as a productive input, which is homogenous of degree one, within the dynamic production function. Public services are trivially produced and completely funded by a proportional income tax. For all tax rates, $\tau > 0$, the private return on investment is lower than the social return and the decentralized economy grows slower than is socially optimal. The optimal tax rate and consequent size of government, using the notation from above, is simply $\tau^* = g/y = \beta$.

Appendix 2 describes the analytical solution of a productive government with decentralized agents within an endogenous growth model. The model has labor and capital as in Lucas [1988] while public services are subject to diminishing returns as in Barro [1990]. Therefore, suppose there exist two separable agents with identical preferences whose competition results in the allocation of the economy's available labor and capital. The agents maximize welfare, which is a function of consumption per worker. Upper case characters represent levels and lower case represent per effective capita. n is the exogenous growth rate of population and χ is the exogenous growth rate of technology.

$$
\begin{aligned}
Max\ W &= \int_{t=0}^{\infty}\left[U\left(\frac{C_{gt}}{L_{Gt}}\right)\cdot L_{Gt} + U\left(\frac{C_{yt}}{L_{Yt}}\right)\cdot L_{Yt}\right]e^{-\rho t}dt \\
&= \int_{t=0}^{\infty}\left(\frac{c_{gt}^{1-\theta}-1}{1-\theta}\cdot A_0^{1-\theta}L_{G0} + \frac{c_{yt}^{1-\theta}-1}{1-\theta}\cdot A_0^{1-\theta}L_{Y0}\right)e^{[(1-\theta)\chi+n-\rho]t}dt
\end{aligned}
\tag{4.18}
$$

The representative private agent, denoted by subscript y, owns the representative firm and receives income from wages, rental capital and sales of output to the entire economy. Taxes are assessed on wage and capital income. I assume that all capital is ultimately owned by the private sector. After tax income from final good sales accounts for private sector resource income but does not account for capital rental by the public sector.

$$Y_t = K_{Yt}^{\alpha} G_t^{\beta} \left(A_t L_{Yt}\right)^{1-\alpha-\beta} = r_t K_{Yt} + w_t L_{Yt} + P_{Gt} G_t \tag{4.19}$$

$$\left(Y_t + r_t K_{Gt}\right)\left(1-\tau\right) = P_{Yt} \cdot C_{Yt} + S_{Yt} \tag{4.20}$$

The price of y must be explicitly specified since it is possible to have greater dollar income than physical output. Thus $P_Y = \dfrac{Total\ Economywide\ Income}{Y}$.[27]

The representative public agent, denoted by subscript g, receives wage income which is taxed plus whatever public goods premium that she can garner from the administration of the public sector. Public goods are produced by the government at resource cost.

$$\Psi_t = P_{Gt} G_t - r_t\left(1-\tau\right) K_{Gt} - w_t\left(1-\tau\right) L_{Gt} \tag{4.21}$$

$$G_t = \tilde{G}_t + \frac{\tau Y_t}{P_{Gt}} = \tilde{G}_t + \frac{\tau G_t}{\beta} = \frac{\beta}{\beta-\tau}\tilde{G}_t = \frac{\beta}{\beta-\tau} K_{Gt}^{\gamma}\left(A_t L_{Gt}\right)^{1-\gamma} \tag{4.22}$$

$$\Psi_t + w_t\left(1-\tau\right) L_{Gt} = P_{Yt} \cdot C_{Gt} + S_{Gt} \tag{4.23}$$

The two representative agents independently choose consumption and consequent saving to maximize their independent optimal consumption paths. Capital evolves as a result of the sum total of savings. Since the two agents have identical preferences, they necessarily have equal saving rates as well.[28] Thus the growth rate of consumption per effective capita for either agent is defined by a modified golden rule.

$$\xi = \frac{\dot{c}_y}{c_y} = \frac{\dot{c}_g}{c_g} = \frac{1}{\theta}\left[r\left(1-\tau\right) - \rho - \theta\chi\right] \tag{4.24}$$

$$\dot{K}_t = S_{Yt} + S_{Gt} \tag{4.25}$$

The dynamic adjustment process is similar to Lucas [1988]. The results may be summarized as follows.

$$\frac{\dot{c}_{it}}{c_{it}} = \frac{\dot{k}_{it}}{k_{it}} = \frac{\dot{k}_t}{k_t} = \xi\,,\ \frac{\dot{y}_t}{y_t} = \frac{\dot{\psi}_t}{\psi_t} = \xi\left(\alpha + \beta\gamma\right) \text{ and } \frac{\dot{g}_t}{g_t} = \xi\gamma \tag{4.26}$$

---

[27] If taxes are set optimally at $\tau^* = \beta$, then the $P_Y = 1$.

[28] See Appendix 2 for proof of this assertion.

There are some points worth noting. The relationship between the growth of output and that of consumption is independent of the effects of decentralized public agents. The further the country is from the competitive benchmark, the smaller is the proportion of public to private capital, and the lower is the marginal product of private capital. To understand the significance of equation (4.26), consider the Lucas [1988] model altered to include a Barro [1990] type government that is trivially produced from taxes such that $g = \tau y$. The dynamics of a Barro-Lucas framework are summarized follows.[29]

$$\frac{\dot{c}_t}{c_t} = \frac{\dot{k}_t}{k_t} = \xi \text{ and } \frac{\dot{y}_t}{y_t} = \frac{\dot{g}_t}{g_t} = \frac{\xi\alpha}{(1-\beta)} \tag{4.27}$$

The differences between the model with a productive government and Lucas-Barro model lie in the capital labor ratios at the steady state and in the rate of adjustment that leads to the steady state. For any set of values for α, β, γ and ϕ, the steady state capital labor ratio, given the explicitly specified public sector, is far greater than the Lucas-Barro framework predicts. For example, consider a hypothetical starting point of one unit of capital and one unit of labor with the technology parameter, A, also equal to one, such that the initial effective capital labor ratio is $K_0 / A_0 L_0 = k_0 = 1$. It is important to remember that that the transition to the steady state is unique.[30] Figure 2 plots the simulation results from three separate experiments, a Lucas-Barro model, a Lucas model with a productive albeit decentralized public sector (i.e. ϕ=2) and a Lucas model with a decentralized competitive public sector (i.e. ϕ=1). The coefficients on K and G are α=.35 and β=.25 respectively and the tax rate is τ=.24.[31] In each case, the heavy line is the unique saddle path to the steady state and the lighter line is the reference describing all points in which the growth of effective per capita capital is zero.

The models each converge to their respective steady states defined by modified golden rules. The simulation values at the steady state equilibrium are summarized in Table 5. Notice that the steady state effective capital labor ratio is k^*=6.73, k^*=39.54 and k^*=56.16 respectively. The saddle path is much steeper in the Lucas model and the steady state consequently occurs much sooner. Another way to compare transitions to the steady states is to consider the growth rates at any point away from the steady state. Figures 3 plots the changing growth rate of consumption per effective capita as each model converges to its steady state. Again, it is quite evident that the trivializing assumption that $G_t = \tau Y_t$ implies a much quicker transition to the steady state with a lower capital labor ratio and lower per capita consumption. A productive albeit decentralized government model predicts almost six times more capital per unit of effective labor at the steady state than the Barro-Lucas model.

---

[29] Equation (4.10) results from a single infinitely lived agent that maximizes $\int_{t=0}^{\infty} e^{-\rho t} U\left(\frac{C_t}{L_t}\right) L_t dt$ subject to, $Y_t = K_t^{\alpha} G_t^{\beta} (A_t L_t)^{1-\alpha-\beta}$, $G_t = \tau Y_t$, and $Y_t(1-\tau) = C_t + \dot{K}_t$.

[30] See the textbook by Romer [2001] for details.

[31] The other relevant coefficient values pertaining to figures 2, 3 and 4 are the coefficient on public capital, γ=.5, the growth rate of technology, χ=.03, the growth rate of population, n=.02, the coefficient of relative risk aversion, θ=.99, and the discount rate, ρ=.03.

The competitive benchmark predicts over nine times more capital per unit of effective labor at the steady state. In general, this suggests that government efficiency is reflected by a higher effective capital labor ratio.

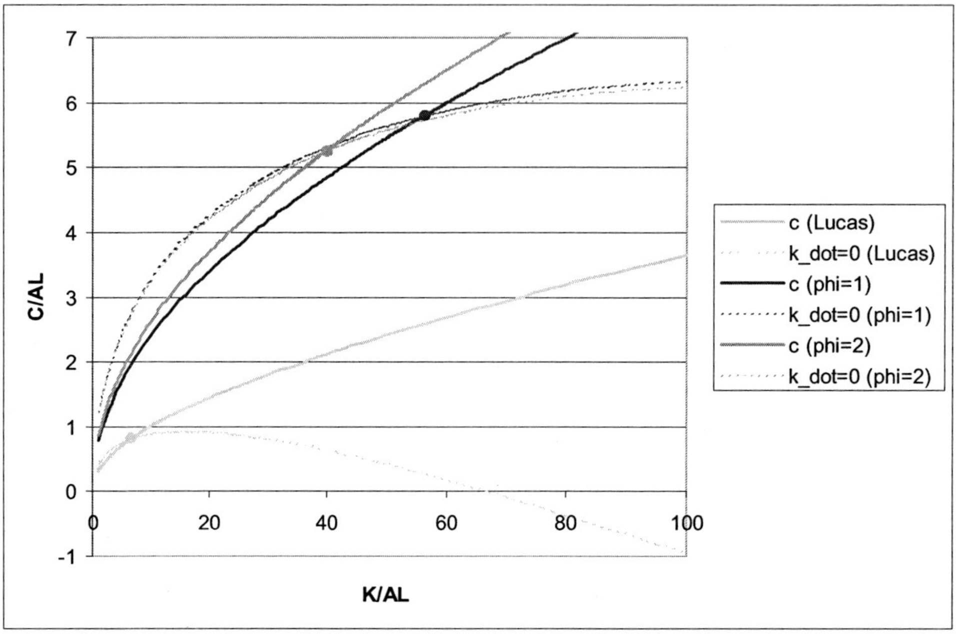

Figure 2: Simulation Results: Saddle Path Comparisons $\{\alpha = .35, \beta = .25, \gamma = .50, \tau = .24\}$

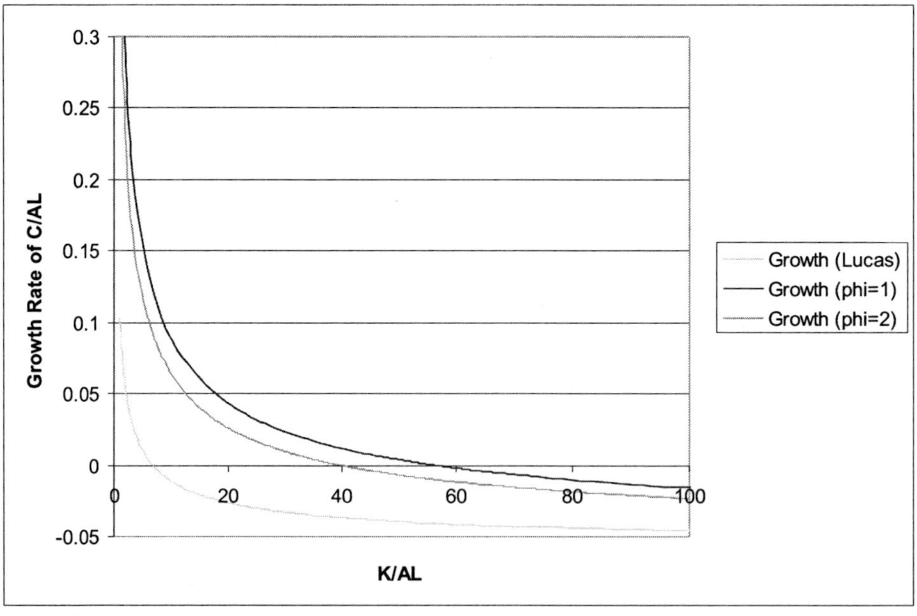

Figure 3: Simulation Results: Growth Path Comparisons $\{\alpha = .35, \beta = .25, \gamma = .50, \tau = .24\}$

Table 5: Simulation results at the steady state

		1	2	3	4	5	6
	Coeficient values	$\alpha=.35$ $\beta=.25$ $\tau=.24$	$\alpha=.35$ $\beta=.25$ $\gamma=.50$ $\tau=.24$ $\phi=1$	$\alpha=.35$ $\beta=.25$ $\gamma=.50$ $\tau=.24$ $\phi=2$	$\alpha=.35$ $\beta=.25$ $\gamma=.50$ $\tau=.20$ $\phi=2$	$\alpha=.30$ $\beta=.25$ $\gamma=.50$ $\tau=.24$ $\phi=2$	$\alpha=.30$ $\beta=.25$ $\gamma=.50$ $\tau=.20$ $\phi=2$
1	ccg = CG / (A * LY)		2.46	5.70	2.74	4.38	2.24
2	ccy = CY / (A * LG)		7.17	5.14	2.46	3.51	1.79
3	cc = C / (A * L)	0.81	5.79	5.24	2.51	3.65	1.85
4	kkg = KG / (A * LG)		61.62	44.11	22.06	32.53	17.28
5	kky = KY / (A * LY)		53.92	38.60	19.30	21.68	11.52
6	kk = K / (A * L)	6.73	56.16	39.54	19.75	23.36	12.37
7	gg = G / (A * LG)	0.36	196.24	166.04	23.48	142.58	20.78
8	yy = Y / (A * LY)		12.10	8.68	4.12	5.69	2.87
9	Y / (A * L)	1.51	8.57	7.20	3.45	4.81	2.44
10	Y/LY		4856	3484	1655	2282	1151
11	Y/L	607	3441	2890	1385	1929	981
12	L	54.48	54.48	54.48	54.48	54.48	54.48
13	K	147119	1227792	864407	431879	510707	270429
14	A	401.32	401.32	401.32	401.32	401.32	401.32
15	Growth Rate	0.00	0.00	0.00	0.00	0.00	0.00
16	Ψ		23375	29495	14132	19691	10013
17	LG		15.87	9.29	8.90	8.42	8.06
18	LY		38.60	45.19	45.58	46.06	46.42
19	LG/L		0.291	0.171	0.163	0.155	0.148
20	KG		392517	164461	78810	109877	55874
21	KY		835275	699946	353069	400830	214555
22	KG/K		0.320	0.190	0.182	0.215	0.207
23	Total Income	25136	189341	159010	79207	106158	56117
24	Public Income		23433	29519	14144	19708	10021
25	Private Income		165908	129491	65063	86451	46096
26	C	17766	126684	114531	54818	79780	40545
27	S	7371	61390	43334	21648	25580	13544
28	Y	33074	187466	157436	75435	105107	53445
29	r	0.08	0.08	0.08	0.07	0.08	0.07
30	w	720712	4.84	3.47	1.65	2.56	1.29
31	PG	1.04	0.04	0.06	0.22	0.05	0.20
32	G	7938	1250103	619049	83895	481641	67213
33	Pub Util per capita		107.14	108.04	107.25	107.76	107.04
34	Priv Util per capita	5.96	108.29	107.93	107.14	107.52	106.80
35	Pub Welfare		1701	1004	955	907	863
36	Priv welfare		4180	4877	4883	4952	4957
37	Total welfare	325	5881	5881	5838	5859	5820

In each of the above simulations, an initial effective capital labor ratio of 1 is imposed and the model is allowed to "grow" for 200 periods such that the level of labor and technology are predetermined by their exogenous growth rates while saving and consequently capital growth is endogenous.

The empirical results herein reinforce the results of Nourzad [2001] in that only α differs across countries, while β and γ are constant. Figure 4 depicts the saddle path with a lower elasticity of private capital ceteris paribus, a lower tax rate ceteris paribus and a lower private capital elasticity combined with a lower tax rate. As the productivity of private capital relative to private labor falls, so does the steady state effective capital labor ratio and the per capita consumption. Therefore, if developing countries suffer from lower private capital productivity, then one would expect tendency toward a lower steady state effective capital labor ratio and a quicker transition to the steady state. Furthermore, a shock to an LDC should have a more pronounced growth effect but a shorter life span.

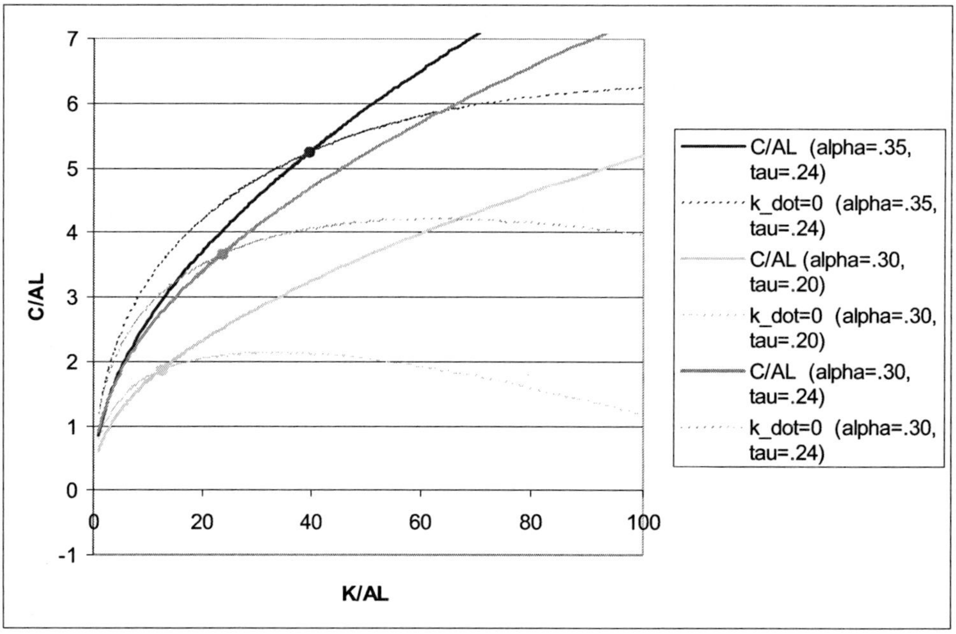

Figure 4: Simulation Results: Saddle Path Comparisons $\{\alpha = \hat{\alpha}, \beta = .25, \gamma = .50, \tau = \hat{\tau}, \phi = 2\}$

Lower private capital productivity combined with a tax that is relatively further from its optimal rate reinforce each other by both implying lower steady state effective capital labor ratios. If one assumes that industrialized countries also have more efficient resource allocations between sectors (i.e. ϕ is closer to 1 than to 2), then developing countries tend toward a steady state at far lower effective capital labor ratio and per capita consumption than do industrialized ones.

Finally, consider the steady state equilibrium values across the various scenarios summarized in Table 5. There are several points worth noting. The effective capital labor ratio in row 6 decreases as the scenario differs from the benchmark competitive equilibrium with optimal taxes. Although lower private capital productivity (i.e. columns 5 & 6) lowers the consumption per effective capita (i.e. row 3) and consequently the welfare per capita (i.e. rows 33 & 34), the implications of sub-optimal taxation are greater (i.e. compare columns 3 & 4 versus columns 3 & 5). This is also evident in the effect of taxation on the level of public goods per effective capita (i.e. row 7).

CONCLUSION

This paper brings to light the problems resulting from the generally accepted, although wholly inadequate convention of assuming that publicly produced goods are provided to the private sector at zero user cost and funded solely by tax revenues. The assumption completely ignores the public-private accounting constraint over resources. As a result the relative level of G versus L and K within a constant returns production function, $Y=F(G,K,L)$, is significantly lower and its estimated productivity is consequently significantly higher. Empirical estimates herein suggest that the elasticity of public goods is closer to .13, far lower than that found by Ashauer [1989] and others. From the theoretical standpoint, the assumption greatly skews the equilibrium capital labor ratio as well as the per effective capita consumption. The inclusion of the accounting constraint dramatically changes the relative price of private versus public goods and consequently the relative price of consumption and saving. The transition to the steady state becomes more gradual and the resulting equilibrium is characterized by relatively more capital per unit of effective labor at a higher level of consumption per effective capita.

There are several conclusions that may be drawn from the preceding analysis. First, any degree of decentralization that may be exploited by government agents will necessarily lead to sub-optimal allocations of labor and capital between the public and private sectors. Therefore less publicly produced goods will be offered to the private sector at a higher price. The resulting rent accrued by public agents is spent along with private sector income on private sector output. This effectively means more nominal income chasing less real goods. Second, the principle agent problem may be effectively addressed by a concerned central government by setting the income tax rate exactly equal to the productivity of public goods within the private production function. Unfortunately, imperfect information by government makes this highly unlikely. There are two caveats to this conclusion. One, tax substitution and the ability to levy consumption taxes would likely lower the optimal income tax rate.[32] Two, the government could set the tax rate above the estimated optimum. Although inefficient, the principal agent problem effectively disappears irrespective of the degree of decentralization as the price of public goods approaches zero.

The model predicts the more inefficient the allocation of resources and the further the tax rate is from optimal, the lower is the steady state effective capital labor ratio and the steeper is the saddle path to the equilibrium. Therefore, if governments in developing countries are less able or desirous to control their agents, they are effectively more decentralized and thus have greater freedom to exploit their positions of power. In such cases, we should expect a steeper saddle path to a steady state defined by less capital and consumption per capita. An intuitive interpretation is that business cycles in developing countries are shorter than those in industrialized countries but have higher amplitudes, or simply are more volatile.

The policy implications are quite straightforward. To an economy on the saddle path somewhere to the left of the steady state, an injection of either technology or labor would decrease the effective capital labor ratio, push the economy further left along the saddle path and manifest itself in the form of temporarily higher growth rates. The steeper the saddle path, the more pronounced is the growth effect of a shock but the shorter its life span. Therefore if a goal of an LDC is to lengthen the business cycle and decrease its amplitude, i.e.

stabilization, then assuming the empirical results herein are correct, the only options are either to increase the productivity of private capital or set the tax rate at its optimum.

The paper implicitly assumes that allocation of capital and labor across the two sectors is determined via some kind of long run institutional process. In the model, this is represented by the coefficient ϕ approaching 1. Any improvement in resource allocation improves private agents' welfares at the expense of public agents' in the sense that public agents get a relative smaller piece of a bigger pie. Since only private sector output may ultimately be consumed, it is a positive sum gain for the whole economy. In other words, the model conforms to the stylized fact regarding institutional development in which governments of industrialized countries tend to better serve their respective populations while governments of developing countries tend to better serve themselves. Moreover, the model depicts how industrialized countries not only tend to higher equilibrium capital labor ratio and per capita consumption, but they do so via business cycles that are longer and more stable.

Appendix 1
Derivation of Allocation Rules (2.6), (2.7), (2.8) and (2.9)

$Y = F(L,K,G) = AK_Y^{\alpha} G^{\beta} L_Y^{1-\alpha-\beta}$ subject to

$$G = H(\tau, K_G, L_G) = \tilde{G} + \frac{\tau Y}{P_G} = \tilde{G} + \frac{\tau Y}{\beta \frac{Y}{G}} = \frac{\beta}{\beta - \tau}\tilde{G} = \frac{\beta}{\beta - \tau} AK_G^{\gamma} L_G^{1-\gamma}$$

where $\tilde{G} = AK_G^{\gamma} L_G^{1-\gamma}$

Decentralized Government Agent Maximization Problem:

$$\begin{aligned} Max\Psi &= P_G G - wL_G - rK_G > 0 \\ &= (MPL_G - MPL_Y)L_G + (MPK_G - MPK_Y)K_G > 0 \end{aligned}$$

Given the equilibrium condition: $\frac{\partial \Psi}{\partial L_G} = \frac{\partial Y}{\partial L_Y}$ and $\frac{\partial \Psi}{\partial K_G} = \frac{\partial Y}{\partial K_Y}$

$$\frac{\partial \Psi}{\partial L_G} = (MPL_G - MPL_Y) = MPL_Y = w(1-\tau)$$

[32] See Barreto and Alm [2002].

$$MPL_G = 2MPL_Y \rightarrow \frac{\beta(1-\gamma)}{L_G} = \frac{2(1-\alpha-\beta)(1-\tau)}{L_Y}$$

$$\therefore L_G{}^* = \frac{\beta(1-\gamma)}{2(1-\alpha-\beta)(1-\tau)+\beta(1-\gamma)} \cdot \overline{L} \quad \textbf{(2.6)}$$

$$\rightarrow \frac{L_G{}^*}{\overline{L}} = z_L{}^*(\alpha,\beta,\gamma,\tau,\phi=2)$$

$$\frac{\partial \Psi}{\partial K_G} = MPK_G - MPK_Y = MPK_Y = r(1-\tau)$$

$$MPK_G = 2MPK_Y \rightarrow \frac{\beta\gamma}{K_G} = \frac{2\alpha(1-\tau)}{K_Y}$$

$$\therefore K_G{}^* = \frac{\beta\gamma}{2\alpha(1-\tau)+\beta\gamma} \cdot \overline{K} \quad \textbf{(2.8)}$$

$$\rightarrow \frac{K_G{}^*}{\overline{K}} = z_K{}^*(\alpha,\beta,\gamma,\tau,\phi=2)$$

Competitive Equilibrium in G Solution $\rightarrow$ $\Psi = 0$

$$\Psi = P_G G - wL_G - rK_G = 0$$
$$= (MPL_G - MPL_Y)L_G + (MPK_G - MPK_Y)K_G = 0$$

Given the equilibrium condition: $\frac{\partial \Psi}{\partial L_G} = \frac{\partial Y}{\partial L_Y}$ and $\frac{\partial \Psi}{\partial K_G} = \frac{\partial Y}{\partial K_Y}$

$$\frac{\partial \Psi}{\partial L_G} = MPL_G - MPL_Y = 0$$

$$MPL_G = MPL_Y \rightarrow \frac{\beta(1-\gamma)}{L_G} = \frac{(1-\alpha-\beta)(1-\tau)}{L_Y}$$

$$\therefore L_G{}^{pc} = \frac{\beta(1-\gamma)}{(1-\alpha-\beta)(1-\tau)+\beta(1-\gamma)} \cdot \overline{L} \quad \textbf{(2.10)}$$

$$\Rightarrow \frac{L_G^{\ pc}}{\bar{L}} = z_L^{\ pc}\left(\alpha,\beta,\gamma,\tau,\phi=1\right)$$

$$\frac{\partial \Psi}{\partial K_G} = MPK_G - MPK_Y = 0$$

$$MPK_G = MPK_Y \Rightarrow \frac{\beta\gamma}{K_G} = \frac{\alpha\left(1-\tau\right)}{K_Y}$$

$$\therefore K_G^{\ pc} = \frac{\beta\gamma}{\alpha\left(1-\tau\right)+\beta\gamma}\cdot \bar{K} \tag{2.12}$$

$$\Rightarrow \frac{K_G^{\ pc}}{\bar{K}} = z_K^{\ pc}\left(\alpha,\beta,\gamma,\tau,\phi=1\right)$$

Appendix 2
Lucas [1988] Endogenous Growth Model with Decentralized Government

$$Max\ W = \int_{t=0}^{\infty}\left[U\left(\frac{C_{Gt}}{L_{Gt}}\right)\cdot L_{Gt} + U\left(\frac{C_{Yt}}{L_{Yt}}\right)\cdot L_{Yt}\right]e^{-\rho t}dt$$

where $c_{gt} = \dfrac{C_{Gt}}{A_t L_{Gt}}$ and $c_{yt} = \dfrac{C_{Yt}}{A_t L_{Yt}}$

If $L_t = L_{Yt} + L_{Gt}$, then one may define $z_L = \dfrac{L_{Gt}}{L_t}$, $\left(1-z_L\right) = \dfrac{L_{Yt}}{L_t}$ and $B_L = \dfrac{\left(1-z_L\right)}{z_L}$

$$Max\ W = A_0^{1-\theta}L_0\int_{t=0}^{\infty}\left[\frac{c_{gt}^{1-\theta}}{1-\theta}\cdot z_L + \frac{c_{yt}^{1-\theta}}{1-\theta}\cdot\left(1-z_L\right)\right]e^{-\left[\rho-n-(1-\theta)\chi\right]t}dt \tag{A.2.28}$$

subject to

$$Y_t = F\left(L_{Yt},K_{Yt},G_t\right) = K_{Yt}^{\alpha}G_t^{\beta}\left(A_t L_{Yt}\right)^{1-\alpha-\beta} \tag{A.2.29}$$

$$y_t = \frac{Y_t}{A_t L_{Yt}} = k_{yt}^{\alpha}\left(\frac{g_t}{B_L}\right)^{\beta}$$

$$\left(Y_t + rK_{Gt}\right)\left(1-\tau\right) = P_{Yt}\cdot C_{Yt} + S_{Yt} \tag{A.2.30}$$

$$\left(y_t + \frac{r_t k_{gt}}{B_L}\right)\left(1-\tau\right) = P_{Yt}\cdot c_{yt} + s_{yt}$$

$$\Psi_t = P_{Gt}G_t - r_t K_{Gt} - w_t L_{Gt} \geq 0 \tag{A.2.31}$$

$$\psi_t = \frac{\Psi_t}{A_t L_{Gt}} = B_L P_{gt} g_t - r_t k_{gt} - \frac{w_t}{A_t} \geq 0$$

$$\Psi_t + w_t\left(1-\tau\right)L_{Gt} = P_{Yt}\cdot C_{Gt} + S_{Gt} \tag{A.2.32}$$

$$\psi_t + \frac{w_t\left(1-\tau\right)}{A_t} = P_{Yt}\cdot c_{gt} + s_{gt}$$

$$G_t = \tilde{G}_t + \frac{\tau Y_t}{P_{Gt}} = K_{Gt}^{\gamma}\left(A_t L_{Gt}\right)^{1-\gamma} + \frac{\tau G_t}{\beta} = \frac{\beta}{\beta-\tau}K_{Gt}^{\gamma}\left(A_t L_{Gt}\right)^{1-\gamma} \tag{A.2.33}$$

$$g_t = \frac{G_t}{A_t L_{Gt}} = \frac{\beta}{\beta-\tau}k_{gt}^{\gamma}$$

$$K_t = K_{Yt} + K_{Gt} \tag{A.2.34}$$

$$k_t = \frac{K_t}{A_t L_t} = \frac{K_{Yt}}{A_t L_{Yt}}\left(1-z_L\right) + \frac{K_{Gt}}{A_t L_{Gt}}z_L = k_{yt}\left(1-z_L\right) + k_{gt}z_L$$

$$\dot{K}_t = S_{Yt} + S_{Gt} \tag{A.2.35}$$

$$\dot{k}_t = \left[y_t\left(1-\tau\right) - P_{Yt}c_{yt}\right]\left(1-z_L\right) + \left(B_L P_{gt} g_t - P_{Yt}c_{gt}\right)z_L - \left(\chi+n\right)k_t$$

$$L_t = L_{Yt} + L_{Gt} \tag{A.2.36}$$

$$L_t = L_0 e^{nt} \tag{A.2.37}$$

$$A_t = A_0 e^{\chi t} \tag{A.2.38}$$

Optimization:

$$L = U\left(c_g\right) + U\left(c_y\right) + \mu_t\left(\dot{k}\right) + \lambda_t\left[k - k_y\left(1 - z_L\right) - k_g z_L\right]$$

$$\frac{\partial L}{\partial c_y} = \frac{\partial U\left(c_y\right)}{\partial c_y} - \mu_t P_Y\left(1 - z_L\right) = 0 \rightarrow \frac{\dot{c}_y}{c_y} = -\frac{1}{\theta} \cdot \frac{\dot{\mu}_t}{\mu_t}$$

$$\frac{\partial L}{\partial c_g} = \frac{\partial U\left(c_g\right)}{\partial c_g} - \mu_t P_Y z_L = 0 \rightarrow \frac{\dot{c}_g}{c_g} = -\frac{1}{\theta} \cdot \frac{\dot{\mu}_t}{\mu_t}$$

$$\frac{\partial L}{\partial k_t} = -\mu_t\left(n + \chi\right) + \lambda_t = -\mu_t\left[n + \left(1 - \theta\right)\chi - \rho\right] - \dot{\mu}_t \rightarrow \frac{\lambda_t}{\mu_t} = \rho + \theta\chi - \frac{\dot{\mu}_t}{\mu_t}$$

$$\frac{\partial L}{\partial k_g} = \mu_t \frac{\partial \psi}{\partial k_g} z_L - \lambda_t z_L = 0 \rightarrow \frac{\lambda_t}{\mu_t} = \frac{\partial \psi}{\partial k_g} = \frac{B_L \beta \gamma y}{k_g} - r\left(1 - \tau\right)$$

$$\frac{\partial L}{\partial k_y} = \mu_t \frac{\partial y}{\partial k_y}\left(1 - \tau\right)\left(1 - z_L\right) - \lambda_t\left(1 - z_L\right) = 0 \rightarrow \frac{\lambda_t}{\mu_t} = \frac{\partial y}{\partial k_y}\left(1 - \tau\right) = r\left(1 - \tau\right)$$

Growth:

$$\frac{\lambda_t}{\mu_t} = \frac{\partial \psi}{\partial k_g} = \frac{\partial y}{\partial k_y}\left(1 - \tau\right) = \rho + \theta\chi - \frac{\dot{\mu}_t}{\mu_t}$$

$$\therefore \xi = \frac{\dot{c}_y}{c_y} = \frac{\dot{c}_g}{c_g} = \frac{1}{\theta}\left[r\left(1 - \tau\right) - \rho - \theta\chi\right] = \frac{1}{\theta}\left[\frac{B_L \beta \gamma y}{k_g} - r\left(1 - \tau\right) - \rho - \theta\chi\right] \tag{A.2.39}$$

Dynamic Analysis:

$$\frac{\dot{G}}{G} = \gamma \frac{\dot{K}_G}{K_G} + \left(1 - \gamma\right)\left(\chi + n\right) \tag{A.2.40}$$

$$\frac{\dot{g}}{g} = \gamma \frac{\dot{k}_g}{k_g} \tag{A.2.41}$$

$$\frac{\dot{Y}}{Y} = (\alpha + \beta\gamma)\frac{\dot{K}}{K} + (1 - \alpha - \beta\gamma)(\chi + n) \tag{A.2.42}$$

$$\frac{\dot{y}}{y} = (\alpha + \beta\gamma)\frac{\dot{k}_i}{k_i} \tag{A.2.43}$$

$$\frac{\dot{\Psi}}{\Psi} = \frac{\dot{Y}}{Y} = \frac{\dot{y}}{y} + \chi + n \tag{A.2.23}$$

$$\frac{\dot{\psi}}{\psi} = \frac{\dot{y}}{y}$$

$$\frac{\dot{K}}{K} = \xi + \chi + n \tag{A.2.45}$$

$$\frac{\dot{k}}{k} = \frac{\dot{k}_i}{k_i}\left[\frac{k_y}{k}(1 - z_L) + \frac{k_g}{k} z_L\right] \rightarrow \frac{\dot{k}}{k} = \frac{\dot{k}_i}{k_i} \Leftrightarrow \frac{k_y}{k}(1 - z_L) + \frac{k_g}{k} z_L = 1$$

$$\frac{\dot{C}_i}{C_i} = \xi + \chi + n \tag{A.2.46}$$

Effective Per Capita Growth:

$$\therefore \frac{\dot{y}}{y} = \frac{\dot{\psi}}{\psi} = \xi(\alpha + \beta\gamma) \tag{A.2.47}$$

$$\therefore \frac{\dot{c}_i}{c_i} = \frac{\dot{k}_i}{k_i} = \frac{\dot{k}}{k} = \xi \tag{A.2.48}$$

$$\therefore \frac{\dot{g}}{g} = \xi\gamma \tag{A.2.49}$$

Levels Growth:

$$\therefore \frac{\dot{\Psi}}{\Psi} = \frac{\dot{Y}}{Y} = \xi\left(\alpha + \beta\gamma\right) + \chi + n \tag{A.2.50}$$

$$\therefore \frac{\dot{C}_i}{C_i} = \frac{\dot{K}}{K} = \frac{\dot{K}_i}{K_i} = \xi + \chi + n \tag{A.2.51}$$

$$\therefore \frac{\dot{G}}{G} = \xi\gamma + \chi + n \tag{A.2.52}$$

Saving Rate:

$$\therefore \overline{s} = \overline{s}_Y = \overline{s}_G = \frac{\left[\phi\alpha\left(1-\tau\right) + \beta\gamma\right]\left(\xi + \chi + n\right)}{\phi\left(\xi\theta + \rho + \chi\theta\right)P_Y} \tag{A.2.53}$$

REFERENCES

Alm, James and R. Barreto, "Optimal Taxation in the presence of Corruption," forthcoming in *Public Finance Review*, 2003.

Aschauer, David A., "Is public expenditure productive?" *The journal of Monetary Economics*, 23, 1989, 177-200.

Bardhan, P. and D. Mookherjee, "Decentralized anti-poverty program delivery in developing countries," unpublished, University of California, Berkeley, 2000a.

Bardhan, P. and D. Mookherjee, "Relative capture of government at local and national levels," *American Economic Review*, 90(2), 2000b.

Bardhan, P. and D. Mookherjee, "Corruption and decentralization of infrastructure delivery in developing countries," unpublished, University of California, Berkeley, 2001.

Bardhan, Pranab, "Decentralization of governance and development," *Journal of Economic Perspectives*, 16(4), 2002.

Barreto, Raul A., "Endogenous corruption in a neoclassical growth model," *The European Economic Review*, 44, 2000, 35-60.

Barreto, Raul A., "Institutional corruption, the public sector, and economic development: institutional corruption and Paraguayan economic development, corruption in a simple endogenous growth model, endogenous corruption, income inequality, and growth: econometric evidence," Ph.D. Thesis, The University of Colorado at Boulder, 1996.

Barro, Robert J., "Government spending in a simple model of economic growth," *Journal of Political Economy*, 98-5, pt. 2, 1990, S103-S125.

Berndt, E. and B. Hansson, "Measuring the contribution of public infrastructure in Sweden," NBER Working Paper 3842, 1991.

Besley, T. and A. Case, "Incumbent behavior: vote-seeking, tax-setting, and yardstick competition," *The American Economic Review*, 85(1), 1995.

Besley, T. and S. Coate, "Centralized versus decentralized provision of public goods: a political economy analysis," NBER Working Paper 7084, 1999.

Cass, David, "Optimum growth in an aggregate model of capital accumulation," *Review of Economic Studies*, 1965, *32*, 233-240.

Crook, R. and J. Manor, *Democracy and Decentralization in South Asia and West Africa*, Cambridge University Press, Cambridge, 1998.

Dasgupta, Dipankar, "Growth versus welfare in a model of non-rival infrastructure," *Journal of Development Economics*, 58, 1999, 359-85.

Diamond, Peter A., "National debt in a neoclassical growth model," *American Economic Review*, 55, 1955, 1126-1150.

Eberts, R., "Public infrastructure and regional economic development," *Economic Review*, Federal Reserve Bank of Cleveland, 26, 1990, 15-27.

Felipe, Jesus, "Aggregate production functions and the measurement of infrastructure productivity: a reassessment," *Eastern Economic Journal*, Vol. 27, No. 3, Summer 2001, 323-44.

Fisher, F. M., "Embodied technical change and the existence of aggregate capital stock," *Review of Economic Studies*, October 1965, 263-288.

__________, "Aggregate production functions and the explanation of wages," *The Review of Economics and Statistics*, November 1971, 305-25.

__________, "On the simultaneous existence of full and partial capital aggregates," *Review of Economic Studies*, January 1983, 197-208.

__________, "The existence of aggregate production functions," *Econometrica*, October 1969, 553-77.

Ford, R. and P. Poret, "Infrastructure and private-sector productivity," *OECD Economic Studies*, 17, Autumn 1991, 63-90.

Flores de Frotus, R. and A. M. Pereira, "Public capital and aggregate growth in the United States: is public capital productive?" unpublished, discussion paper 93-31, University of California, San Diego, July 1993.

Futagami, Koishi, Yuichi Morita and Akihisa Sibata, "Dynamic analysis of an endogenous growth model with public capital," *Scandinavian Journal of Economics*, 95 (4), 1993, 607-625.

Garcia-Mila, T. and T. J. McGuire, "The contribution of publicly provided inputs to to states' economies," *Regional Science and Urban Economics*, 22(2), 1992, 229-42.

Geddes, Barbara and Neto, Artur Ribeiro, (1992), "Institutional sources of corruption in Brazil", *Third World Quarterly,* 13(4), 641-61.

Holtz-Eakin, D. and Schwartz, A. E., "Spatial productivity and spillovers from public infrastructure: evidence from state highways," *International and Public Finance*, 76(1), 1994, 459-68.

Hulten, C. R. and R. M. Schwab, "Regional productivity growth in U.S. manufacturing," *The American Economic Revie*, 74(1), 1984, 152-62.

__________, "Public capital formation and the growth of regional manufacturing industries," *National Tax Journal*, 44(4), 1991, 121-34.

Koopmans, Tjalling, "On the concept of optimal economic growth," *The Econometric Approach to Development Planning*, North Holland, Amsterdam, 1965.

Lucas, Robert E., "On the mechanics of economic development," *Journal of Monetary Economics*, 22, 1988, 3-42.

Lynde, C. and J. Richmond, "The role of public capital in production," *The Review of Economics and Statistics*, 74(1), 1992, 37-44.

Mauro,Paulo, "Corruption and Growth," *Quarterly Journal of Economics*, August 1995, 110(3), 681-712.

Morrison, C. J. and A. E. Schwartz, "State infrastructure and productive performance," *The American Economic Review*, 86(5), 1996,1095-111.

Munnell, Alicia H., "How does public infrastructure affect regional economic performance?" *New England Economic Review*, Sept./Oct., 1990, 11-32.

Nadiri, I. and T. Mamuneas, "The effect of public infrastructure and R&D capital on thye cost structure and performance of U.S. manufacturing industries," NBER Working Paper 3887, 1991.

Nourzad, Farrokh, "The productivity effect of government capital in developing and industrialized countries," *Applied Economics*, 32(9), 2000, 1181-91.

OECD, "Measuring Capital: OECD Manual; Measurement of capital stocks, consumption of fixed capital and capital services," Organization for Economic Cooperation and Development, Paris and Washington D.C., 2001.

Qian, Y. and B.R. Weingast, "Federalism as a commitment to preserving market incentives," *Journal of Economic Perspectives*, 11(4), 1997, 83-92.

Ramsey, F. P., "A mathematical theory of Saving," *Economic Journal*, 38, December 1928, 543-559.

Samuelson, Paul A., "Parable and realism in capital theory: the surrogate production function," *Review of Economic Studies*, June 1962, 193-206.

Samuelson, Paul A., "The Pure Theory of Public Expenditure", *Review of Economics and Statistics*, 36, November 1954, 387-389.

Schliefer, A. and R.W. Vishny, "Corruption," *The Quarterly Journal of Economics*, 108 (3), 1993, 599-617.

Seabright, P., "Accountability and decentralization in government: an incomplete contracts model," *European Economic Review*, 40(1), 1996.

Solow, Robert M., "A Contribution to the theory of economic growth", *Quarterly Journal of Economics*, LXX, 1956, 65-94.

Swan, Trevor, "On Golden ages and Production Functions", in K. Beril, ed., *Economic Development with Social Reference to Southeast Asia*, London: Macmillan, 1956, 3-18.

Tommasi, M. and F. Weinschelbaum, "A principal agent building block for the study of decentralization and integration," unpublished, Universidad de San Andrés, Argentina, 1999.

Turnovsky, Stephen J., "Optimal Tax, Debt, and Expenditure in a Growing Economy", *The Journal of Political Economy*, 60 (1), 1996, 21-44.

In: Economic Growth Issues
Editor: L. A. Finley, pp. 105-153
ISBN 1-59454-555-3

Chapter 5

How are Survival-Efficiency Profiles Related to Retirement Rates and Capital Vintage Prices?

Erik Biørn[1]

University of Oslo, Department of Economics, P.O. Box 1095 Blindern,

0317 Oslo, Norway

Abstract

The decline in the service flow from a stock of capital goods with age, due to the physical retirement of capital units and the gradual loss of efficiency of each unit remaining, can be described by survival curves and efficiency curves. We discuss the relationship between the retirement process of the capital, as formalized by these curves, and the average retirement rate, and how this relationship is affected by changes in the investment growth path. The effect of changes in the survival and efficiency curves on the age distribution of the capital goods, those existing as well as those retired in each period, is also considered. We next reconsider the relationship between these curves and the vintage prices of capital under neo-classical assumptions about perfect second-hand markets and malleability, using duality between quantities and prices. Three examples with parametric survival and efficiency curves are presented. The retirement rate is a declining function of the growth rate of investment (except in the exponential decay case) and quite sensitive to this growth rate over a reasonable interval. Approximating the retirement rate by the inverse of the capital's maximal life-time or twice this value ('double declining balance') will frequently produce very inaccurate results. The response of the capital/investment ratio and the retirement/investment ratio to changes in the investment growth rate and in the curvature of the survival function is also investigated. Concavity of the survival and efficiency curves may be compatible with convexity of the age-price profile. This approach for making inference on survival and efficiency functions from vintage price data is contrasted with the frequently cited Hulten-Wykoff approach. Our estimates give evidence less strongly in favour of convex efficiency and survival curves than is often believed.

[1] E-mail: erik.biorn@econ.uio.no Tel: +47 22 85 51 20. Fax: +47 22 85 50 35

INTRODUCTION

The process determining capital retirement is of considerable interest in economics, and retirement rates are important for several purposes. Replacement investment usually accounts for a substantial part of gross investment and GDP, and the process describing how capital retires in combination with the growth path of new investment are basic determinants of the capital's age distribution. Using demographic analogues, we may associate (gross) investment with the birth of capital and retirement with death. From basic demography we know that the age specific mortality rates of a population of persons and the time profile of the births jointly determine the age distribution of the population (when adjusting for migrations). Similarly, changes in the retirement process and in the time path of new investments change the average age of the capital and other characteristics of its age distribution (when purchases and sales of used capital are adjusted for).

In this article, two related topics are addressed. First, we discuss the relationship between the retirement process of the capital and the average retirement rate, and how this rate is affected by changes in the investment growth path. The retirement process is formalized by two functions, one, the *survival curve*, describing the physical disappearance of capital goods with age, the other, the *efficiency curve*, representing the loss of efficiency of the goods remaining. The average retirement rate of capital goods corresponds to the average mortality rate of a population of persons, and the ratio between gross investment and capital stock corresponds to the birth rate.

The second, related, focus is on the relationship between the retirement process and the age profile of capital vintage prices and what observations on second-hand capital prices can tell us about this process. If time series of capital stocks measured in physical well as in efficiency-corrected units and corresponding series for the gross investment flows were available, empirical analyses of the decline in capital efficiency with age could have been conducted by means of econometric techniques based on lag distributions. Such a favourable situation very rarely occurs. However, observations of *prices of capital goods in second-hand markets* may be available. It is possible – by exploiting the *duality* that exists between quantities and prices in a *neo-classical* market for capital goods [cf. Jorgenson (1974); see also Jorgenson (1980, 1989)] – to indirectly obtain inference on the survival and efficiency pattern of capital from second-hand prices. We propose a way of exploiting neo-classical assumptions in order to establish an *econometrically applicable* relationship between the second-hand prices on the one hand and the efficiency and survival curves, provided some not unreasonable assumptions are made about the functioning of the market.

It is well known that the average rate of capital retirement will be a constant independent of the time path of gross investment in the particular case where the survival function is exponentially declining in the age of the capital (exponential decay, declining balance). Exponential decay is the *only* case in which changes in the investment profile do not affect the average retirement rate; see Feldstein and Rothschild (1974, section 2). Often exponential decay is considered a benchmark case of capital retirement, and it has been argued to be an acceptable simplification for long-term analysis, for instance in modelling economic growth, cf. Jorgenson (1963, p. 251, 1974). Yet, average retirement rates are applied by researchers even if exponential decay is not warranted, for instance in the calculation of capital service prices. This practise may be criticized, see Biιιrn (1989, section 11.7). Retirement, as the term is being used here, is distinctly different from *depreciation*, which is related to the decline in the *value* of the capital, rather than to its deterioration as an input in production.

An examination of the relationship between the form of the retirement process and the average retirement rate of capital under non-exponential decay is interesting for several purposes. We may, for example, wish to interpret time series for retirement rates calculated from investment data by the perpetual inventory method with a given retirement process on a 'scale' comparable with the retirement rate under exponential decay. Which is the appropriate 'translation' of the retirement rate, δ, if the retirement pattern of the capital corresponds to, say, simultaneous retirement at a fixed age N, or to linear retirement up to a fixed life-time, N? Often $\delta = 1/N$ is used for the former and $\delta = 2/N$ for the latter. The latter is often denoted as the 'double declining balance' pattern; cf., *e.g.*, Fraumeni and Jorgenson (1980, p. 24). Under which conditions are these translation rules valid, or acceptable, approximations? If direct registrations of the capital stock are available, when will constancy of the implied retirement rate hold as a satisfactory approximation? A further, more basic question is: How will the changes in the curvature of the survival function affect the average retirement rate for different growth profiles of gross investment? In empirical and theoretical studies, *exponential decay* – assuming the survival curve or the efficiency curve, or both, to be exponentially declining functions of age – has frequently been adopted. In several respects, however, this assumption is open to critique [cf., *e.g.*, Biørn (1989, pp. 4–5)].

Jorgenson (1996) surveys empirical studies of depreciation based on the econometric model of asset prices introduced by Hall (1971); see also Hall (1968). Seminal articles exploiting the basic ideas of this model are Hulten and Wykoff (1981a, b, c), and several researchers have followed, more or less, their approach. Jorgenson states that "As a consequence of the rapid assimilation of the results of Hulten and Wykoff, depreciation has been transformed from one of the most contentious and problematic areas in economic measurement to one of the best understood and most useful" [Jorgenson (1994, p. 25)]. The present approach departs in significant ways from that of Hulten and Wykoff, in that we (i) follow explicitly neo-classical assumptions about the functioning of the market for capital goods, including their assumed malleability, and (ii) make use of two distinct capital vintage price concepts, one observable, one unobservable, and corresponding quantity variables. We conclude, from an econometric investigation using this framework with three parametric specifications and a data set also investigated by Hulten, Robertson, and Wykoff (1989), that the evidence in favour of convex efficiency and survival curves is less obvious than may seem from the Hulten-Wykoff studies.

The following sections are disposed as follows. In Section 2, we describe the model and define the basic concepts. Section 3 considers the age distribution of the capital and the related age distribution of retirement. We next derive the relationship between the overall retirement rates, the hazard rate of the mortality distribution of the capital, and its age distribution. The hazard rates can be interpreted as age specific retirement rates. In Section 4, we establish from neo-classical non-arbitrage conditions econometrically applicable relationships between the second-hand prices on the one hand and the efficiency and survival curves.

Next, in Section 5, three parametric survival functions are defined, characterized by, respectively, exponentially declining survival and efficiency functions with infinite maximal life-time (exponential decay), convex survival and efficiency functions with finite maximal life-time, and concave survival and efficiency functions with finite maximal life-time. We discuss the way in which the curvature of the survival function interferes with the growth rate of investment in determining the age distribution of the capital and its average retirement rate. Numerical illustrations of the sensitivity of the retirement rate and properties of the age distribution to changes in the curvature of the survival function and the growth pattern of investment are given in Section 6. A main conclusion is that the retirement rate is a declining function of the growth rate of investment and is quite sensitive to the value of this growth rate over a reasonable interval. If, for example, the (continuous) growth rate of investment increases from 0 to 5 per cent and all capital retires simultaneously at age 20, the retirement rate decreases from 5 per cent to 2.9 per cent. With linear retirement over 20 years, the corresponding retirement rate decreases from 10 per cent to 8.6 per cent.

BASIC TERMINOLOGY AND VARIABLES

Let $J(t)$ denote the quantity of capital of a certain kind invested at time t, where time is considered as continuous. The investment brings an increase in the production capacity at time t, which gradually disappears as the capital becomes older. This is characterized by the function $B_S(s) \in [0,1]$, indicating the proportion of the capacity of a capital stock, measured in physical units (*e.g.*, the number of identical machines or automobiles), which survives at age $s(\geq 0)$, denoted as the *survival curve*. It has the following properties

$$B_S'(s) \leq 0, B_S(0) = 1, B_S(\infty) = 0. \tag{2.1}$$

The capital volume of of age s at time t, measured in *physical* units, is then

$$C(t,s) = B_S(s)\,J(t\text{–}s). \tag{2.2}$$

The efficiency of each remaining capital unit, *i.e.*, each unit in $C(t,s)$, also declines over time: one machine of age s' at time t is in general less efficient than machine of age $s(s' > s)$ at time t. To indicate this decline, we introduce the function $B_E(s) \in [0,1]$, denoted as the *efficiency curve*, indicating the efficiency of one *physical* capital unit existing at age s relative to its efficiency as new. It has the same general properties as the survival curve,

$$B_E'(s) \leq 0, B_E(0) = 1, B_E(\infty) = 0, \tag{2.3}$$

but their specific forms usually differ. The volume of the capital stock which is of age s at time t, measured in *efficiency* units, then can be written as

$$K(t,s) = B_E(s)\,C(t,s). \tag{2.4}$$

Combining (2.2) and (2.4), we get

$$K(t,s) = B(s)\,J(t-s), \tag{2.5}$$

where

$$B(s) = B_S(s)\,B_E(s). \tag{2.6}$$

Eqs. (2.1)–(2.4) imply $K(t,s) \le C(t,s) \le J(t-s)$ for all t and $s \ge 0$, *i.e.*, capital measured in efficiency units can never exceed capital measured in physical units, which in turn can never exceed the number of units originally invested.

We make the familiar assumption that capital in efficiency units is measured such that *one unit of capital produces one unit of capital services per unit of time*. This normalization implies that $K(t,s)$ has not only a stock interpretation, but also represents the instantaneous flow of capital services produced at time t by the stock of capital which is of age s. Correspondingly, the efficiency curve, $B_E(s)$, represents the (intensity of the) flow of capital services at age s per physical capital unit existing at this age, and $B(s)$, denoted as the combined *efficiency-survival function*, represents the (intensity of the) flow of capital services at age s per unit of capital originally invested. It follows from (2.6) that the latter function represents both the disappearance of capital goods and their loss of efficiency with age and has the same general properties as its two components [cf. (2.1) and (2.3)]. It is, however, possible for $B_S(s)$ and $B_E(s)$ to be concave while $B(s)$ is convex (at least on a certain interval). An example will be given in Section 5.

According to *neo-classical* production theory, capital is malleable, *i.e.*, capital efficiency units belonging to different vintages are perfectly substitutable inputs at any point in time, so that the total capital input at time t as an argument in a production function can be represented by

$$K(t) = \int_0^\infty K(t,s)ds = \int_0^\infty B(s)J(t-s)ds. \tag{2.7}$$

This variable, the *gross capital stock*, has the joint interpretation as the total number of capital efficiency units at time t and the instantaneous flow of services 'produced' by these units at time t. This contrasts with the *'putty-clay' approach* in which (i) each capital vintage is assumed to have its specific input coefficients *ex post*, determined at the time of investment [cf. Johansen (1959, 1972)], (ii) capital is not malleable, and (iii) (planned and realized) retirement of capital is determined from profitability conditions, *e.g.*, formalized by means of a quasi-rent criterion [cf. Biørn and Frenger (1992)].

The flow of capital retired at time t, measured in efficiency units, is, by definition, the difference between gross investment and the increase in the gross capital stock. Using (2.6) and (2.7), *retirement* at time t can be expressed as

$$D(t) = J(t) - \dot{K}(t) = \int_0^\infty b(s)J(t-s)\,ds, \tag{2.8}$$

where

$$b(s) = -B'(s) = b_E(s)B_S(s) + b_S(s)B_E(s), b_i(s) = -B_i'(s)(i = S, E), \tag{2.9}$$

The function $b(s)$, denoted as the *(relative) retirement function, or retirement (mortality) curve*, of the retirement process: $b(s)ds$ is the share of an *initial investment* of one unit, still measured in efficiency units, which disappears from s to $s+ds$ years after installation. From (2.1), (2.2), and (2.9) it follows that $b(s)$, $b_S(s)$, and $b_E(s)$ are non-negative with $\int_0^\infty b(s)ds = \int_0^\infty b_S(s)ds = \int_0^\infty b_E(s)ds = 1$.

Let

$$\beta(s) = \frac{b(s)}{B(s)} = -\frac{d\ln B(s)}{ds} = \beta_E(s) + \beta_S(s), \beta_i(s) = = -\frac{d\ln B_i(s)}{ds}(i = S, E), \tag{2.10}$$

so that $\beta(s)ds$ is the share of the *remaining capital* at age s, measured in efficiency units, which disappears from s to $s + ds$ years after installation. The difference between $b(s)$ and $\beta(s)$ follows from their different normalization: $b(s)$ assumes normalization with respect to the *initial* investment, $\beta(s)$ assumes normalization with respect to the capital *remaining*. The latter corresponds to *age specific mortality rates* in demography. In a probabilistic setting, $B(s)$ can be interpreted as the survival probability, $1 - B(s)$ as the non-survival probability, $b(s)$ as the density function and $\beta(s)$ as the *hazard rate, or failure rate, function* of capital measured in efficiency units; see Barlow and Proschan (1975, section 3.1) and Kalbfleisch and Prentice (1980, section 1.2).

Retirement at time t, given by (2.8), can be decomposed by vintages, such that

$$D(t,s) = b(s)J(t-s) = \beta(s)K(t,s) \tag{2.11}$$

denotes the retirement of capital of age s at time t, *i.e.*, belonging to vintage $t-s$ at time t. Then (2.8) can be written as

$$D(t) = \int_0^\infty D(t,s)ds. \tag{2.12}$$

Age Distribution of Capital and Retirement

We next consider the age distributions of capital and retirement. Using (2.5) and (2.7), the *age distribution of the gross capital stock* at time t can be described by

$$k(t,s)=\frac{K(t,s)}{K(t)}=\frac{B(s)J(t-s)}{\int_0^\infty B(s)J(t-s)ds}, s\geq 0, \int_0^\infty k(t,s)ds=1. \tag{3.1}$$

From (2.11) and (2.12) it follows, in a similar way, that the *age distribution of retirement* at time t can be described by

$$d(t,s)=\frac{D(t,s)}{D(t)}=\frac{b(s)J(t-s)}{\int_0^\infty b(s)J(t-s)ds}, s\geq 0, \int_0^\infty d(t,s)ds=1. \tag{3.2}$$

Eq. (2.11) implies that the *age specific retirement rate* for age s at time t, $D(t,s)/K(t,s)=\beta(s)$, is time invariant, whereas (2.7), (2.10), (2.12), and (3.1) imply that the *overall retirement rate* becomes

$$\delta(t)=\frac{D(t)}{K(t)}=\frac{\int_0^\infty b(s)J(t-s)ds}{\int_0^\infty B(s)J(t-s)ds}=\int_0^\infty \beta(s)k(t,s)ds$$
$$=\int_0^\infty [\beta_S(s)+\beta_E(s)]k(t,s)ds. \tag{3.3}$$

This rate is an average of the age specific retirement rates, weighted by the age distribution of gross capital at time t. It will therefore, in general, be *time dependent.* If, however, *either* $\beta(s)$ is age invariant *i.e.*, both $\beta_S(s)$ and $\beta_E(s)$ are time invariant, *or* the age distribution $k(t,s)$ is time invariant, then $\delta(t)$ will be a constant independent of t. These are the only two cases in which $\delta(t)$ will be time invariant.

From (3.1)–(3.3) it follows that the relationship between the age distributions of retirement and of capital can be expressed as

$$d(t,s)=\frac{\beta(s)k(t,s)}{\int_0^\infty \beta(s)k(t,s)ds}\Longleftrightarrow\frac{d(t,s)}{k(t,s)}=\frac{\beta(s)}{\delta(t)}, \tag{3.4}$$

i.e., the ratio between the shares of retirement and of capital at time t which have age s equals the ratio between the age specific retirement rate at age s and the overall retirement rate at time t.

Let now $\gamma(t,s)=J(t-s)/J(t)(s\geq 0)$ denote the *growth path of gross investment* up to time t. The rates $k(t,s)$, $d(t,s)$, and $\delta(t)$ then can be reexpressed in terms of, respectively, the survival function $B(s)$ and the growth path of investment $\gamma(t,s)$:

$$k(t,s)=\frac{B(s)\gamma(t,s)}{\int_0^\infty B(s)\gamma(t,s)ds}, \tag{3.5}$$

the retirement function $b(s)$ and the growth path of investment $\gamma(t,s)$:

$$d(t,s) = \frac{b(s)\gamma(t,s)}{\int_0^\infty b(s)\gamma(t,s)ds}, \tag{3.6}$$

and the survival function $B(s)$, the retirement function $b(s)$, and the growth path $\gamma(t,s)$:

$$\begin{aligned}\delta(t) &= \frac{\int_0^\infty b(s)\gamma(t,s)ds}{\int_0^\infty B(s)\gamma(t,s)ds} = \frac{\int_0^\infty \beta(s)B(s)\gamma(t,s)ds}{\int_0^\infty B(s)\gamma(t,s)ds} \\ &= \frac{\int_0^\infty [\beta_S(s)+\beta_E(s)]B_S(s)B_E(s)\gamma(t,s)ds}{\int_0^\infty B_S(s)B_E(s)\gamma(t,s)ds}.\end{aligned} \tag{3.7}$$

Eqs. (3.5)–(3.7) show that $k(t,s)$, $d(t,s)$, *and* $\delta(t)$ *are all time invariant for any* $B(s)$ *if and only if* $\gamma(t,s)$ *is time invariant.* The demographic analogue is that of a *stable population*; cf. Coale (1972) and Keyfitz (1977). For $\gamma(t,s) = J(t-s)/J(t)$ to be independent of t for all t and s, it must be an *exponential function* of the form $\gamma(t,s) = e^{-\alpha s}$. The latter assumption will be considered specifically in Sections 5–7. If $\beta(s) = -d\ln[B(s)]/ds$ is constant, which implies that $B(s)$ is an exponential function of the form $B(s) = e^{-\delta s}$ (exponential decay), $\delta(t)$ will be time invariant and equal to the constant δ for any $\gamma(t,s)$. *To summarize, constancy of* $\delta(t)$ *implies that at least one of the functions* $B(s)$ *or* $\gamma(t,s)$ *must be exponential functions in* s.

Nickell comments on the latter result by saying that if $\delta(t)$ "is to settle down to a constant level in the long run in the absence of exponential decay, investment must settle to an exponential growth path in the long run. This is, in fact the result of renewal theory which has been quoted ..... as a justification for assuming that the potential replacement-capital ratio is constant. Now, if investment was indeed moving on a fixed exponential growth path, a proliferation of investment equations would hardly be required to explain this movement and consequently any serious theoretical justification of the assumption of a fixed potential replacement-capital ratio for empirical work must fall back on exponential decay" [Nickell (1978, p. 119)].

If gross investment is constant, i.e., $\gamma(t,s) = 1$ for all t and s, the age distributions of capital and retirement and the overall retirement rates will be stationary, depending on the form of the survival function only. Let us take a look at this case.

Let Φ denote the total flow of services produced by one capital efficiency unit during its entire life-time, *i.e.*,

$$\Phi = \int_0^\infty B(s)ds = \int_0^\infty B_S(s)B_E(s)ds. \tag{3.8}$$

If gross investment is constant and equal to J, it follows from from (2.7) and (2.8) that

$$K(t) = K = \Phi J, \tag{3.9}$$

$$D(t) = D = J. \tag{3.10}$$

Then the (constant) capital stock equals the (constant) gross investment times the per unit of capital service flow during the unit's life-time; net investment, $\dot{K}$, is zero. This corresponds to a *stationary population* in demography. Hence,

$$\delta(t) = \delta = \frac{D}{K} = \frac{1}{\Phi}, \tag{3.11}$$

i.e., under constant gross investment, the overall retirement rate is constant and equal to the inverse of the total service flow per capital efficiency unit during its life-time. If the survival function declines so rapidly that $\Phi < 1$ – which is rather unlikely to occur in practice – the overall retirement rate, given our continuous time formulation of the retirement process will exceed 1.

From (3.1), (3.2), and (3.8) we find, furthermore, that under constant gross investment, the age distribution of capital and retirement are stationary and given by

$$k(t,s) = \frac{B(s)}{\Phi}, \tag{3.12}$$

$$d(t,s) = b(s), \tag{3.13}$$

respectively, for all t. Then we have

$$\frac{d(t,s)}{k(t,s)} = \frac{b(s)}{B(s)}\Phi = \beta(s)\Phi, \tag{3.14}$$

so that the two age distributions will coincide if and only if the hazard rate $\beta(s)$ is constant and equal to the inverse of the total service flow per capital unit during its life-time. This is the 'exponential decay' case, which will be discussed in Section 5.

How Does the Vintage Price Structure Depend on the Retirement Process?

We now demonstrate how it is possible, by exploiting neo-classical assumptions, to establish an econometrically applicable relationship between the second-hand prices on capital goods on the one hand and the efficiency and survival curves $B_E(s)$ and $B_S(s)$ on the other.

Consider a stock of capital goods which have attained age s. Let $\Phi_\rho(s)$ be the *future service flow per efficiency unit of capital which is s years of age*, discounted at the rate ρ. It can be expressed in terms of the efficiency-survival function $B(s)$ as [cf. Biшrn (1989, section 3.3.1)]

$$\Phi_\rho(s) = \frac{\int_s^\infty e^{-\rho(z-s)} B(z)\,dz}{B(s)} = \frac{\int_s^\infty e^{-\rho(z-s)} B_S(z) B_E(z)\,dz}{B_S(s) B_E(s)}. \tag{4.1}$$

In particular, $\Phi = \Phi_0(0)$. The numerator of this expression represents the flow of capital services produced by one *new* capital unit from the time it is s years old until it is scrapped, discounted to the time when it attains age s. Since the service flow is a quantity concept, we interpret the rate of discount ρ as a real interest rate. The denominator represents the share of the initial investment, measured in efficiency units, which attains age s.

Let $q(t)$ denote the *investment price, i.e.*, the price of a new capital unit, at time t. The value of the new investment at time t is $V(t,0) = q(t)J(t) = q(t)C(t,0) = q(t)K(t,0)$. Corresponding to the two quantity measures of capital, $K(t,s)$ and $C(t,s)$, we define two *vintage price* variables: $q(t,s)$ is the price *per efficiency unit* of capital of age s at time t, and $p(t,s)$ is the corresponding capital price measured *per physical unit* remaining at age s. The former is, in general, unobservable, while the latter can be observed from transactions in second-hand markets. The latter may be the price of an office building which is 20 years old, the price of an automobile which is 5 years old, etc. From the above assumptions it follows in particular that $q(t,0) = p(t,0) = q(t)$, and $V(t,0) = q(t)J(t) = p(t,0)C(t,0) =$ $= q(t,0)\,K(t,0)$.

The value of the capital stock which is s years of age at time t can be written as

$$V(t,s) = p(t,s)\,C(t,s) = q(t,s)\,K(t,s). \tag{4.2}$$

Combining (2.4) and (4.2), we see that the two vintage prices are related by

$$p(t,s) = B_E(s)\,q(t,s) \text{ for all } t \text{ and all } s \geq 0. \tag{4.3}$$

We assume that the system of vintage prices measured *per efficiency unit* satisfies the following *perfect market assumption* [cf. Biшrn (1989, sections 3.5.2 and 3.5.4)]

$$\frac{q(t,s)}{\Phi_\rho(s)} = \frac{q(t)}{\Phi_\rho(0)} \text{ for all } t \text{ and all } s \geq 0. \tag{4.4}$$

This assumption postulates a 'law of indifference', or non-arbitrage condition, to exist between different capital vintages, in the sense that a firm which buys one *efficiency* unit of capital of age s at time t at the price $q(t,s)$ pays the same price per unit of *prospective* discounted capital services as a firm buying one new unit at the price $q(t)$. This equality holds for all ages at any point in time and is strongly related to the malleability assumption for capital, since when (4.4) is satisfied and capital can be moved freely, there is no possibility of arbitrage between vintages. Eq. (4.4) is related to, but is not identical to, the condition that the acquisition price of a capital asset shall be equal to the (present value of the) future rental prices of the capital weighted by the relative efficiency of the capital in each future period. Cf. Jorgenson (1989, section 1.2), as well as Hotelling (1925) and Hicks (1973, chapter II). Our way of formalizing the 'law of indifference' is more convenient for econometric applications. Expressed in terms of the (observable) second-hand prices $p(t,s)$, (4.4) says

$$\frac{p(t,s)}{B_E(s)\Phi_\rho(s)} = \frac{q(t)}{\Phi_\rho(0)} \text{ for all } t \text{ and all } s \geq 0. \tag{4.5}$$

From (2.2), (2.4), (4.2), and (4.4) it follows that the vintage specific capital value can be written as

$$\begin{aligned} V(t,s) &= q(t)\frac{\Phi_\rho(s)}{\Phi_\rho(0)}K(t,s) = q(t)\,B_E(s)\frac{\Phi_\rho(s)}{\Phi_\rho(0)}C(t,s) = \\ &= B_E(s)\,B_S(s)\frac{\Phi_\rho(s)}{\Phi_\rho(0)}q(t)\,J(t-s). \end{aligned} \tag{4.6}$$

The expression after the last equality sign is the capital value written in terms of the replacement value of the capital originally invested, $q(t)J(t-s)$, the survival curve, $B_S(s)$, the efficiency curve, $B_E(s)$, and the ratio between the discounted per unit service flow function at age s and at age 0. Inserting for $\Phi_\rho(s)$ from (4.1), we find

$$V(t,s) = \frac{\int_s^\infty e^{-\rho(z-s)}\,B_S(z)\,B_E(z)\,dz}{\int_0^\infty e^{-\rho z}\,B_S(z)\,B_E(z)\,dz}q(t)\,J(t-s), \tag{4.7}$$

which shows that the capital value of age s at time t can be interpreted simply as the product of the replacement value of the capital originally invested and the discounted share of the capital service flow, in volume terms, from one new capital unit which it 'produces' after age s.

Combining (4.1) and (4.5), it follows that at time t the ratio between the second-hand price at age s and the investment price is

$$\frac{p(t,s)}{q(t)} = \frac{\int_s^\infty e^{-\rho(z-s)} B_S(z) B_E(z)\, dz}{B_S(s) \int_0^\infty e^{-\rho z} B_S(z) B_E(z)\, dz}, \tag{4.8}$$

whose right-hand side is a function of s, ρ, and the parameters of the B_S and B_E functions. Hence, our assumption about the market for capital goods implies (i) that the second-hand price $p(t,s)$, for any given age s and rate of discount, ρ, changes in proportion to the corresponding price of a new capital unit, $q(t)$, and (ii) that there is a relationship between the price ratio $p(t,s)/q(t)$ on the one hand, and the survival curve $B_S(s)$ and the efficiency curve $B_E(s)$ of the capital on the other. Eq. (4.8) may therefore, in principle, be the basis for estimating survival and efficiency curves from second-hand price data when suitable parametrizations of $B_E(s)$ and $B_S(s)$ have been chosen. If, less likely, both these functions and the second-hand prices were completely known, (4.8) could be used to test the perfect capital market assumption econometrically.

In the usual case where $B_S(s)$ and $B_E(s)$ contain unknown parameters, application of (4.8) for estimation purposes has the inconvenience that it contains two integrals, one being a function of age s. For certain parametric forms of $B_S(s)$ and $B_E(s)$, however, the integrals can be written as rather simple closed form expressions; see Section 5. But in general, a reformulation may be needed. Below, we indicate one possible way to proceed. From (4.3) and (4.4) it follows, by differentiation with respect to s, that the rate of decline of the second-hand price with age at age s is independent of current time t and is equal to

$$\frac{\frac{\partial p(t,s)}{\partial s}}{p(t,s)} = \frac{\frac{\partial q(t,s)}{\partial s}}{q(t,s)} + \frac{B_E'(s)}{B_E(s)} = \frac{\Phi_\rho'(s)}{\Phi_\rho(s)} - \beta_E(s). \tag{4.9}$$

Now, since (4.1) implies $B(s)\Phi_\rho(s) = \int_s^\infty e^{-\rho(z-s)} B(z)dz$, it follows, by differentiation, that

$$B'(s)\Phi_\rho(s) + B(s)\Phi_\rho'(s) = \rho \int_s^\infty e^{-\rho(z-s)} B(z)\, dz - B(s).$$

Dividing by $B(s)\Phi_\rho(s)$ and using (2.10), we get

$$\frac{\Phi_\rho'(s)}{\Phi_\rho(s)} = \rho + \beta_S(s) + \beta_E(s) - \frac{1}{\Phi_\rho(s)}.$$

Inserting this in (4.9), we obtain

$$\frac{\frac{\partial p(t,s)}{\partial s}}{p(t,s)} = \rho + \beta_S(s) - \frac{1}{\Phi_\rho(s)},$$

where $\Phi_\rho(s)$ can be eliminated in the following way. Multiplication by $p(t,s)$, while using (4.5), yields a relationship between $\partial p(t,s)/\partial s$, $p(t,s)$, and $q(t)$,

$$\frac{\partial p(t,s)}{\partial s} = \lambda_1(s)\,p(t,s) + \lambda_2(s)\,q(t),$$

or

$$\frac{\frac{\partial p(t,s)}{\partial s}}{q(t)} = \lambda_1(s)\frac{p(t,s)}{q(t)} + \lambda_2(s), \tag{4.10}$$

where

$$\lambda_1(s) = \rho + \beta_S(s), \lambda_2(s) = -\frac{B_E(s)}{\Phi_\rho(0)}. \tag{4.11}$$

Hence, a basic implication of the 'perfect market assumption' (4.4) is that $\lambda_1(s)$ and $\lambda_2(s)$ in (4.10) are age dependent, but time invariant, parameters. Specifying $\lambda_1(s)$ and $\lambda_2(s)$ as unrestricted functions would be inappropriate. The former is the sum of the rate of discount and the rate of decline of the survival curve and is non-negative. The latter depends on the shape of the efficiency curve and, via $\Phi_\rho(0)$, also on the shape of the survival curve and the discount rate, and is non-positive. An econometric analysis of vintage price data under neo-classical assumptions should take account of this.

Parametric Survival and Efficiency Functions

In this section, we describe three examples, characterized by, respectively, exponentially declining survival function with infinite maximal life-time, convex survival function with finite maximal life-time, and concave survival function with finite maximal life-time. The first example is one-parametric, the second and third are two-parametric, with one parameter representing the maximal life-time and the other describing the curvature of the function.

Example 1: Exponential Decay

We first assume that the survival curve and the efficiency curve are both exponentially declining, with rates of decline $\delta_S (\geq 0)$ and $\delta_E (\geq 0)$, respectively, *i.e.*,

$$B_S(s) = e^{-\delta_S s}, B_E(s) = e^{-\delta_E s}, s \geq 0. \tag{5.1}$$

Using (2.6), (2.9) and (2.10) this implies

$$B(s) = e^{-\delta s}, \tag{5.2}$$

and

$$\begin{array}{lll} b_S(s) = \delta_S e^{-\delta_S s}, & b_E(s) = \delta_E e^{-\delta_E s}, & b(s) = \delta e^{-\delta s}, \\ \beta_S(s) = \delta_S, & \beta_E(s) = \delta_E, & \beta(s) = \delta, \end{array}$$

where

$$\delta = \delta_S + \delta_E. \tag{5.3}$$

The combined retirement-efficiency distribution thus has a *constant hazard rate*, equal to δ. Therefore, the combined efficiency-survival function is also exponential, and the discounted per unit service flow function (4.1) is age independent and equal to

$$\Phi_\rho(s) = \frac{1}{\rho + \delta_S + \delta_E} = \frac{1}{\rho + \delta}. \tag{5.4}$$

Inserting this in (4.3) and (4.4) it follows that

$$q(t,s) = q(t), \tag{5.5}$$

$$p(t,s) = e^{-\delta_E s} q(t). \tag{5.6}$$

Hence, the exponential decay assumption for both the survival and the efficiency curves has the particular implication that the efficiency unit price $q(t,s)$ is independent of age and is equal to the investment price. The second-hand price is, for $\delta_E > 0$, an exponentially declining function of age, with a rate of decline equal to the rate of decline of the efficiency curve. The expression for the latter price does not contain the rate of decline of the survival curve, δ_S. *Consequently, the shape of the survival curve cannot be identified from data on second-hand prices in this case.* Only the rate of decline of the efficiency curve, δ_E, is identifiable.

Combining (4.6), (5.1), and (5.4), it follows that the vintage capital values can be written simply as

$$V(t,s) = e^{-(\delta_S+\delta_S)s}\, q(t)\, J(t-s) = e^{-\delta s}\, q(t)\, J(t-s), \tag{5.7}$$

where the factor $e^{-\delta_E s}$ can be interpreted as 'belonging to' the price component and the factor $e^{-\delta_S s}$ as 'belonging to' the volume component. Eq. (2.2) in this case reads

$$C(t,s) = e^{-\delta_S s}\, J(t-s), \tag{5.8}$$

which implies that observations on $C(t,s)$, *i.e.*, capital measured in physical units, would be needed, in addition to the observations on gross investment, to identify δ_S.

The parameters (4.11) have the form

$$\lambda_1(s) = \rho + \delta_S, \lambda_2(s) = -(\rho + \delta_S + \delta_E)e^{-\delta_E s}.$$

Both are functions of δ_S, but $\lambda_1(s)$ is independent of s. However, since $p(t,s)$ satisfies (5.6), it follows that all terms containing ρ and δ_S in (4.10) vanish, and we get simply

$$\frac{\partial p(t,s)}{\partial s} = -\delta_E\, e^{-\delta_E s}\, q(t).$$

This expression is the derivative of (5.6) with respect to age, which confirms our conclusion that in this exponential decay case the rate of decline of the *survival* curve cannot be identified from data on second-hand prices.

We also find from (3.5) and (3.6)

$$k(t,s) = d(t,s) = \frac{e^{-\delta s}\gamma(t,s)}{\int_0^\infty e^{-\delta s}\gamma(t,s)ds},$$

$$\delta(t) = \delta,$$

so that this survival function is characterized by identical age distributions of capital and retirement and a constant overall retirement rate.

Assume now *constant rate of investment growth* at the rate α, $J(t-s) = J(t)e^{-\alpha s}$ for all t and s. Then we get

$$K(t) = \int_0^\infty e^{-(\delta+\alpha)s} ds = \frac{J(t)}{\delta+\alpha},$$

$$D(t) = \delta \int_0^\infty e^{-(\delta+\alpha)s} ds = \frac{\delta J(t)}{\delta+\alpha} = \delta K(t).$$

It is easy to show that net investment then equals

$$\dot{K}(t) = \alpha \int_0^\infty e^{-(\delta+\alpha)s} ds = \frac{\alpha J(t)}{\delta+\alpha} = \alpha K(t),$$

which implies that the net investment/gross investment ratio is larger the larger is the growth rate of the investment. There is proportionality between $K(t)$, $D(t)$, $\dot{K}(t)$, and $J(t)$. If δ and α are positive, the net investment/retirement ratio equals α/δ. The capital/gross investment ratio and the retirement/gross investment ratio are smaller the larger is the past growth rate of the investment. If investment is declining, with $\delta > -\alpha$, retirement will exceed gross investment, *i.e.*, net investment will be negative. The two age distributions coincide in this case,

$$k(t,s) = d(t,s) = (\delta+\alpha)e^{-(\delta+\alpha)s}$$

i.e., the age specific shares are time invariant and have the same form as an exponential decay retirement function with δ replaced by $(\delta+\alpha)$.

Example 2: Convex Survival and Efficiency Functions

In our second example, we assume that the maximal service life of the capital is a finite constant, N, and that the survival curve and the efficiency curve are both convex functions of age up to this maximal age. Their parametric forms are

$$B_S(s) = \left(1-\frac{s}{N}\right)^{\tau_S}, B_E(s) = \left(1-\frac{s}{N}\right)^{\tau_E}, 0 \le s \le N, \tag{5.9}$$

where $\tau_S(\ge 1)$ and $\tau_E(\ge 1)$ are constants, to be denoted as 'curvature parameters'. The functions are *strictly* convex for $\tau_S > 1$ and $\tau_E > 1$. If $\tau_S \in (0,1)$ and $\tau_E \in (0,1)$, the functions are concave. For brevity, we denote the functions as convex even if they are concave for certain parameter values. Using (2.6) it follows that the combined efficiency-survival function has the same parametric form as its components, with a 'curvature parameter' which is the sum of the 'curvature parameters' of its two components, *i.e.*,

$$B(s) = \left(1-\frac{s}{N}\right)^{\tau_S+\tau_E}, 0 \le s \le N. \tag{5.10}$$

The fact that $B(s)$ belongs to the same class of functions as $B_S(s)$ and $B_E(s)$ is a property which this example shares with the exponential decay example, cf. (5.2).

Using (2.9) and (2.10) we also obtain

$$b_S(s) = \frac{\tau_S}{N}\left(1 - \frac{s}{N}\right)^{\tau_S - 1}, \quad b_E(s) = \frac{\tau_E}{N}\left(1 - \frac{s}{N}\right)^{\tau_E - 1}, \quad b(s) = \frac{\tau}{N}\left(1 - \frac{s}{N}\right)^{\tau - 1},$$

$$\beta_S(s) = \frac{\tau_S}{N - s}, \qquad \beta_E(s) = \frac{\tau_E}{N - s}, \qquad \beta(s) = \frac{\tau}{N - s},$$

where

$$\tau = \tau_S + \tau_E. \tag{5.11}$$

In describing the properties of the convex survival and efficiency functions we need the function

$$F(i,z) = \int_0^1 e^{z\theta}(1-\theta)^i d\theta = \sum_{j=1}^{\infty} \frac{i!\, z^{j-1}}{(i+j)!}, i = 0,1,2,..., \tag{5.12}$$

where the second equality is explained in the Appendix. Other properties of this function to be used below are also proved in the Appendix. This function is also useful in describing properties of the concave survival and efficiency functions.

The general expression for $\Phi_\rho(s)$ for arbitrary s and ρ is a bit complicated. For $s = 0$ and ρ arbitrary, we obtain by substituting $\theta = s/N, i = \tau, z = -\rho N$ in (5.12),

$$\Phi_\rho(0) = \int_0^N e^{-\rho s}(1 - s/N)^\tau ds = NF(\tau, -\rho N) = \frac{N}{\tau + 1}[1 - \rho N F(\tau + 1, -\rho N)], \tag{5.13}$$

where the last equality is shown in (A.5). For $\rho = 0$, *i.e.*, no discounting of the capital service flow and s arbitrary, it follows, by using (4.1) and (5.10), that the per unit service flow function is

$$\Phi_0(s) = \frac{N - s}{\tau_S + \tau_E + 1}. \tag{5.14}$$

From (4.3), (4.4), (5.9), and (5.14) we find that the vintage prices satisfy

$$q(t,s) = \left(1 - \frac{s}{N}\right) q(t), \tag{5.15}$$

$$p(t,s) = \left(1 - \frac{s}{N}\right)^{\tau_E} \frac{N - s}{N} q(t) = \left(1 - \frac{s}{N}\right)^{\tau_E + 1} q(t). \tag{5.16}$$

The efficiency unit price $q(t,s)$ is a linearly declining function of age, regardless of τ_S and τ_E, while the second-hand price $p(t,s)$ is, for $\tau_E > 0$, a degressively declining function of age, with a curvature parameter equal to the curvature parameter of the efficiency curve increased by one. The expression for the latter price does not contain τ_S. *Consequently, the shape of the survival curve cannot be identified from data on second-hand prices in this case*, only τ_E is identifiable from such data. We obtained a similar conclusion in the exponential decay example.

Combining (4.4), (4.6), (5.9), and (5.14), it follows that the vintage specific capital value can be written simply as

$$V(t,s) = p(t,s)C(t,s) = \left(1-\frac{s}{N}\right)^{\tau_E+\tau_S+1} q(t)J(t-s), \tag{5.17}$$

where the factor $(1-s/N)^{\tau_E+1}$ can be interpreted as 'belonging to' the price component and the factor $(1-s/N)^{\tau_S}$ as 'belonging to' the volume component. Since (2.2) in this case reads

$$C(t,s) = \left(1-\frac{s}{N}\right)^{\tau_S} J(t-s), \tag{5.18}$$

observations on $C(t,s)$, *capital measured in physical units, would be needed, in addition to observations on gross investment, to identify* τ_S.

The parameters (4.11) have the form

$$\lambda_1(s) = \frac{\tau_S}{N-s}, \lambda_2(s) = -\frac{\tau_S+\tau_E+1}{N}\left(1-\frac{s}{N}\right)^{\tau_E},$$

both of which are functions of τ_S. However, since $p(t,s)$ satisfies (5.16), it follows that all terms containing τ_S in (4.10) vanish, and we get simply

$$\frac{\partial p(t,s)}{\partial s} = -\frac{\tau_E+1}{N}\left(1-\frac{s}{N}\right)^{\tau_E} q(t).$$

This expression is the derivative of (5.16) with respect to age. This confirms our conclusion that the curvature parameter of the *survival* curve cannot be identified from data on second-hand prices in this case.

Inserting (5.10) into (3.5)–(3.7), we find the following expressions for the age distributions of capital and retirement and the (time dependent) overall retirement rate for an arbitrary growth path of investment, $\gamma(t,s)$:

$$k(t,s)=\frac{\left(1-\frac{s}{N}\right)^{\tau}\gamma(t,s)}{\int_0^N\left(1-\frac{s}{N}\right)^{\tau}\gamma(t,s)ds},.$$

$$d(t,s)=\frac{\left(1-\frac{s}{N}\right)^{\tau-1}\gamma(t,s)}{\int_0^N\left(1-\frac{s}{N}\right)^{\tau-1}\gamma(t,s)ds},$$

$$\delta(t)=\frac{\tau}{N}\frac{\int_0^N\left(1-\frac{s}{N}\right)^{\tau-1}\gamma(t,s)ds}{\int_0^N\left(1-\frac{s}{N}\right)^{\tau}\gamma(t,s)ds}$$

If τ is large, $k(t,s)$ and $d(t,s)$ are approximately equal, but they may be very different for small τ.

Let us again assume exponentially growing investment at the rate α. Since by substituting $\theta = s/N, i = \tau, z = -\alpha N$ in (5.12), we obtain [cf. (5.13)]

$$\int_0^N\left(1-\frac{s}{N}\right)^{\tau}e^{-\alpha s}ds = NF(\tau,-\alpha N)=\frac{N}{\tau+1}[1-\alpha NF(\tau+1,-\alpha N)].$$

We then can write the relationship between capital, gross investment, and retirement at time t as

$$K(t)=J(t)NF(\tau,-\alpha N)=J(t)\frac{N}{\tau+1}[1-\alpha NF(\tau+1,-\alpha N)],$$
$$D(t)=J(t)\tau F(\tau-1,-\alpha N)=J(t)[1-\alpha NF(\tau,-\alpha N)],$$

when again using (A.5). Eqs. (3.5) and (3.6) then yield

$$k(t,s)=\frac{e^{-\alpha s}}{NF(\tau,-\alpha N)}\left(1-\frac{s}{N}\right)^{\tau},$$
$$d(t,s)=\frac{e^{-\alpha s}}{NF(\tau-1,-\alpha N)}\left(1-\frac{s}{N}\right)^{\tau-1},$$

and hence *the overall retirement rate is time invariant* and can be written as the following function of $N, \tau = \tau_S + \tau_E$, and α :

$$\delta(t) = \delta = \frac{\tau}{N}\frac{F(\tau{-}1,-\alpha N)}{F(\tau,-\alpha N)} = \frac{\tau{+}1}{N}\frac{1-\alpha NF(\tau,-\alpha N)}{1-\alpha NF(\tau{+}1,-\alpha N)}. \tag{5.19}$$

Numerical illustrations will be given in Section 6.

In the particular case where $\tau = 1$, the expressions for capital, retirement, and the overall retirement rate become

$$K(t) = J(t)NF(1,-\alpha N) = J(t)\frac{1}{\alpha}\left[1-\frac{1}{\alpha N}(1-e^{-\alpha N})\right],$$

$$D(t) = J(t)F(0,-\alpha N) = J(t)\frac{1}{\alpha N}(1-e^{-\alpha N}),$$

$$\delta = \frac{1}{N}\frac{F(0,-\alpha N)}{F(1,-\alpha N)} = \frac{1}{N}\frac{1-e^{-\alpha N}}{1-\frac{1}{\alpha N}(1-e^{-\alpha N})},$$

when again using (A.5).

If we in (5.19) approximate $F(\tau,-\alpha N)$ and $F(\tau{+}1,-\alpha N)$ by the *first* term in their Taylor expansions, which are $1/(\tau{+}1)$ and $1/(\tau{+}2)$, respectively [cf. (A.6)], we find the following approximation formula for the retirement rate, provided that αN is not too large:

$$\delta \approx \frac{\tau{+}1}{N}\frac{1-\frac{\alpha N}{\tau+1}}{1-\frac{\alpha N}{\tau+2}} \approx \frac{\tau{+}1}{N}\left[1-\left(\frac{1}{\tau{+}1}-\frac{1}{\tau{+}2}\right)\alpha N\right] = \frac{\tau{+}1}{N}-\frac{\alpha}{\tau{+}2}. \tag{5.20}$$

Under *constant investment* ($\alpha = 0$), this class of survival-efficiency functions imply

$$K(t) = J(t)\frac{N}{\tau{+}1}, \qquad \delta = \frac{\tau{+}1}{N},$$

$$k(t,s) = \frac{\tau{+}1}{N}\left(1-\frac{s}{N}\right)^{\tau}, \quad d(t,s) = \frac{\tau}{N}\left(1-\frac{s}{N}\right)^{\tau-1}.$$

Comparing the expression $\delta = (\tau+1)/N$ with (5.19), we see that the retirement rate when gross investment grows at the rate α can be interpreted as obtained by multiplying its value under constant investment by a correction factor which is one for $\alpha = 0$ and in general depends on αN. Approximately, when α is not too large, (5.20) says that this correction simply leads to deducting a share $1/(\tau+2)$ of the growth rate of investment. This share declines from $1/3$ to zero as τ increases from 1 to infinity.

Example 2 contains efficiency-survival profiles frequently discussed in the literature as special cases. Let us consider two.

(a) $\tau_E = 0$**:** Then the efficiency curve has the *'one-hoss-shay'* pattern, *i.e.*, the efficiency is constant and equal to 1 up to the service life N and then drops to zero. In this case, (5.15) and (5.16) imply

$$\frac{q(t,s)}{q(t)} = \frac{p(t,s)}{q(t)} = 1 - \frac{s}{N},$$

i.e., the second-hand price $p(t,s)$, like the efficiency unit price $q(t,s)$, is a linearly declining function of age on $(0,N)$.

(b) $\tau_E = 1$**:** Then the efficiency of each capital unit is *linearly declining* with age up to the service life. Eqs. (5.15) and (5.16) then give

$$\frac{q(t,s)}{q(t)} = 1 - \frac{s}{N}, \frac{p(t,s)}{q(t)} = \left(1 - \frac{s}{N}\right)^2.$$

Now, the second-hand price $p(t,s)$ is a quadratically declining, convex function of age, whereas the efficiency unit price $q(t,s)$ is still linearly declining.

Example 3: Concave Survival and Efficiency Functions

In our third example we again assume that the maximal service life of the capital is a finite constant N, but now the survival curve and the efficiency curve are both concave functions of age up to this maximal age. Their parametric forms are

$$B_S(s) = 1 - \left(\frac{s}{N}\right)^{\sigma_S}, B_E(s) = 1 - \left(\frac{s}{N}\right)^{\sigma_E}, 0 \le s \le N, \tag{5.21}$$

where $\sigma_S(\ge 1)$ and $\sigma_E(\ge 1)$ are constants, to be denoted, like τ_S and τ_E, as 'curvature parameters'. The two functions are *strictly* concave for $\sigma_S > 1$ and $\sigma_E > 1$. If $\sigma_S \in (0,1)$ and $\sigma_E \in (0,1)$ the functions are convex. For brevity, we denote the functions as concave even if they are convex for certain parameter values.

Using (2.6), it follows that the combined efficiency-survival function is

$$B(s) = 1 - \left(\frac{s}{N}\right)^{\sigma_S} - \left(\frac{s}{N}\right)^{\sigma_E} + \left(\frac{s}{N}\right)^{\sigma_S+\sigma_E}, 0 \le s \le N. \tag{5.22}$$

This function does not, in general, belong to the same parametric class as its two components, which distinguishes this example from Examples 1 and 2. It may be concave on a certain interval and convex on another, as shown by the following illustrations:

1. $(\sigma_S,\sigma_E)=(1,2),(2,1)$: $B''(s)<0$ for $0\le s/N\le\frac{1}{3}$; $B''(s)>0$ for $\frac{1}{3}<s/N\le 1$.
2. $(\sigma_S,\sigma_E)=(2,2)$: $B''(s)<0$ for $0\le s/N\le 1/\sqrt{3}$; $B''(s)>0$ for $1/\sqrt{3}<s/N\le 1$.
3. $(\sigma_S,\sigma_E)=(1,3),(3,1)$: $B''(s)<0$ for $0\le s/N\le\frac{1}{2}$; $B''(s)>0$ for $\frac{1}{2}<s/N\le 1$.

If, however, $\sigma_E\to\infty, 1<\sigma_S<\infty$, then $B(s)=B_S(s)$, which is concave, and if $\sigma_S\to\infty, 1<\sigma_E<\infty$, then $B(s)=B_E(s)$, which is also concave. In the first case, the efficiency function has the 'one-hoss-shay' form, and in the second case, the survival function has the 'one-hoss-shay' form, since $\lim_{\sigma\to\infty}(s/N)^\sigma=0$ for $s<N$ and $=1$ for $s=N$.

Using (2.9) and (2.10) we obtain

$$b_S(s)=\frac{\sigma_S}{N}\left(\frac{s}{N}\right)^{\sigma_S-1}, b_E(s)=\frac{\sigma_E}{N}\left(\frac{s}{N}\right)^{\sigma_E-1},$$

$$\beta_S(s)=\frac{\sigma_S}{N}\frac{(s/N)^{\sigma_S-1}}{1-(s/N)^{\sigma_S}}, \beta_E(s)=\frac{\sigma_E}{N}\frac{(s/N)^{\sigma_E-1}}{1-(s/N)^{\sigma_E}},$$

$$b(s)=\frac{\sigma_S}{N}\left(\frac{s}{N}\right)^{\sigma_S-1}+\frac{\sigma_E}{N}\left(\frac{s}{N}\right)^{\sigma_E-1}-\frac{\sigma}{N}\left(\frac{s}{N}\right)^{\sigma-1},$$

$$\beta(s)=\frac{\frac{\sigma_S}{N}\left(\frac{s}{N}\right)^{\sigma_S-1}+\frac{\sigma_E}{N}\left(\frac{s}{N}\right)^{\sigma_E-1}-\frac{\sigma}{N}\left(\frac{s}{N}\right)^{\sigma-1}}{1-\left(\frac{s}{N}\right)^{\sigma_S}-\left(\frac{s}{N}\right)^{\sigma_E}+\left(\frac{s}{N}\right)^{\sigma}},$$

$$0<s<N, \sigma_S>1, \sigma_E>1,$$

where

$$\sigma=\sigma_S+\sigma_E. \tag{5.23}$$

Let

$$H(s,m)=\frac{1}{m}\left[1-\left(\frac{s}{N}\right)^m\right], m=1,2,\ldots,$$

$$\mu(\sigma_S,\sigma_E)=1-\frac{1}{\sigma_S+1}-\frac{1}{\sigma_E+1}+\frac{1}{\sigma+1}$$
$$=1-H(0,\sigma_S+1)-H(0,\sigma_E+1)+H(0,\sigma+1),$$

so that

$$\int_s^N \left[1-\left(\frac{z}{N}\right)^{\sigma_S}\right]\left[1-\left(\frac{z}{N}\right)^{\sigma_E}\right]dz$$
$$= N\left[1-\frac{s}{N}-H(s,\sigma_S+1)-H(s,\sigma_E+1)+H(s,\sigma+1)\right].$$

From (4.1), (4.3), (4.4), (5.22), and (5.24), assuming again that the rate of discount ρ is zero, and using $\Phi_0(0)=N\mu(\sigma_S,\sigma_E)$, we get

$$\Phi_0(s)=\frac{N\left[1-\frac{s}{N}-H(s,\sigma_S+1)-H(s,\sigma_E+1)+H(s,\sigma+1)\right]}{\left[1-\left(\frac{s}{N}\right)^{\sigma_S}\right]\left[1-\left(\frac{s}{N}\right)^{\sigma_E}\right]}, \tag{5.24}$$

$$q(t,s)=\frac{1-\frac{s}{N}-H(s,\sigma_S+1)-H(s,\sigma_E+1)+H(s,\sigma+1)}{\mu(\sigma_S,\sigma_E)\left[1-\left(\frac{s}{N}\right)^{\sigma_S}\right]\left[1-\left(\frac{s}{N}\right)^{\sigma_E}\right]}q(t), \tag{5.25}$$

$$p(t,s)=\frac{1-\frac{s}{N}-H(s,\sigma_S+1)-H(s,\sigma_E+1)+H(s,\sigma+1)}{\mu(\sigma_S,\sigma_E)\left[1-\left(\frac{s}{N}\right)^{\sigma_S}\right]}q(t). \tag{5.26}$$

Both of these price equations contain the curvature parameters of the survival curve and the efficiency curve. The corresponding equations in Examples 1 and 2, (5.5)–(5.6) and (5.15)–(5.16), did not have this property. *As a consequence, it is possible to identify both σ_S and σ_E from data on second-hand prices.* Note that σ_S and σ_E enter symmetrically in (5.24) and (5.25), but not in (5.26).

Combining (4.6) and (5.24) it follows that when $\rho=0$, the vintage specific capital value can be written as

$$V(t,s)=\frac{1-s/N-H(s,\sigma_S+1)-H(s,\sigma_E+1)+H(s,\sigma+1)}{\mu(\sigma_S,\sigma_E)}q(t)J(t-s). \tag{5.27}$$

In this case, we cannot split the ratio between the vintage capital value at age s, time t and the replacement value of the original investment, $V(t,s)/[q(t)J(t-s)]$, into two factors, a function of the curvature parameter of the efficiency curve, σ_E 'belonging to' the capital price component, and a function of the curvature parameter of the survival curve, σ_S 'belonging to' the volume component. This is a basic difference between Example 3 and Examples 1 and 2.

The parameters (4.11) have the form

$$\lambda_1(s) = \frac{\sigma_S}{N}\frac{(s/N)^{\sigma_S-1}}{1-(s/N)^{\sigma_S}}, \lambda_2(s) = -\frac{1-(s/N)^{\sigma_E}}{N\mu(\sigma_S,\sigma_E)},$$

both of which are functions of σ_S, and hence (4.10) becomes

$$\frac{\partial p(t,s)}{\partial s} = \frac{\sigma_S}{N}\frac{(s/N)^{\sigma_S-1}}{1-(s/N)^{\sigma_S}} p(t,s) - \frac{1-(s/N)^{\sigma_E}}{N\,\mu(\sigma_S,\sigma_E)} q(t). \tag{5.28}$$

This equation can be used, instead of (5.26), for making inference on σ_S and σ_E (and N) from data on second-hand prices.

We next consider the age distribution of capital and retirement, confining attention to the case where the *combined survival-efficiency function* is concave. We represent this by letting either σ_S or σ_E go to infinity and instead of (5.23) let σ symbolize the curvature parameter which is finite and larger than 1. From (5.22) we then get Again, one parameter, N, is the maximal life-time, the other, σ, characterizes the curvature of the survival function. It is given by [cf. Biuurn (1989, section 11.2.1)]

$$B(s) = 1 - \left(\frac{s}{N}\right)^{\sigma}, N > 0, \sigma \geq 1, 0 \leq s \leq N, \tag{5.29}$$

$$b(s) = \frac{\sigma}{N}\left(\frac{s}{N}\right)^{\sigma-1}, \beta(s) = \frac{\frac{\sigma}{N}\left(\frac{s}{N}\right)^{\sigma-1}}{1-\left(\frac{s}{N}\right)^{\sigma}}.$$

In this case, $B(s)$ and $b(s)$ do *not* belong to the same class of functions. The hazard rate is a monotonically increasing function of the capital's age and goes to infinity at the maximal age N. The survival function is strictly concave for $\sigma > 1$ and linear for $\sigma = 1$.

Inserting these functions into (3.5)–(3.7), we find the following expressions for the age distributions of capital and retirement and the (time dependent) overall retirement rate for an arbitrary growth path of investment, $\gamma(t,s)$:

$$k(t,s)=\frac{\left[1-\left(\frac{s}{N}\right)^{\sigma}\right]\gamma(t,s)}{\int_0^N\left[1-\left(\frac{s}{N}\right)^{\sigma}\right]\gamma(t,s)ds},$$

$$d(t,s)=\frac{\left(\frac{s}{N}\right)^{\sigma-1}\gamma(t,s)}{\int_0^N\left(\frac{s}{N}\right)^{\sigma-1}\gamma(t,s)ds},$$

$$\delta(t)=\frac{\sigma}{N}\frac{\int_0^N\left(\frac{s}{N}\right)^{\sigma-1}\gamma(t,s)ds}{\int_0^N\left[1-\left(\frac{s}{N}\right)^{\sigma}\right]\gamma(t,s)ds}.$$

We again assume exponentially growing investment at the rate α. Since, from (A.1) and (A.5), by substituting $\lambda = s/N$ and $i=\sigma$,

$$\int_0^N\left(\frac{s}{N}\right)^{\sigma}e^{-\alpha s}ds=Ne^{-\alpha N}F(\sigma,\alpha N)=\frac{N}{\sigma+1}e^{-\alpha N}[1+\alpha NF(\sigma+1,\alpha N)],$$

so that

$$\int_0^N\left[1-\left(\frac{s}{N}\right)^{\sigma}\right]e^{-\alpha s}ds=Ne^{-\alpha N}[F(0,\alpha N)-F(\sigma,\alpha N)],$$

we can write the relationship between capital, gross investment, and retirement at time t as

$$K(t)=J(t)Ne^{-\alpha N}[F(0,\alpha N)-F(\sigma,\alpha N)],$$
$$D(t)=J(t)\sigma e^{-\alpha N}F(\sigma-1,\alpha N)=J(t)e^{-\alpha N}[1+\alpha NF(\sigma,\alpha N)].$$

It also follows that

$$k(t,s)=\frac{e^{-\alpha s}}{Ne^{-\alpha N}[F(0,\alpha N)-F(\sigma,\alpha N)]}\left[1-\left(\frac{s}{N}\right)^{\sigma}\right],$$

$$d(t,s)=\frac{e^{-\alpha s}}{Ne^{-\alpha N}F(\sigma-1,\alpha N)}\left(\frac{s}{N}\right)^{\sigma-1}.$$

Hence, *the overall retirement rate is time invariant* and can be written as the following function of N, σ, and α:

$$\delta(t) = \delta = \frac{\sigma}{N}\frac{F(\sigma-1,\alpha N)}{F(0,\alpha N) - F(\sigma,\alpha N)}. \tag{5.30}$$

Simultaneous retirement: This case can be considered the special case of the concave survival function (5.29) where $\sigma \to \infty$:

$$B(s) = 1 - \lim_{\sigma\to\infty}\left(\frac{s}{N}\right)^{\sigma} = \begin{cases} 1, & s < N, \\ 0, & s = N. \end{cases}$$

It then follows, by using (A.3) and (A.4), that capital and retirement becomes

$$K(t) = J(t)Ne^{-\alpha N}F(0,\alpha N) = J(t)NF(0,-\alpha N),$$
$$D(t) = J(t-N) = J(t)e^{-\alpha N}.$$

The overall retirement rate, obtained from (5.30), is

$$\delta = \frac{1}{NF(0,\alpha N)} = \frac{e^{-\alpha N}}{NF(0,-\alpha N)}.$$

Immediate retirement: This case, in which all capital goods vanish immediately after investment, may be considered the special case of simultaneous retirement where the life-time is $N = 1$. We then get

$$K(t) = J(t)e^{-\alpha}F(0,\alpha) = J(t)F(0,-\alpha),$$
$$D(t) = J(t)e^{-\alpha},$$

and the overall retirement rate becomes

$$\delta = \frac{1}{F(0,\alpha)} = \frac{e^{-\alpha}}{F(0,-\alpha)}.$$

If we let α go to zero – which has the interpretation that investment is constant over the age interval $(0,1)$ – we simply get $K(t) = D(t) = J(t)$ and $\delta = 1$, which agree with our intuitive understanding of immediate retirement when the life-time is arbitrarily short.

If we approximate $F(\sigma-1,\alpha N)$, $F(0,\alpha N)$ and $F(\sigma,\alpha N)$ by the *first and second* term in their Taylor expansions, which are $(1/\sigma)[1+\alpha N/(\sigma+1)]$, $1+\alpha N/2$ and $[1/(\sigma+1)][1+\alpha N/(\sigma+2)]$, respectively, [cf. (A.6)] we find the following approximation formula for the retirement rate provided that αN is not too large:

$$\delta \approx \frac{\sigma}{N}\frac{\frac{1}{\sigma}+\frac{\alpha N}{\sigma(\sigma+1)}}{\left(1+\frac{\alpha N}{2}\right)-\left(\frac{1}{\sigma+1}+\frac{\alpha N}{(\sigma+1)(\sigma+2)}\right)}$$

$$=\frac{1}{N}\frac{1+\frac{\alpha N}{\sigma+1}}{\frac{\sigma}{\sigma+1}+\left(\frac{1}{2}-\frac{1}{(\sigma+1)(\sigma+2)}\right)\alpha N}=\frac{\sigma+1}{\sigma N}\frac{1+\frac{\alpha N}{\sigma+1}}{1+\frac{\sigma+3}{2(\sigma+2)}\alpha N} \tag{5.31}$$

$$\approx\frac{\sigma+1}{\sigma N}\left[1-\left(\frac{\sigma+3}{2(\sigma+2)}-\frac{1}{\sigma+1}\right)\alpha N\right]=\frac{\sigma+1}{\sigma N}-\left(\frac{(\sigma+1)(\sigma+3)}{2\sigma(\sigma+2)}-\frac{1}{\sigma}\right)\alpha.$$

Under *constant investment* ($\alpha = 0$), when we use (A.2), this survival function implies

$$K(t)=J(t)\frac{N\sigma}{\sigma+1},$$

$$k(t,s)=\frac{\sigma+1}{N\sigma}\left[1-\left(\frac{s}{N}\right)^{\sigma}\right],$$

$$d(t,s)=\frac{\sigma}{N}\left(\frac{s}{N}\right)^{\sigma-1},$$

$$\delta=\frac{\sigma+1}{N\sigma}.$$

Comparing the last expression with (5.30) and using (A.2), we see that we can interpret the retirement rate when gross investment grows at the rate α as obtained by multiplying its value under constant investment by a correction factor which is one for $\alpha = 0$ and in general depends on αN. Approximately, when α is not too large, this correction implies that we should deduct a share of the growth rate of investment which increases from $1/3$ to $1/2$ as σ increases from 1 to infinity. Numerical illustrations are given in Section 7.

It is informative to consider special cases of Example 3. We let, for brevity, $x = s/N$.

(a) $\sigma_S \to \infty, \sigma_E \to \infty$**:** In this case, the survival curve and the efficiency curve both follow the *'one-hoss-shay'* pattern, since $\lim_{\sigma\to\infty}(s/N)^{\sigma} = 0$ for $s < N$ and $=1$ for $s = N$. This case coincides with Example 2 when $\tau_S = \tau_E = 0$. Since $H(s,\infty) = 0$ and $\mu = 1$, (5.25) and (5.26) then give

$$\frac{q(t,s)}{q(t)} = \frac{p(t,s)}{q(t)} = 1-x.$$

(b) $\sigma_S = 1, \sigma_E \to \infty$**:** In this case, the efficiency curve follows the 'one-hoss-shay' pattern, while the survival curve, and hence also the combined survival-efficiency curve, are linearly declining. This case coincides with Example 2 when $\tau_S = 1, \tau_E = 0$. Then $\mu = 1/2$, and we get from (5.25) and (5.26)

$$\frac{q(t,s)}{q(t)} = \frac{p(t,s)}{q(t)} = \frac{1-x-\frac{1}{2}(1-x^2)}{\frac{1}{2}(1-x)} = 1-x.$$

(c) $\sigma_S \to \infty, \sigma_E = 1$**:** In this case, the survival curve follows the 'one-hoss-shay' pattern, while the efficiency curve, and hence also the combined survival-efficiency curve, are linearly declining. This case coincides with Example 2 when $\tau_S = 0, \tau_E = 1$. Then $\mu = 1/2$, and we get from (5.25) and (5.26)

$$\frac{q(t,s)}{q(t)} = \frac{1-x-\frac{1}{2}(1-x^2)}{\frac{1}{2}(1-x)} = 1-x,$$

$$\frac{p(t,s)}{q(t)} = \frac{1-x-\frac{1}{2}(1-x^2)}{\frac{1}{2}} = (1-x)^2.$$

(d) $\sigma_S = \sigma_E = 1$**:** In this case, both the survival curve and the efficiency curve are linearly declining. This case coincides with Example 2 for $\tau_S = \tau_E = 1$. Then $\mu = 1-1/2-1/2+1/3 = 1/3$, and we get from (5.25) and (5.26)

$$\frac{q(t,s)}{q(t)} = \frac{1-x-2\frac{1}{2}(1-x^2)+\frac{1}{3}(1-x^3)}{\frac{1}{3}(1-x)^2} = 1-x,$$

$$\frac{p(t,s)}{q(t)} = \frac{1-x-2\frac{1}{2}(1-x^2)+\frac{1}{3}(1-x^3)}{\frac{1}{3}(1-x)} = (1-x)^2.$$

Cases **(a)** and **(b)** give identical age-price profiles, which is also true for cases **(c)** and **(d)**. This may seem surprising, but follows from the fact that $(\sigma_S, \sigma_E) = (\infty,\infty), (1,\infty), (\infty,1), (1,1)$ correspond to $(\tau_S, \tau_E) = (0,0), (1,0), (0,1), (1,1)$, respectively, in Example 2, where all age-price profiles are independent of the curvature parameter of the survival curve, τ_S.

(e) $\sigma_S = 2, \sigma_E \to \infty$**:** In this case, the efficiency curve follows the 'one-hoss-shay' pattern, while the survival curve, and hence also the combined survival-efficiency curve, are strictly concave. Then $\mu = 1-1/3 = 2/3$, and we get from (5.25) and (5.26)

$$\frac{q(t,s)}{q(t)} = \frac{p(t,s)}{q(t)} = \frac{1-x-\frac{1}{3}(1-x^3)}{\frac{2}{3}(1-x^2)} = \frac{(1-x)(2+x)}{2(1+x)}.$$

By comparing this case with **(b)**, we see that the effect of increasing σ_S from 1 to 2, when $\sigma_E \to \infty$, is to *reduce* $q(t,s)/q(t) = p(t,s)/q(t)$ by a factor $(2+x)/(2+2x)$. The age-price profiles are both *convex* functions of age: we find

$$\frac{\partial^2 q(t,s)}{\partial x^2} = \frac{\partial^2 p(t,s)}{\partial x^2} = \frac{2}{(1+x)^3} q(t),$$

which is positive for $0 < x \le 1$.

(f) $\sigma_S \to \infty, \sigma_E = 2$**:** In this case, the survival curve follows the 'one-hoss-shay' pattern, while the efficiency curve, and hence also the combined survival-efficiency curve, are strictly concave. Then $\mu = 1 - 1/3 = 2/3$, and we get from (5.25) and (5.26)

$$\frac{q(t,s)}{q(t)} = \frac{1-x-\frac{1}{3}(1-x^3)}{\frac{2}{3}(1-x^2)} = \frac{(1-x)(2+x)}{2(1+x)},$$

$$\frac{p(t,s)}{q(t)} = \frac{1-x-\frac{1}{3}(1-x^3)}{\frac{2}{3}} = \frac{1}{2}(1-x)^2(2+x).$$

Comparing this case with **(c)**, we see that the effect of increasing σ_E from 1 to 2, when $\sigma_S \to \infty$, is to *reduce* $q(t,s)/q(t)$ by a factor $(2+x)/(2+2x)$ and to *increase* $p(t,s)/q(t)$ by a factor $(2+x)/2$. As in case **(e)**, the age-price profiles are both *convex* functions of age, since

$$\frac{\partial^2 q(t,s)}{\partial x^2} = \frac{2}{(1+x)^3} q(t), \frac{\partial^2 p(t,s)}{\partial x^2} = 3xq(t),$$

both of which are positive for $0 < x \le 1$.

In cases **(e)** and **(f)**, the shape of the age-price profile differs substantially from the shape of the survival and the efficiency curves: the age-price profile is convex, while the combined efficiency-survival function is concave, since in both cases, $B(s) = 1 - (s/N)^2$ for $0 \le s \le N$. *Hence, concluding from convexity of the age-price profiles that the decline in capital efficiency with age follows a convex function is unwarranted.*

RETIREMENT RATES. NUMERICAL ILLUSTRATIONS

We next give numerical illustrations of retirement rates and related ratios, under exponential investment growth, relating to Examples 2 and 3 in Section 5. Using a demographic analogue, what we describe are characteristics of a *stable population* of capital assets for different parameter values. Six values of the maximal life-time N, between 6 and 100 years, are considered, and four values of the curvature parameters τ, given by (5.11), and σ, with the survival-efficiency function given by (5.29), are specified for each class of functions. Panels a–d of Tables 1–6 represent the four values of the curvature parameters. Seven values of the (continuous) growth rate of investment, α, are considered, ranging from -5 to +15 per cent. Tables 1–3 illustrate the convex class, Tables 4–6 illustrate the concave class of survival-efficiency functions. The function $F(i,z)$ is evaluated by means of (A.6) (by truncating the expansion after a suitable number of terms), and the calculations are performed by means of routines in the Gauss software code.

Tables 1 and 4 contain retirement rates (in per cent). Tables 2, 3, 5, and 6 describe properties of the implied age distributions. Tables 2 and 5 give capital/investment ratios (K/J) – which are analogous to the inverse birth rate of capital – and Tables 3 and 6 give retirement/investment ratios (D/J) – which are analogous to the death to birth ratio.

Retirement Rates

From Tables 1 and 4 we see that the retirement rate under exponential investment growth shows considerable *sensitivity to the growth rate.* The relative sensitivity is larger the higher is the maximal life-time. In the concave class with the curvature parameter $\sigma = 2$ and the maximal life time $N = 6$, for example, the retirement rate declines from $\delta = 27.3$ per cent for $\alpha = -0.05$, via $\delta = 25$ per cent for $\alpha = 0$ to $\delta = 19.2$ per cent for $\alpha = 0.15$. With $\sigma = 2, N = 50$, the retirement rate declines from $\delta = 5.97$ per cent for $\alpha = -0.05$, via $\delta = 3$ per cent for $\alpha = 0$ to $\delta = 0.55$ per cent for $\alpha = 0.15$. For each value of the maximal life time N, the sensitivity of δ to changes in α is smaller the higher is the curvature parameter τ for the convex class of functions, and larger the higher is the curvature parameter σ for the concave class.

The rows for $\alpha = 0$ in Tables 1 and 4, which represent the *constant investment case*, give the value $\delta = (\tau + 1)/N$ for the convex class of survival functions [cf. 5.19)] and the value $\delta = (\sigma + 1)/(\sigma N)$ for the concave class, as can be easily checked. The 'double declining balance' hypothesis, corresponding to $\delta = 2/N$, is represented by the $\alpha = 0$ rows for $\tau = 1$ in Table 1 and for $\sigma = 1$ in Table 4 (linear retirement). The 'inverse life-time' hypothesis, corresponding to $\delta = 1/N$, is represented by the $\alpha = 0$ rows for $\tau = 0$ in Table 1 and (approximately) for $\sigma = 1000$ in Table 4 (simultaneous retirement).

Table 1. Retirement rate for convex survival functions, per cent. Curvature Parameter $= \tau$. Maximal life time $= N$. Rate of investment growth, per cent $= \alpha$

a. $\tau = 0$

α	$N=6$	$N=10$	$N=20$	$N=30$	$N=50$	$N=100$
-5	19.29148	12.70747	7.90988	6.43608	5.44713	5.03392
-1	17.17167	10.50833	5.51666	3.85830	2.54149	1.58198
0	16.66667	10.00000	5.00000	3.33333	2.00000	1.00000
1	16.17167	9.50833	4.51666	2.85830	1.54149	0.58198
5	14.29148	7.70747	2.90988	1.43608	0.44713	0.03392
10	12.16369	5.81977	1.56518	0.52396	0.06784	0.00045
15	10.27677	4.30825	0.78594	0.16851	0.00830	0.00000

b. $\tau = 1$

α	$N=6$	$N=10$	$N=20$	$N=30$	$N=50$	$N=100$
-5	35.08496	21.80997	11.96106	8.78465	6.43968	5.17555
-1	33.67001	20.33893	10.34459	7.01699	4.36199	2.39221
0	33.33333	20.00000	10.00000	6.66667	4.00000	2.00000
1	33.00332	19.67218	9.67763	6.34966	3.69348	1.71828
5	31.74829	18.46742	8.59141	5.37158	2.90097	1.23949
10	30.31943	17.18282	7.61594	4.63567	2.47898	1.11106
15	29.03567	16.11473	6.95350	4.22470	2.30622	1.07143

c. $\tau = 3$

α	$N=6$	$N=10$	$N=20$	$N=30$	$N=50$	$N=100$
-5	67.70771	41.06957	21.14513	14.56018	9.40887	5.95496
-1	66.86827	40.20269	20.20543	13.54154	8.21391	4.22903
0	66.66667	40.00000	20.00000	13.33333	8.00000	4.00000
1	66.46826	39.80264	19.80524	13.14113	7.81277	3.82447
5	65.70565	39.06386	19.12235	12.50917	7.26932	3.44133
10	64.81863	38.24470	18.44938	11.95350	6.88267	3.26259
15	63.99986	37.52750	17.93025	11.57137	6.66214	3.18427

d. $\tau = 5$

α	$N=6$	$N=10$	$N=20$	$N=30$	$N=50$	$N=100$
-5	100.73780	60.75411	30.79721	20.84382	12.94851	7.28450
-1	100.14378	60.14440	30.14597	20.14756	12.15082	6.15944
0	100.00000	60.00000	30.00000	20.00000	12.00000	6.00000
1	99.85806	59.85866	29.86016	19.86163	11.86450	5.87130
5	99.30814	59.32250	29.35648	19.38789	11.44380	5.55167
10	98.65903	58.71297	28.83385	18.93737	11.10334	5.36570
15	98.04970	58.16366	28.40606	18.59937	10.88266	5.27054

Table 2. Capital/Investment ratio for convex survival functions. Curvature Parameter $= \tau$. Maximal life time $= N$. Rate of investment growth, per cent $= \alpha$

a. $\tau = 0$

α	$N = 6$	$N = 10$	$N = 20$	$N = 30$	$N = 50$	$N = 100$
-5	6.99718	12.97443	34.36564	69.63378	223.64988	2948.26318
-1	6.18365	10.51709	22.14028	34.98588	64.87213	171.82818
0	6.00000	10.00000	20.00000	30.00000	50.00000	100.00000
1	5.82355	9.51626	18.12692	25.91818	39.34693	63.21206
5	5.18364	7.86939	12.64241	15.53740	18.35830	19.86524
10	4.51188	6.32121	8.64665	9.50213	9.93262	9.99955
15	3.95620	5.17913	6.33475	6.59261	6.66298	6.66666

b. $\tau = 1$

α	$N = 6$	$N = 10$	$N = 20$	$N = 30$	$N = 50$	$N = 100$
-5	3.32392	5.94885	14.36564	26.42252	69.45995	569.65264
-1	3.06091	5.17092	10.70138	16.61960	29.74425	71.82818
0	3.00000	5.00000	10.00000	15.00000	25.00000	50.00000
1	2.94089	4.83742	9.36538	13.60607	21.30613	36.78794
5	2.72121	4.26123	7.35759	9.64174	12.65668	16.02695
10	2.48019	3.67879	5.67668	6.83262	8.01348	9.00005
15	2.27089	3.21391	4.55508	5.20164	5.77827	6.22222

c. $\tau = 3$

α	$N = 6$	$N = 10$	$N = 20$	$N = 30$	$N = 50$	$N = 100$
-5	1.59470	2.77242	6.19382	10.46006	22.68155	104.71663
-1	1.51818	2.55085	5.20686	7.97350	13.86210	30.96910
0	1.50000	2.50000	5.00000	7.50000	12.50000	25.00000
1	1.48218	2.45082	4.80648	7.07157	11.34717	20.72766
5	1.41431	2.26943	4.14553	5.71129	8.15041	11.84647
10	1.33657	2.07277	3.51501	4.55508	5.92323	7.54000
15	1.26582	1.90376	3.03672	3.76345	4.61635	5.49926

d. $\tau = 5$

α	$N = 6$	$N = 10$	$N = 20$	$N = 30$	$N = 50$	$N = 100$
-5	1.04452	1.79359	3.87639	6.31161	12.58097	43.77331
-1	1.00864	1.69078	3.43101	5.22260	8.96795	19.38194
0	1.00000	1.66667	3.33333	5.00000	8.33333	16.66667
1	0.99149	1.64315	3.24042	4.79349	7.77333	14.55329
5	0.95870	1.55467	2.91066	4.10040	6.08132	9.47717
10	0.92031	1.45533	2.57507	3.45574	4.73859	6.50800
15	0.88457	1.36680	2.30383	2.97625	3.86359	4.93327

Table 3. Retirement/Investment ratio for convex survival functions. Curvature Parameter $= \tau$. Maximal life time $= N$. Rate of investment growth, per cent $= \alpha$

a. $\tau = 0$

α	$N=6$	$N=10$	$N=20$	$N=30$	$N=50$	$N=100$
-5	1.34986	1.64872	2.71828	4.48169	12.18249	148.41316
-1	1.06184	1.10517	1.22140	1.34986	1.64872	2.71828
0	1.00000	1.00000	1.00000	1.00000	1.00000	1.00000
1	0.94176	0.90484	0.81873	0.74082	0.60653	0.36788
5	0.74082	0.60653	0.36788	0.22313	0.08208	0.00674
10	0.54881	0.36788	0.13534	0.04979	0.50337	0.00005
15	0.40657	0.22313	0.04979	0.01111	0.00055	0.00000

b. $\tau = 1$

α	$N=6$	$N=10$	$N=20$	$N=30$	$N=50$	$N=100$
-5	1.16620	1.29744	1.71828	2.32113	4.47300	29.48263
-1	1.03061	1.05171	1.10701	1.16620	1.29744	1.71828
0	1.00000	1.00000	1.00000	1.00000	1.00000	1.00000
1	0.97059	0.95163	0.90635	0.86394	0.78694	0.63212
5	0.86394	0.78694	0.63212	0.51791	0.36717	0.19865
10	0.75198	0.63212	0.43233	0.31674	0.59933	0.10000
15	0.65937	0.51791	0.31674	0.21975	0.13326	0.06667

c. $\tau = 3$

α	$N=6$	$N=10$	$N=20$	$N=30$	$N=50$	$N=100$
-5	1.07974	1.13862	1.30969	1.52300	2.13408	6.23583
-1	1.01518	1.02551	1.05207	1.07974	1.13862	1.30969
0	1.00000	1.00000	1.00000	1.00000	1.00000	1.00000
1	0.98518	0.97549	0.95194	0.92928	0.88653	0.79272
5	0.92928	0.88653	0.79272	0.71444	0.59248	0.40768
10	0.86634	0.79272	0.64850	0.54449	0.70384	0.24600
15	0.81013	0.71444	0.54449	0.43548	0.30755	0.17511

d. $\tau = 5$

α	$N=6$	$N=10$	$N=20$	$N=30$	$N=50$	$N=100$
-5	1.05223	1.08968	1.19382	1.31558	1.62905	3.18867
-1	1.01009	1.01691	1.03431	1.05223	1.08968	1.19382
0	1.00000	1.00000	1.00000	1.00000	1.00000	1.00000
1	0.99009	0.98357	0.96760	0.95207	0.92227	0.85447
5	0.95207	0.92227	0.85447	0.79498	0.69593	0.52614
10	0.90797	0.85447	0.74249	0.65443	0.76307	0.34920
15	0.86731	0.79498	0.65443	0.55356	0.42046	0.26001

Table 4. Retirement rate for concave survival functions, per cent. Curvature Parameter $= \tau$. Maximal life time $= N$. Rate of investment growth, per cent $= \alpha$

a. $\sigma = 1$

α	$N=6$	$N=10$	$N=20$	$N=30$	$N=50$	$N=100$
-5	35.08496	21.80997	11.96106	8.78465	6.43968	5.17555
-1	33.67001	20.33893	10.34459	7.01699	4.36199	2.39221
0	33.33333	20.00000	10.00000	6.66667	4.00000	2.00000
1	33.00332	19.67218	9.67763	6.34966	3.69348	1.71828
5	31.74829	18.46742	8.59141	5.37158	2.90097	1.23949
10	30.31943	17.18282	7.61594	4.63567	2.47898	1.11106
15	29.03567	16.11473	6.95350	4.22470	2.30622	1.07143

b. $\sigma = 2$

α	$N=6$	$N=10$	$N=20$	$N=30$	$N=50$	$N=100$
-5	27.27980	17.34218	10.00000	7.65851	5.96757	5.10736
-1	25.44116	15.44361	7.94977	5.45596	3.46844	2.00000
0	25.00000	15.00000	7.50000	5.00000	3.00000	1.50000
1	24.56615	14.56857	7.07460	4.58057	2.59237	1.12081
5	22.90287	12.96184	5.60405	3.23783	1.47723	0.41574
10	20.98180	11.20811	4.22469	2.16496	0.83149	0.20398
15	19.22876	9.71349	3.24744	1.53313	0.55030	0.13453

c. $\sigma = 4$

α	$N=6$	$N=10$	$N=20$	$N=30$	$N=50$	$N=100$
-5	23.33183	15.06714	8.98805	7.07225	5.72011	5.07212
-1	21.31660	12.98600	6.74284	4.66637	3.01343	1.79761
0	20.83333	12.50000	6.25000	4.16667	2.50000	1.25000
1	20.35826	12.02764	5.78443	3.70785	2.05458	0.83728
5	18.53924	10.27291	4.18638	2.25894	0.87506	0.14521
10	16.44555	8.37275	2.72774	1.16724	0.29043	0.02381
15	14.54601	6.77681	1.75087	0.60052	0.10782	0.00711

d. $\sigma = 1000$

α	$N=6$	$N=10$	$N=20$	$N=30$	$N=50$	$N=100$
-5	19.30802	12.71726	7.91448	6.43886	5.44834	5.03409
-1	17.18833	10.51832	5.52164	3.86160	2.54345	1.58290
0	16.68333	10.01000	5.00500	3.33667	2.00200	1.00100
1	16.18833	9.51832	4.52164	2.86160	1.54345	0.58290
5	14.30802	7.71727	2.91449	1.43886	0.44835	0.03409
10	12.17987	5.82898	1.56880	0.52561	0.06818	0.00046
15	10.29236	4.31658	0.78842	0.16928	0.00836	0.00000

Table 5. Capital/Investment ratio for concave survival functions. Curvature Parameter $= \tau$. Maximal life time $= N$. Rate of investment growth, per cent $= \alpha$

a. $\sigma = 1$

α	$N=6$	$N=10$	$N=20$	$N=30$	$N=50$	$N=100$
-5	3.32392	5.94885	14.36564	26.42252	69.45995	569.65264
-1	3.06091	5.17092	10.70138	16.61960	29.74425	71.82818
0	3.00000	5.00000	10.00000	15.00000	25.00000	50.00000
1	2.94089	4.83742	9.36538	13.60607	21.30613	36.78794
5	2.72121	4.26123	7.35759	9.64174	12.65668	16.02695
10	2.48019	3.67879	5.67668	6.83262	8.01348	9.00005
15	2.27089	3.21391	4.55508	5.20164	5.77827	6.22222

b. $\sigma = 2$

α	$N=6$	$N=10$	$N=20$	$N=30$	$N=50$	$N=100$
-5	4.48837	8.10230	20.00000	37.61501	103.35194	931.44422
-1	4.09146	6.92347	14.38897	22.44185	40.51149	100.00000
0	4.00000	6.66667	13.33333	20.00000	33.33333	66.66667
1	3.91142	6.42320	12.38452	17.91930	27.83679	47.15178
5	3.58386	5.56736	9.43036	12.13912	15.43870	18.46468
10	3.22770	4.71518	7.03003	8.22033	9.23234	9.80010
15	2.92152	4.04637	5.48022	6.04846	6.43074	6.60741

c. $\sigma = 4$

α	$N=6$	$N=10$	$N=20$	$N=30$	$N=50$	$N=100$
-5	5.45499	9.93330	25.07491	48.25666	138.86777	1386.53744
-1	4.92208	8.34307	17.41298	27.27496	49.66652	125.37454
0	4.80000	8.00000	16.00000	24.00000	40.00000	80.00000
1	4.68203	7.67599	14.73964	21.24113	32.73769	54.42842
5	4.24823	6.54754	10.88568	13.77612	17.02110	19.43554
10	3.78135	5.44284	7.85685	8.95476	9.71777	9.97625
15	3.38455	4.59204	5.96984	6.41004	6.61909	6.66351

d. $\sigma = 1000$

α	$N=6$	$N=10$	$N=20$	$N=30$	$N=50$	$N=100$
-5	6.98909	12.95796	34.31138	69.49967	223.04288	2933.51031
-1	6.17729	10.50605	22.11588	34.94544	64.78981	171.55690
0	5.99401	9.99001	19.98002	29.97003	49.95005	99.90010
1	5.81790	9.50722	18.11056	25.89597	39.31662	63.17527
5	5.17919	7.86332	12.63505	15.53070	18.35419	19.86456
10	4.50859	6.31753	8.64394	9.50063	9.93228	9.99954
15	3.95376	5.17690	6.33376	6.59227	6.66295	6.66666

Table 6. Retirement/Investment ratio for concave survival functions. Curvature Parameter $= \tau$. Maximal life time $= N$. Rate of investment growth, per cent $= \alpha$

a. $\sigma = 1$

α	$N=6$	$N=10$	$N=20$	$N=30$	$N=50$	$N=100$
-5	1.16620	1.29744	1.71828	2.32113	4.47300	29.48263
-1	1.03061	1.05171	1.10701	1.16620	1.29744	1.71828
0	1.00000	1.00000	1.00000	1.00000	1.00000	1.00000
1	0.97059	0.95163	0.90635	0.86394	0.78694	0.63212
5	0.86394	0.78694	0.63212	0.51791	0.36717	0.19865
10	0.75198	0.63212	0.43233	0.31674	0.19865	0.10000
15	0.65937	0.51791	0.31674	0.21975	0.13326	0.06667

b. $\sigma = 2$

α	$N=6$	$N=10$	$N=20$	$N=30$	$N=50$	$N=100$
-5	1.22442	1.40511	2.00000	2.88075	6.16760	47.57221
-1	1.04091	1.06923	1.14389	1.22442	1.40511	2.00000
0	1.00000	1.00000	1.00000	1.00000	1.00000	1.00000
1	0.96089	0.93577	0.87615	0.82081	0.72163	0.52848
5	0.82081	0.72163	0.52848	0.39304	0.22806	0.07677
10	0.67723	0.52848	0.29700	0.17797	0.07677	0.01999
15	0.56177	0.39304	0.17797	0.09273	0.03539	0.00889

c. $\sigma = 4$

α	$N=6$	$N=10$	$N=20$	$N=30$	$N=50$	$N=100$
-5	1.27275	1.49667	2.25375	3.41283	7.94339	70.32687
-1	1.04922	1.08343	1.17413	1.27275	1.49667	2.25375
0	1.00000	1.00000	1.00000	1.00000	1.00000	1.00000
1	0.95318	0.92324	0.85260	0.78759	0.67262	0.45572
5	0.78759	0.67262	0.45572	0.31119	0.14895	0.02822
10	0.62186	0.45572	0.21431	0.10452	0.02822	0.00238
15	0.49232	0.31119	0.10452	0.03849	0.00714	0.00047

d. $\sigma = 1000$

α	$N=6$	$N=10$	$N=20$	$N=30$	$N=50$	$N=100$
-5	1.34945	1.64790	2.71557	4.47498	12.15214	147.67552
-1	1.06177	1.10506	1.22116	1.34945	1.64790	2.71557
0	1.00000	1.00000	1.00000	1.00000	1.00000	1.00000
1	0.94182	0.90493	0.81889	0.74104	0.60683	0.36825
5	0.74104	0.60683	0.36825	0.22347	0.08229	0.00677
10	0.54914	0.36825	0.13561	0.04994	0.00677	0.00005
15	0.40694	0.22347	0.04994	0.01116	0.00056	0.00000

The formulae (5.20) and (5.31) give very good approximations to the exact δ value for $\alpha \in (-0.01, +0.01)$, $N \leq 50$ and fairly good approximations for $\alpha \in (-0.05, -0.01)$, $N \leq 20$ and $\alpha \in (0.01, 0.05)$, $N \leq 20$, as shown by the following examples. For $\alpha = 0.01, \tau = 1, N = 30$ in the *convex* class, the exact formula gives for example $\delta = 6.35$ per cent and the approximate formula $\delta = 6.33$ per cent. For $\alpha = 0.05, \tau = 1, N = 20$ the exact formula gives $\delta = 8.59$ per cent and the approximate formula $\delta = 8.33$ per cent. For $\alpha = -0.01, \sigma = 2, N = 30$ in the concave class, the exact formula gives $\delta = 5.46$ per cent and the approximate formula $\delta = 5.44$ per cent. For $\alpha = -0.05, \sigma = 2, N = 20$, the exact formula gives $\delta = 10.00$ per cent and the approximate formula $\delta = 9.68$ per cent.

Capital/Investment Ratios

From Tables 2 and 5 we see how changes in the investment growth rate, for each given maximal life-time and each value of the curvature parameter, affects an important property of the age distribution of the capital, the capital/investment ratio, or the inverse birth ratio of capital. As a benchmark case, we may consider the constant investment case, where $K/J = N/(\tau+1)$ for the convex class and $K/J = N\sigma/(\sigma+1)$ for the concave class. These constants also represent the total flow of services per capital unit during its life time. The latter can be confirmed by comparing the $\alpha = 0$ rows in Tables 2 and 5 with the corresponding rows in Tables 1 and 4.

Increasing α implies a growing and gradually younger stock of capital (decreasing K/J). A few examples illustrate this. In the convex class with $\tau = 3, N = 6$, the capital/investment ratio declines from $K/J = 1.59$ for $\alpha = -0.05$ via $K/J = 1.50$ for $\alpha = 0$ to $K/J = 1.27$ for $\alpha = 0.15$. With $\tau = 3, N = 50$, the ratio declines from $K/J = 22.7$ for $\alpha = -0.05$ via $K/J = 12.5$ for $\alpha = 0$ to $K/J = 4.6$ for $\alpha = 0.15$. In the concave class with $\sigma = 2, N = 6$, the capital/investment ratio declines from $K/J = 4.49$ for $\alpha = -0.05$ via $K/J = 4.00$ for $\alpha = 0$ to $K/J = 2.92$ for $\alpha = 0.15$, whereas with $\sigma = 2, N = 50$, the ratio declines from $K/J = 103.4$ for $\alpha = -0.05$ via $K/J = 33.3$ for $\alpha = 0$ to $K/J = 6.4$ for $\alpha = 0.15$. For each N and α, increasing τ leads to a younger stock of capital for the convex class (decreasing K/J), and increasing σ leads to an older stock of capital for the concave class (increasing K/J).

Retirement/Investment Ratios

Tables 3 and 6 illustrate how changes in the investment growth rate, for each given maximal life-time and each value of the curvature parameter, affect another basic property of the age distribution of the capital, the retirement/investment ratio, or the death to birth ratio of the capital. As a benchmark case, we may consider the constant investment case, in which $D/J = 1$ for any survival functions.

Increasing α leads to a decline in the death to birth ratio. This is also an indication of a gradually younger capital stock. A few examples illustrate this. In the convex class with $\tau = 3, N = 6$, the retirement/investment ratio declines from $D/J = 1.08$ for $\alpha = -0.05$ to $D/J = 0.81$ for $\alpha = 0.15$, whereas with $\tau = 3, N = 50$, the ratio declines from $D/J = 2.13$ for $\alpha = -0.05$ to $D/J = 0.31$ for $\alpha = 0.15$. In the concave class with $\sigma = 2, N = 6$, the retirement/investment ratio declines from $D/J = 1.22$ for $\alpha = -0.05$ to $D/J = 0.56$ for $\alpha = 0.15$, whereas with $\sigma = 2, N = 50$, the ratio declines from $D/J = 6.17$ for $\alpha = -0.05$ to $D/J = 0.04$ for $\alpha = 0.15$. For each N and α, increasing τ leads to a decreasing/increasing D/J ratio for the convex class if α is negative/positive, and increasing σ leads to increasing/decreasing D/J ratio for the concave class if α is negative/positive.

EMPIRICAL EVIDENCE ON SURVIVAL PROFILES

In a frequently cited article, Hulten and Wykoff (1981a) consider the estimation of depreciation by estimating parametrically specified age-price profiles from observed vintage prices of capital goods. Their basic problem is similar to the one considered in Section 4, but the approaches differ in two substantial respects.

Comparison of the Two Approaches

First, Hulten-Wykoff start from a parametrization of the second-hand price of a capital asset as a function of age s and time t. Using the Box-Cox (1964) power transformation, they assume (in our notation) approximately that [cf. Hulten and Wykoff (1981a, p. 373)]

$$\frac{p(t,s)^{\theta_1} - 1}{\theta_1} = \alpha + \beta \frac{s^{\theta_2} - 1}{\theta_2} + \gamma \frac{t^{\theta_3} - 1}{\theta_3}, \tag{7.1}$$

where α, β, γ, θ_1, θ_2, and θ_3 are unknown constants, and hence do not specify an *explicit* relationship between the age-price profiles and the survival and efficiency curves from which these age-price profiles may be derived, as is done in (4.8) above. This has three notable implications.

(A) The Hulten-Wykoff approach does not, in general, imply proportionality between the second-hand price $p(t,s)$ and the corresponding price of a new capital good, $p(t,0) = q(t)$, for a given age. Rather, (7.1) parametrizes $p(t,s)$ as an *explicit* function of both age s and time t, while (4.5) restricts the relative price, $p(t,s)/q(t)$, to be a function of s only. We consider the latter a basic implication of our perfect market assumption (4.4) and the assumed malleability of capital assets. Hence, the second-hand price is a function of current time t only via the price of a new capital good, $p(t,0) = q(t)$. From (7.1) the rate of increase of the second-hand price at time t can be expressed as

$$\frac{\frac{\partial p(t,s)}{\partial t}}{p(t,s)} = \gamma \frac{t^{\theta_3 - 1}}{p(t,s)^{\theta_1}}, \tag{7.2}$$

which is a function not only of time, but also (when $\theta_1 \neq 0$) of age, while (4.5) implies

$$\frac{\frac{\partial p(t,s)}{\partial t}}{p(t,s)} = \frac{\frac{dq(t)}{dt}}{q(t)}, \tag{7.3}$$

which is a time dependent function containing no unknown parameters.

(B) The Hulten-Wykoff approach restricts the time path of the investment price $q(t)$, since (7.1) for $s = 0$ gives

$$p(t,0)^{\theta_1} = q(t)^{\theta_1} = 1 + \alpha\theta_1 - \beta\frac{\theta_1}{\theta_2} - \gamma\frac{\theta_1}{\theta_3} + \gamma\frac{\theta_1}{\theta_3}t^{\theta_3},$$

i.e., $q(t)^{\theta_1}$ is linear in t^{θ_3}. No such restriction is implied by (4.5).

(C) Eq. (7.1) implies that the rate of increase of the second-hand price with age is [cf. Hulten and Wykoff (1981a, eq. (6'))]

$$\frac{\frac{\partial p(t,s)}{\partial s}}{p(t,s)} = \beta \frac{s^{\theta_2 - 1}}{p(t,s)^{\theta_1}}, \tag{7.4}$$

which is a function not only of age, but also of time t (when $\theta_1 \neq 0$), whereas (4.5) implies that this rate is an age dependent function, given by (4.9), in general.

Consider, as an illustration, how two of the most common assumptions, linear depreciation and exponential decay, are represented.

Linear depreciation, according to Hulten-Wykoff, is obtained by letting $\theta_1 = \theta_2 = \theta_3 = 1$ in (7.1), which gives

$$p(t,s) = (\alpha - \beta - \gamma + 1) + \beta s + \gamma t,$$

see Hulten and Wykoff (1981a, eq. (4)), implying $p(t,s) = p(t,0) + \beta s$, where $p(t,0) = (\alpha - \beta - \gamma + 1) + \gamma t$. This equation has the (debatable) implication that the investment price follows a linear time trend. This vintage price function has three unknown parameters, α, β, and γ. In our approach, linear depreciation is represented as

$$p(t,s) = \left(1 - \frac{s}{N}\right) q(t), \text{with } q(t) \text{ free},$$

which has one unknown parameter, N, only; see Section 5, Example 2, case **(a)**. This is obtained by letting $\tau_E = 0$ in (5.16) and corresponds to specifying the underlying efficiency function as 'one-hoss-shay'.

Exponential decay, according to Hulten-Wykoff, is represented by $\theta_1 = 0, \theta_2 = \theta_3 = 1$, which gives

$$\ln(p(t,s)) = (\alpha - \beta - \gamma) + \beta s + \gamma t,$$

see Hulten and Wykoff (1981a, eq. (5)), implying $\ln(p(t,s)) = \ln(p(t,0)) + \beta s$, where $\ln(p(t,0)) = (\alpha - \beta - \gamma) + \gamma t$. This equation has the (debatable) implication that the investment price follows a log-linear time trend. Again, the vintage price function has three unknown parameters, α, β, and γ. In our approach, exponential decay is represented as

$$\ln(p(t,s)) = -\delta_E s + \ln(q(t)), \text{with } q(t) \text{ free},$$

which has δ_E as the only unknown parameter; see Section 5, Example 1, in particular (5.6).

Second, Hulten-Wykoff remark that "any sample of used asset prices has been 'censored' by the retirement process, since assets taken out of service are no longer available for sampling" and that "at any point on the age-price profile the average value of the initial investment cohort is different from the average value of surviving structures" [Hulten and Wykoff (1981a, pp. 376, 377)]. In order to take this 'censoring' effect into account and obtain a valid measure of the 'total' economic depreciation, Hulten-Wykoff multiply each observed second-hand price [$p(t,s)$ in our notation] by a measure of the probability of survival, before using the Box-Cox transformation [cf. Hulten and Wykoff (1981a, pp. 377–379)]. This is related to our distinction between the survival curve $B_S(s)$ and the efficiency curve $B_E(s)$, the former corresponding to the Hulten-Wykoff survival probability. See also Biırn (1989, section 3.4.1).

Define a hypothetical vintage price for capital of age s at time t as

$$p^*(t,s) = \frac{V(t,s)}{J(t-s)} = B_E(s) B_S(s) \frac{\Phi_\rho(s)}{\Phi_\rho(0)} q(t) = B_E(s) B_S(s) q(t,s) = B_S(s) p(t,s),$$

where the second, third, and fourth equality follow from (4.5) and (4.6). It can be interpreted as the *average price* at time t per unit of capital invested s years ago, and representing both the units still remaining [the share $B_S(s)$ with price per physical unit $p(t,s)$ or the share $B_E(s)B_S(s)$ with price per efficiency unit $q(t,s)$] and those retired [the share $1-B_S(s)$, or $1-B_E(s)B_S(s)$, with price zero]. We can then write the value of capital of age s at time t, (4.6), as

$$V(t,s) = p^*(t,s)J(t-s) = \{B_S(s)p(t,s) + [1-B_S(s)]0\}J(t-s)$$
$$= \{B_E(s)B_S(s)q(t,s) + [1-B_E(s)B_S(s)]0\}J(t-s).$$

Taking this point of departure, we may say that a problem with the Hulten-Wykoff 'censoring' correction is that *the second-hand price of the capital units, in physical terms, which are not retired,* $p(t,s)$, *may not be independent of the shape of the survival curve (the survival probability),* $B_S(s)$. This can be seen from the three examples in Section 5. In Examples 1 and 2, changes in $B_S(s)$ will not affect $p(t,s)$, which only depends on the parameters of the efficiency curve, *i.e.*, δ_E and τ_E, respectively [cf. (5.6) and (5.16)]. On the other hand, in Example 3, such separability does not exist. Changes in the parameter of the survival function, σ_S, affect not only the price ratio $p^*(t,s)/p(t,s)$, but also the second-hand price $p(t,s)$, as shown by (5.26). In general, changes in the efficiency curve as well as the survival curve will, via $\Phi_\rho(s)/\Phi_\rho(0)$ [cf. (4.1)], affect both the efficiency unit price $q(t,s)$, the second-hand price $p(t,s)$, and the hypothetical average price $p^*(t,s)$. This is not reflected in the Hulten-Wykoff procedure.

Empirical Illustrations

We next we give some empirical illustrations of our approach based on the parametric survival and efficiency functions considered in Section 5. The data are annual U.S. data on vintage prices for the machine category milling machines, based on auction reports from the years 1954–1983. This data set gives, for $n = 1139$ transactions, information about the year of the second-hand purchase of the assets, t, their age in the year of purchase, s, their second-hand price, $p(t,s)$, and their price after division by an appropriate deflator. The maximal age of the machines is $s = 42$ years, while the minimal age is $s = 0$ years. The earliest year of origin is $t-s = 1938$, the latest is $t-s = 1981$. The data set is described in and used by Hulten, Robertson, and Wykoff (1989) and was kindly given to me by Charles R. Hulten. It contains no information about the price of a new capital unit, $q(t)$, corresponding to each transaction, but we have constructed time series of this variable from the data available in the following way. Let the index used as deflator in year t be denoted by $I(t)$, so that the deflated price is $\overline{p}(t,s) = p(t,s)/I(t)$. Assuming that the deflator properly reflects the development of prices of new capital assets of the type considered and that the assets are fairly homogeneous, we should expect $q(t)$ to be proportional to $I(t)$, *i.e.*, $\overline{p}(t,0) = p(t,0)/I(t) = q(t)/I(t)$ to be approximately constant, say C. The data set contains 11 cases, *i.e.*, about 1 per cent of the observations, in which capital assets are purchased at age 0. These values of $\overline{p}(t,0)$ are not time invariant, but in 9 cases out of 11 they are between 2400 and 3800 dollars and show no systematic variation with the year of purchase. We use their mean value as an estimate of C, which gives $C = 3164.1$ dollars, and can then represent the relative second-hand price $p(t,s)/q(t)$ as

$$y_{ts} = \frac{p(t,s)}{q(t)} = \frac{p(t,s)}{CI(t)} = \frac{\overline{p}(t,s)}{C}.$$

Table 7 gives estimates of the parameter δ_E of the efficiency curve in the exponential decay example (5.1), obtained from (5.6), by using (i) ordinary least squares (OLS), after transformation to logarithms (assuming additive disturbances in log-form), and (ii) non-linear least squares (NLS) based on its original form (assuming additive disturbances in this form). For each method, two versions of the equation are considered, one with a multiplicative intercept term *a priori* set to unity [as in (5.6)] and one treating the intercept term as an unknown constant, A, to be estimated. Assuming A free may also account for a systematic error in assessing the value of the normalization constant C. In this case, which *a priori* restricts the efficiency curve (but not the survival curve) to be convex, and we get an estimate of δ_E in the range 0.04–0.06, *i.e.*, roughly 4–6 per cent of the efficiency of each *remaining* capital unit disappears each year. We are unable to estimate the corresponding parameter, δ_S, of the survival curve, as explained in Section 5, Example 1. When relaxing the $A = 1$ restriction, we get estimates of this parameter significantly below one and lower δ_E estimates than when $A = 1$ is imposed. The sum of squared residuals, defined as $\text{SSR} = \sum_{t,s} (y_{ts} - \hat{y}_{ts})^2$, where $\hat{y}_{ts}$ is the value of $y_{ts}[= p(t,s)/q(t)]$ calculated from the estimated equation, are also recorded.

Table 7. The vintage price equation $p(t,s)/q(t) = A e^{-\delta_E s}$. Parameter estimates (Standard errors in parenthesis)

δ_E	A	$\ln A$	SSR	Method
0.0591	1	0	70.4076	OLS, semilog
(0.0009)				
0.0626	1	0	70.0991	NLS
(0.0015)				
0.0417	0.7628	-0.2708	70.7990	OLS, semilog
(0.0015)		(0.0201)		
0.0499	0.8791	-0.1289	68.0730	NLS
(0.0024)	(0.0194)			

Estimates of the parameter of the efficiency curve in (5.9), τ_E, obtained from (5.16), are given in Table 8. The (potential) maximal age is set to $N = 43$ years *a priori*, which is one year more than the maximal age occurring in the data set. This choice is somewhat arbitrary. Only one asset was sold at the maximal age, $s = 42$ years. Attempts to estimate τ_E and N, simultaneously, using NLS on (5.16) did not succeed. Again, OLS, utilizing that conditional on N (5.16) is linear in $\ln y_{ts}$ and $\ln(1-s/N)$], and NLS are used, and for each method, two versions of the equations are considered, one with a multiplicative intercept *a priori* set to unity and one treating it as an unknown parameter, B, to be estimated. In one of the four cases (NLS with $B=1$ imposed), the estimate of τ_E exceeds unity ($\tau_E = 1.25$), which indicates convexity of the efficiency curve, but concavity (*i.e.*, $\tau_E \in (0,1)$) is indicated in two cases (OLS with $B=1$ and NLS with B unrestricted). All these conclusions are significant at the 1 per cent level. In the final case (OLS with B unrestricted), the estimate of τ_E is significantly negative (-0.18), which is not a meaningful result, but the corresponding estimate of the intercept is as low as $B = 0.63$. On the whole, the SSR statistic, taken as a measure of the goodness of fit, is somewhat higher when assuming this functional form for the efficiency curve than when assuming exponential decay–in the NLS case with B unrestricted, for instance 70.18 against 68.07. Hence, we do not get a clear support of either concavity or convexity of the efficiency curve from the results in Table 8 when restricting the maximal age to $N = 43$ years. We are unable to estimate the corresponding parameter of the survival curve, τ_S, as explained in Section 5, Example 2.

Table 8. The vintage price equation $p(t,s)/q(t) = B\left(1-\frac{s}{N}\right)^{\tau_E+1}$. $N = 43$ Parameter estimates (Standard errors in parenthesis)

$\tau_E + 1$	B	$\ln B$	SSR	Method
1.6016 (0.0337)	1	0	83.7404	OLS, semilog
2.2470 (0.0587)	1	0	74.5695	NLS
0.8200 (0.0406)	0.6301	-0.4619 (0.0180)	78.8958	OLS, semilog
1.5881 (0.0832)	0.8344 (0.0176)	-0.1811	70.1777	NLS

Additional results, illustrating the sensitivity of the estimate of τ_E to the choice of value for N, when the $B=1$ restriction is imposed, are given in Table 9. We find, not surprisingly, that the τ_E estimate is increasing with the value of the parameter that we condition on, N. Using OLS, the curvature changes from concave ($\tau_E < 1$) to convex ($\tau_E > 1$) at a maximal age of about 48 years. Using NLS, we find evidence of convexity of the efficiency curve for all values of N greater than 43.

Table 9. The vintage price equation $p(t,s)/q(t) = \left(1-\frac{s}{N}\right)^{\tau_E+1}$. Parameter estimates for different N (Standard errors in parenthesis)

N	$\tau_E + 1$	SSR	Method
43	1.6016 (0.0337)	83.7404	OLS, semilog
45	1.7960 (0.0350)	80.5941	OLS, semilog
50	2.1652 (0.0390)	77.5604	OLS, semilog
55	2.4960 (0.0433)	76.0884	OLS, semilog
60	2.8137 (0.0476)	75.1579	OLS, semilog
43	2.2470 (0.0587)	74.5695	NLS
45	2.3729 (0.0617)	74.2588	NLS
50	2.6879 (0.0692)	73.6360	NLS
55	3.0026 (0.0768)	73.1716	NLS
60	3.3170 (0.0844)	72.8134	NLS

Table 10. The vintage price equation

$$\frac{p(t,s)}{q(t)} = \frac{1-(s/N)-H(s,\sigma_S+1)-H(s,\sigma_E+1)+H(s,\sigma+1)}{\mu(\sigma_S,\sigma_E)[1-(s/N)^{\sigma_S}]}$$

Estimates of σ_S and σ_E for $N = 43$. B is a multiplicative constant.

σ_S	σ_E	B	SSR	Method
1.236	0.724	1	72.9876	NLS, grid search
1.964	4.029	0.8301	70.2245	NLS, grid search

Finally, Table 10 reports estimates of σ_S and σ_E in (5.21) obtained from the vintage price equation (5.26). This equation is highly non-linear in these two parameters, and we did not obtain convergence when trying to estimate it directly by NLS. A grid search variant of the minimization procedure was chosen. The estimate of σ_S exceeds unity both when the (multiplicative) intercept term is *a priori* set to unity and when it is unrestricted. There is thus evidence of *concavity of the survival curve*. For the efficiency curve, we obtain an ambiguous result. The estimate is $\sigma_E = 0.72$, indicating convexity, when the intercept term is set to unity and is $\sigma_E = 4.03$, indicating concavity, when the intercept term is freely estimated. The goodness of fit is approximately the same as in the corresponding alternatives in Table 8.

We then conclude that from the U.S. price data for milling machines of Hulten, Robertson, and Wykoff (1989) we find some evidence of concavity of the survival curve, but we are not able to draw a firm conclusion regarding the curvature of the efficiency curve. The overall fit is slightly better for the exponential decay model than for the other two functional forms. Overall, our conclusion concerning the appropriate parametric form is far less in favour of exponential decay than the conclusion of Hulten and Wykoff based on the Box-Cox transformation (7.1).

CONCLUDING REMARKS

In this article, we have discussed two related issues. The first is the relationship between the retirement process of the capital and the average retirement rate and how this relationship is affected by changes in the investment path. The second is the relationship between the shape of the survival and efficiency curves of capital input on the one hand and the age profile of the vintage prices of capital on the other.

As is well known, the average retirement rate will be a constant independent of the investment path and equal for all capital vintages only in the particular case where the survival function is exponentially declining (exponential decay). This is often regarded as a benchmark case in the literature. Otherwise, the average retirement rate will depend on both the growth profile of gross investment and the parameters describing the survival function. A pertinent question for many practical purposes is: How sensitive is it? Can constant average retirement rate be defended as a useful practical simplification?

We have emphasized the econometric relevance of distinguishing between (i) the capital stock measured in physical units and its price, denoted as the second-hand price, and (ii) the capital stock measured in efficiency units and its price, denoted as the efficiency unit price. The former price is observable from transactions in a second-hand market, the latter is usually unobservable.

Our numerical illustrations of how the average retirement rate responds to changes in the curvature of survival-efficiency function and to the growth pattern of investment under non-exponential survival functions show considerable sensitivity to both. The functional forms we have considered are two-parametric and characterized by the maximal life-time and a curvature parameter indicating the degree of convexity or concavity. We find that the retirement rate is a declining function of the growth rate of investment and quite sensitive to its value over a reasonable interval. Furthermore, we have illustrated how two basic properties of the age distribution of the capital, the capital/investment ratio and the retirement/investment ratio, are affected by changes in the growth rate of investment and in the form of the survival function.

Simultaneous retirement (sudden death) at a fixed age N, and linear retirement up to a fixed life-time, N are often applied in practical research or in national accounting. Which is the appropriate 'translation' of the retirement rate, δ, in these cases? We have shown, as particular cases of our parametric functions, that the 'translation' rules $\delta = 1/N$ for the former and $\delta = 2/N$ for the latter hold under constant investment, but may be very inaccurate otherwise.

It is not always possible, in a neo-classical framework, to simultaneously identify the shape of the survival and efficiency curves from observations on second-hand prices by using the non-arbitrage condition or relationships derived from it. We have demonstrated, by two examples – one based on exponential decay for both the survival and the efficiency curves (Example 1), and one based on a two-parametric convex form for both curves (Example 2) – that sometimes it is only possible to identify the curvature parameter of the efficiency curve from second-hand prices. Additional quantity information will then be needed to identify the survival curve. In our third example, based on concave survival and efficiency curves (Example 3), however, both curvature parameters can be identified from data on second-hand prices. As the vintage prices are rather complicated functions of the curvature parameters, numerical difficulties may arise when solving the estimation problems. The latter example also demonstrates that, under neo-classical perfect market and malleability assumptions, concavity of the survival and efficiency curves may be compatible with observed convexity of the age profile of second-hand prices. There is no contradiction between assuming concavity of the former and observing convexity of the latter. In Biuurn (1992) it is demonstrated that age-price profiles obtained from concave survival and efficiency curves can, to a satisfactory degree of approximation, be represented by two simple parametric convex functions, one of which is exponential decay. If the survival and efficiency curves satisfy exponential decay *exactly*, the age-price profile will have *exactly* the exponential decay form, and vice versa. But from the fact that a given set of second-hand prices give an age-price profile which can be *approximated* to exponential decay, we cannot conclude that the underlying survival and efficiency curves also have the exponential decay form.

Using U.S. data for one category of machines, also analyzed by Hulten, Robertson, and Wykoff (1989), we find evidence of concavity of the survival curve. But we are unable to draw a firm conclusion regarding convexity versus concavity of the efficiency curve. Our conclusion in this respect is far less obvious than those of Hulten and Wykoff and most of their followers, based on similar data, but different price-age profiles. In particular, we cannot exclude that both the survival of capital units and the efficiency of each remaining unit follow concave functions of age, as researchers assuming exponential decay *a priori* do. As our tentative conclusion is confined to one asset type and three functional forms only (one one-parametric and two two-parametric), more econometric research, based on vintage prices for other asset types and functional forms, and maybe other estimation procedures, is needed.

On the methodological side, the article challenges the frequently cited approach of Hulten and Wykoff (1981a, b, c), based on the Box-Cox power transformation. A basic difference is that Hulten and Wykoff start from a parametrization of the second-hand capital price (and hence also the price of new assets) as a function of age and time, whereas we *derive* this function from the survival and efficiency curves in combination with a perfect market assumption for the transaction prices of new and old capital goods and the malleability of capital under a neo-classical production technology which is assumed to hold in the absence of possibilities of arbitrage between different capital vintages. Finally, the article gives a reinterpretation of the 'censoring' correction recommended by Hulten and Wykoff, and subsequently referred to and adopted by several authors, in analyzing economic depreciation from vintage price data. The approach proposed here involves no such correction, as both the survival curve and the efficiency curve of the capital are included in the model from the start.

Neither of the two approaches pay regard to the often made suggestion that retirement of capital is not a purely mechanistic process, but is endogenous, determined by, *e.g.*, (expected and realized) profits and (non-capital) factor costs. Pursuing this idea econometrically, however, and abandoning the neo-classical malleability assumption, is hardly possible when only observations on realized second-hand capital prices are available.

APPENDIX

Properties of the Function $F(i,z) = \int_0^1 e^{z\theta}(1-\theta)^i d\theta$

In this appendix, we prove some useful properties of the auxiliary function (5.12), defined by the intergral

$$F(i,z) = \int_0^1 e^{z\theta}(1-\theta)^i d\theta = \int_0^1 e^{z(1-\lambda)}\lambda^i d\lambda, i = 0,1,2,.... \quad \text{(A.1)}$$

It is straightforward to show that

$$F(i,0) = \frac{1}{i+1}, \quad \text{(A.2)}$$

$$\lim_{i\to\infty} F(i,z) = 0 \text{for all } z, \quad \text{(A.3)}$$

$$\lim_{i\to\infty}(i+1)F(i,z) = 1 \text{for all } z. \quad \text{(A.4)}$$

If $z \neq 0$, the function satisfies the recursion

$$\left.\begin{aligned} F(0,z) &= \frac{1}{z}(e^z - 1) \\ F(i,z) &= \frac{1}{z}[iF(i-1,z) - 1] \end{aligned}\right\} \Longleftrightarrow \left\{\begin{aligned} F(0,-z) &= e^{-z}F(0,z) = \frac{1}{z}(1-e^{-z}) \\ F(i,-z) &= \frac{1}{z}[1 - iF(i-1,-z)], \end{aligned}\right.$$

$$i = 1,2,..., \quad \text{(A.5)}$$

which can be shown by integration by parts. In particular,

$$F(1,z)=\frac{1}{z}\left[\frac{1}{z}(e^{z}-1)-1\right]\Longleftrightarrow F(1,-z)=\frac{1}{z}\left[1-\frac{1}{z}(1-e^{-z})\right],$$

$$F(2,z)=\frac{1}{z}\left[\frac{2}{z}\left(\frac{1}{z}(e^{z}-1)-1\right)-1\right]\Longleftrightarrow F(2,-z)=\frac{1}{z}\left[1-\frac{2}{z}\left(1-\frac{1}{z}(1-e^{-z})\right)\right].$$

If z is small and i is large, the recursion (A.5) may give inaccurate results in numerical calculations. A better way of keeping the accuracy under control is to represent $F(i,z)$ by its Taylor expansion. Expanding e^{z} by Taylor's formula, we get, for $i=0$,

$$F(0,z)=\frac{1}{z}(1+z+\frac{z^{2}}{2!}+\frac{z^{3}}{3!}+\cdots-1)=1+\frac{z}{1\cdot 2}+\frac{z^{2}}{1\cdot 2\cdot 3}+\frac{z^{3}}{1\cdot 2\cdot 3\cdot 4}+\cdots.$$

Substituting this expression in (A.5), it follows that

$$F(1,z)=\frac{1}{z}[F(0,z)-1]=\frac{1}{2}+\frac{z}{2\cdot 3}+\frac{z^{2}}{2\cdot 3\cdot 4}+\frac{z^{3}}{2\cdot 3\cdot 4\cdot 5}+\cdots,$$

$$F(2,z)=\frac{1}{z}[2F(0,z)-1]=\frac{1}{3}+\frac{z}{3\cdot 4}+\frac{z^{2}}{3\cdot 4\cdot 5}+\frac{z^{3}}{3\cdot 4\cdot 5\cdot 6}+\cdots,$$

and in general,

$$F(i,z)=\frac{1}{i+1}+\frac{z}{(i+1)(i+2)}+\frac{z^{2}}{(i+1)(i+2)(i+3)}+\cdots=\sum_{j=1}^{\infty}\frac{i!\,z^{j-1}}{(i+j)!}, \qquad i=0,1,2,..., \tag{A.6}$$

which can be verified by induction.

REFERENCES

[1] Statistical Theory of Reliability and Life Testing. New York: Holt, Rinehart and Winston.

[2] *Taxation, Technology and the User Cost of Capital*. Amsterdam: North-Holland.

[3] Expectations, Substitution, and Scrapping in a Putty-Clay Model. *Journal of Economics* **56**, 157–184.

[4] Concave Survival and Efficiency Curves for Capital and the Form of Age-Price Profiles. Memorandum from the Department of Economics, University of Oslo, No. 6/1992.

[5] Survival and Efficiency Curves for Capital and the Time-Age-Profile of Vintage Prices. *Empirical Economics* **23**, 611–633.

[6] An Analysis of Transformations. *Journal of the Royal Statistical Society, Series B* **26**, 211 - 243.
[7] *The Growth and Structure of Human Populations.* Princeton: Princeton University Press.
[8] Towards an Economic Theory of Replacement Investment. *Econometrica* **42**, 393–423.
[9] The Role of Capital in U.S. Economic Growth, 1948–1976. Chapter 2 in: G.M. von Furstenberg (ed.): *Capital, Efficiency and Growth.* Cambridge, Mass.: Ballinger.
[10] Technical Change and Capital from the Point of View of the Dual. *Review of Economic Studies* **35**, 36–46.
[11] The Measurement of Quality Change from Vintage Price Data. In *Price Indexes and Quality Change*, ed. by Z. Griliches. Cambridge, Mass.: Harvard University Press, pp. 240–271.
[12] *Capital and Time.* Oxford: Clarendon Press.
[13] A General Mathematical Theory of Depreciation. *Journal of the American Statistical Association* **20**, 340–353.
[14] Energy, Obsolescence, and the Productivity Slowdown. In *Technology and Capital Formation*, ed. by D.W. Jorgenson and R. Landau. Cambridge, Mass: The MIT Press, pp. 225–258.
[15] Economic Depreciation and the Taxation of Structures in United States Manufacturing Industries: An Empirical Analysis. In *The measurement of Capital*, ed. by D. Usher. Chicago: University of Chicago Press, pp. 83–120.
[16] The Estimation of Economic Depreciation. Using Vintage Asset Prices: An Application of the Box-Cox Power Transformation. *Journal of Econometrics* **15**, 367–396.
[17] The Measurement of Economic Depreciation. In *Depreciation, Inflation, and the Taxation of Income from Capital*, ed. by C.R. Hulten. Washington: The Urban Institute Press, pp. 81–125.
[18] Substitution versus Fixed Production Coefficients in the Theory of Economic Growth: A Synthesis. *Econometrica* **27**, 157–176.
[19] *Production Functions*. Amsterdam: North-Holland.
[20] Capital Theory and Investment Behavior. *American Economic Review* **53**, 247–259.
[21] The Economic Theory of Replacement and Depreciation. In: Sellekaerts, W. (ed.): *Econometrics and Economic Theory. Essays in Honour of Jan Tinbergen*. London: Macmillan, pp. 189–221.
[22] : Accounting for Capital. In *Capital, Efficiency and Growth.*, ed. by G.M. von Furstenberg. Cambridge, Mass.: Ballinger Publishing Company, pp. 251–319.
[23] Capital as a Factor of Production. In *Technology and Capital Formation*, ed. by D.W. Jorgenson and R. Landau. Cambridge, Mass: The MIT Press, pp. 1–35.
[24] Empirical Studies of Depreciation. *Economic Inquiry* **34**, 24–42.
[25] *The Statistical Analysis of Failure Time Data.* New York: Wiley, 1980.
[26] *Introduction to the Mathematics of Population.* Reading, Mass.: Addison-Wesley.
[27] *The Investment Decisions of Firms*. Cambridge: Cambridge University Press.

In: Economic Growth Issues
Editor: L. A. Finley, pp. 155-169
ISBN 1-59454-555-3

Chapter 6

On the Relationship between Telecommunications Investment and Economic Growth: Three Empirical Studies

Richard O. Beil*, George S. Ford[#] and John D. Jackson*

*Department of Economics, Auburn University, Alabama 36849.

[#]Applied Economic Studies, Tampa, Florida 33635.

Abstract

This study begins by posing the question of what is the relationship between telecommunications investment and regional economic development. After providing a theoretical basis for each of the three potential relationships, i.e., growth causes investment, investment causes growth, and growth and investment are jointly determined, we review the statistical methodology involved in testing for Granger causality and look at some recent applications in the development economics literature. Next, we present results from three different causality analyses. First, we present the results of causality tests performed on a panel of six states from the southern Unites States over the year 1983 - 1992. Next, a straightforward application of causality testing using fifty years of data (1947-1996) for the United States is presented. The third analysis employs time series data from 25 OECD countries for the years 1980 – 1996. The results of these distinct analyses are consistent and indicate that economic growth causes telecommunications investment but not conversely.

1. Introduction

The longest economic expansion in the developed world ended in 2001 (NBER 2002). During the previous decade, developed countries had seen rapid advances in both real per capita income and real telecommunications investment. While there are sound theoretical arguments that suggest these two phenomena are not unrelated, it is by no means precisely clear what their relationship is. Some insight into the true nature of this relationship could shed considerable light on important questions concerning development policy as well as competition policy to the extent investment and competition are interdependent. For example, if increases in telecommunications investment — through some multiplier process — result in increased real per capita personal incomes, then policies that encourage telecommunications investment (e.g., investment tax credits) will be effective spurs to economic development. On the other hand, if the relationship is one in which increases in per capita income induce increases in telecommunications investment – perhaps by creating a market for the new telecommunications products — then policies which encourage or require additional telecommunications investment will be ineffective in expanding growth; alternative policies such as government investment in social infrastructure may be superior. Finally, it may be that telecommunications investment and economic development (as measured by real per capita income) are jointly, or simultaneously, determined so that each type of policy will provide an effective impetus for regional development.

Clearly, the important question is "what causes what?" Does telecommunications investment cause economic development? Does development cause telecommunications investment? Are the two determined simultaneously? Unless they are totally unrelated, one of the above options must be correct, and knowledge of which is the case, opens the door to appropriate development policy. If telecommunications investment causes economic development or if the two are jointly determined, it then becomes interesting to inquire into the relative magnitudes of the various growth determinants. It makes little sense to orient policy toward a minor factor when a major one is available. Alternatively, if increases in per-capita income cause additional telecommunications investment but not vice versa, policies targeting telecommunications investment *as a development stimulus* are not warranted.

This study proceeds as follows: the next section presents a naïve theoretical foundation for each of the potential behavioral relationships. Then a discussion of the methodology employed in empirically testing for causality, with particular reference to its role in the economic development literature, is presented. The subsequent three sections of the paper present the results of empirical analysis, from three similar but separate studies followed by conclusions for each study; the final section summarizes our findings and relates them to public policy for development.

2. What CausesWhat?

As indicated in our introductory remarks, sound arguments can be made in support of the notions that development causes investment, that investment causes development, and that the two are determined jointly. Consider first the proposition that investment [specifically, private net-investment — later, we will address the question of a subset of aggregate net investment; i.e., telecommunications investment] causes economic growth, as measured by the rate of change in output. Define the aggregate production function

$$Y = f(K, L, G) \tag{1}$$

where Y is aggregate output, K is the existing private capital stock, L is the amount of labor employed, and G is government spending (which we treat as an input in the production of total output). Totally differentiating (1) and then expressing the result in rate of change form, we have

$$\Delta Y = MP_K \Delta K + MP_L \Delta L + MP_G \Delta G \tag{2}$$

or

$$\dot{Y} = \beta_K \dot{K} + \beta_L \dot{L} + \beta_G \dot{G} \tag{3}$$

so that

$$\dot{Y} = \alpha_K \left(\frac{1}{Y}\right) + \beta_L \dot{L} + \alpha_G \left(\frac{\Delta G}{Y}\right) \tag{4}$$

where the α_i's are marginal productivities ($\partial Y/\partial z$), the β_j's are partial output elasticities [$\partial Y/\partial z_j \times (z_j/Y)$], and the dot over-script indicates that the variable is measured in rate of change form $\dot{z} = (dz/z)$. It should be noted that the level of private net investment, $I = \Delta K$ above, is defined implicitly as the change in the capital stock.

Models such as the ones in equations (3) and (4) are rife throughout modern development literature. A classic example of such models was proposed by Ram (1986). In a considerably more general analysis geared toward analyzing the effect of the government sector on growth, he derived a broad model specification of which both equations (3) and (4) can be considered special cases. Ram's model has become the standard for the empirical literature on economic development, with other researchers building off of its foundations. For example Hwa (1988) adds the rate of growth in exports, domestic prices, and agricultural output to the basic Ram model to determine the contribution of agricultural output to economic growth.

It is worth noting that economic growth need not be defined as the rate of growth in output; many times — particularly for developed countries — it is more appropriate to consider the level of output. But this view does not diverge from the basic framework. This can be seen by rewriting equation (2) and subtracting Y from both sides so that

$$Y_t = \alpha_K I + \alpha_L \Delta L + \alpha_G \Delta G + \gamma Y_{t-1} \tag{5}$$

where the α_i's are again marginal productivities, $\Delta K = I$, $\Delta Z = z_t - z_{t-1}$, and $\gamma = 1$ is a test of the appropriateness of the model. Thus the functional form taken by this basic growth model is an empirical question. The data could enter in rate of change, absolute change, or level form; the coefficients could be marginal products, output elasticities, or some combination of the two.

One aspect of the model that is consistent, regardless of how the model is written, is the implied relationship between economic growth (however written) and the level of investment. Since α_K is the marginal product of K (capital), it should be non-negative in the economic region of production. Thus increases in investment must increase economic growth. This is the important result of Ram's (and many other related models) model for this study: investment causes economic growth.

This view is contradicted by an alternative explanation proposed by many, relatively recently by Cullem (1988) but most recently by Ramirez (1994), which is known as the acceleration principle. To use this relationship, assume that the desired capital stock (K^*) is proportional to current output (Y_t)

$$K_t^* = \alpha Y_t \tag{6}$$

where α_t is a constant (the "desired" capital output ratio). Assume further that the actual capital stock (K_t) adjusts to its desired level with a one period lag

$$K_t = K_{t-1}^* \tag{7}$$

Finally, define investment in period t as the difference between the desired and actual capital stock in that period.

$$I_t = K_t^* - K_t \tag{8}$$

Substituting (7) and then (6) into (8) and rewriting yields one version of the accelerator model

$$\begin{aligned} I_t &= K_t^* - K_{t-1}^* \\ &= \alpha Y_t - \alpha T_{t-1} \\ &= \alpha(Y_t - T_{t-1}) \\ &= \alpha(\Delta Y) \end{aligned} \tag{9}$$

This model clearly indicates that the level of investment is determined by the change in income, and not conversely as equation (2) suggests.

An empirical problem that plagues the accelerator is that equation (9) indicates that investment should be negative when Y is falling ($\Delta Y < 0$) and zero when Y is constant ($\Delta Y = 0$), but we observe positive net investment even under these conditions. Some explanation of this phenomenon include investment being determined by expected (rather than actual) demand increases, by expanded market size due to technological advance, a decrease in the rate of change of K, and/or by the level of retained earnings. All of these propositions suggest that investment is determined by the level of output rather than its change. This phenomenon is sometimes called "induced" investment: increases in income induce business to further increase investment

$$I = g(Y) \tag{10}$$

and it clearly has some theoretical validity and empirical support. For this study, the important implication is that (10) directly contradicts (5) from a causality perspective.

Now consider the implication if a simplified version of (5) and (10) both hold, i.e.

$$Y = h(I) \tag{5'}$$

$$I = g(Y) \tag{10}$$

By (5') an increase in investment causes income/output to grow. But from (10) this increased output will result in increased investment, which via (5') will increase output, which via (10) will increase, and so forth. Thus when both relationships hold jointly the effect of one relation feeds back onto the other, and the other then feeds back onto the one. In this particular case, a very simplified view of an internally generated business cycle results.

Ideally, we would prefer to determine causality by theoretical means. Unfortunately, each of the three causal scenarios has a reasonable theoretical underpinning. Thus, we must rely on empirical means to consider which of the three views, if any, are supported by the data.

3. EMPIRICAL TESTS OF CAUSALITY

According to Granger (1969), the causal relationship between two variables can be determined by examining the way they move with respect to each other over time. Specifically, Granger suggested that a variable X_t causes another variable Y_t if, given a universe of information on all factors affecting both X_t and Y_t, the present value of Y (i.e. Y_t) can be predicted better using past values of X (*i.e.* X_{t-j}, $j = 1, \ldots n$) than by not using them. In a statistical sense, this means that the mean squared (prediction) errors of Y, given all information affecting $\{Y_t\}$ except information on $\{X_t\}$ -- call this information set $\{A_t\}$, i.e. MSE = $\sigma^2(Y_t|A_t)$ -- is larger than the mean square (predictions) error of Y, given information on both $\{A_t\}$ and $\{X_t\}$, i.e. MSE = $\sigma^2(Y_t|A_t, X_t)$. Thus, "Granger causality" states that X causes Y if

$$\sigma^2(Y_t|A_t, X_t) < \sigma^2(Y_t|A_t). \tag{11}$$

Since a significant reduction in error variance will result within a least squares framework when a statistically significant variable (or set of variables) is added to the model, a simple statistical test for this requirement is available.

Thus, if $\{X_t\}$ and $\{Y_t\}$ are a pair of linear covariance stationary time series processes, then each can be written, respectively, as

$$X_t = \sum_{j=1}^{k} \alpha_j X_{t-j} + \sum_{j=1}^{k} \beta_j Y_{t-j} + \varepsilon_t \tag{12}$$

and

$$Y_t = \sum_{j=1}^{k} \gamma_j Y_{t-j} + \sum_{j=1}^{k} \delta_j X_{t-j} + \mu_t. \tag{13}$$

Causality tests based on these models are then straightforward: (i) X causes Y if H_o: $\delta_1 = \delta_2 = \ldots \delta_k = 0$ can be rejected based on estimates of equation (13). By similar reasoning, it should be clear that (ii) Y causes X if H_0: $\beta_1 = \beta_2 = \ldots = \beta_k = 0$ can be rejected based on estimates of equation (12). Feedback is implied when the hypotheses in both (i) and (ii) can be rejected.

There are a number of modifications that can be introduced into this methodology. Pierce and Haugh (1977) characterized a number of causal relationships, some of which (e.g., instantaneous causality) have not proven particularly valuable over time. However, one divergence from the above procedure that does appear in the literature from time to time is for other additional variables to be included in the sequels to (12) and (13) [see, e.g. Conte and Darrat (1988)]. This procedure is perfectly justifiable since A_t need not include only past values, of *Y*. However Wold's theorem states that any stationary time series can be characterized by a moving average process of possibly infinite order (i.e., an auto-regressive process). Thus, if $\{Y_t\}$ is stationary, it is possible for A_t to include only past values of *Y*. This probably accounts for the continuing popularity of the original Granger causality testing methodology outlined above. It is certainly this version of the procedure that is finding its way into the newer advanced econometrics texts [see, e.g. Griffiths, et al. (1993) or Greene (2003)].

The tests required by the causality procedure of (12) and (13) are traditional F-tests of the joint hypotheses implied in (i) and (ii) above. As such they should be interpreted with some caution. First, the null hypotheses to be tested assume the relevant parameters are jointly zero. Thus the null being tested is one of Granger non-causality rather than one of Granger causality. This is appropriate however since rejection of the null provides the strong inference that, say, *X* does indeed cause *Y*, i.e., rejecting non-causality implies causality. Second, it is important that $\{X_t\}$ and $\{Y_t\}$ be stationary processes. If the variables are not stationary, one can find perverse causality implications such as business cycles Granger causing sunspots [see, Sheehan and Grieves (1982) and Noble and Fields (1983)]. Third, including additional variables in the regression models (12) and (13) may aid in insuring stationarity but they muddy the causality implications since *X* could influence *Y* through *Z*, rather than directly. Nonetheless, rejection of the hypothesis that *X* does not cause *Y*, if the assumptions of the test are satisfied, provides reasonably strong inferences that *X* causes *Y*.

The profession has not viewed the potential drawbacks of the procedure as particularly limiting since it has found wide application in many areas of economics. Of particular interest to this study is the use of Granger causality in the field of development economics. A number of fairly recent and very interesting studies fall into this category. Jung and Marshall (1985) consider the causal relationships between exports and growth and find no support for the notion that exports cause growth. Joerding (1986) and Kusi (1994) consider the relationship between military spending and economic growth. Joerding (1986) finds that, if anything, economic growth Granger causes military spending and not conversely. Kusi (1994) finds that military spending Granger causes economic growth in only four of the countries considered; the opposite is found for six countries; but no relationship is found for sixty-two of the countries tested. Conte and Darrat (1988) look at the relation between the size of the government sector and rate of real economic growth. While their findings are mixed, there appears to be no causal impact of government growth on economic growth for the majority of OECD countries. More recently Ramirez (1994) has shown that, for Mexico, real government investment Granger causes real private investment, and Walker and Jackson (1998) have shown that some forms of state sponsored gambling cause economic growth.

Clearly, the Granger causality procedure has found wide application in the area of development economics. It is therefore natural to employ it to investigate the question that is central to this study: What is the relationship between telecommunications investment and regional economic growth.

4. A Causality Study for the Southeastern United States

Our initial interest in whether telecommunication investment causes economic growth, or conversely, does economic growth cause investment in telecommunications resulted in an analysis finalized in 1994.[1] The analysis was conducted using data from six states in the southeastern United States and covered the period 1983 through 1992.

BellSouth was (and continues to be) the dominant provider of local telecommunications services in the Southeast, and all states in the sample were located in the BellSouth service area. More specifically, BellSouth is the dominant provider of telephone service in Kentucky, Tennessee, North Carolina, South Carolina, Georgia, Florida, Alabama, Mississippi, and Louisiana. With the exception of Kentucky, BellSouth handled roughly ninety-plus percent of the local telecommunications market in these states at the time. To avoid the statistical anomalies inherent in aggregating across companies for a measure of investment, we treated BellSouth as the "representative firm," with the implicit assumption that other companies exhibit fluctuations about BellSouth's long-term trend.

We initiated the study with an attempt to collect data on telecommunications investment for the period 1983-1992 for each of the nine states in the BellSouth market. For various reasons, we were able to gather the data from the applicable Public Service Commissions for only six states: Louisiana, Florida, Tennessee, Kentucky, Alabama and Georgia. From the data supplied, we chose to represent telecommunications capital stock by a balance sheet item "total plant" and net investment as the difference between plant added in the given year and plant retired in that year. This information was reported on Form M Schedule B-l for the State of Alabama and on similar balance sheet reports in other states. The difference in plant added and plant retired incorporates information on plant in service, property held for future use, plant under construction, plant adjustment, non-operating plant, and goodwill. We deflated this nominal value by using the consumer price index for the largest SMA in the state, and then we divided the result by state population to get real net telecommunications investment per capita (*RPCNET*). It is this variable we employed as a measure of telecommunications investment. Our measure of regional (state) economic activity was personal income, which is also converted into real, per-capita terms (RPCI) using the price index. Increases in this measure, of course, imply economic growth in the region/state. While we started with the potential for sixty observations (10 years, six states), we began our analysis with only 52 observations. We lost five observations due to lack of 1992 population data, and we lost an additional three observations from the Florida (1984) and Tennessee (1985) series beginning later than 1983.

On the question of stationarity, differencing the data was not practical because of the consequent reduction in the number of observations. That is, when we lagged the data one period, we lost six observations (one for each state). In addition we lost two more degrees of freedom per state by adding two more lagged values of each variable to the model. This meant that the degrees of freedom dropped from thirty-five to nineteen as the lag length considered in estimating (12) and (13) rises from 2 to 4. Obviously, considering lag lengths in excess of 4 is not practicable. So, we decided that we were unable to analyze the question of stationarity of {*RPCNET*} and {*RPCI*} using a direct approach because of the sizeable loss of degrees of freedom resulting from only a few lags.

However, Griffiths, et al. (1993) explain that even if ($RPCI_t$) and ($RPCNET_t$) are non-stationary, then a cointegrating vector (i.e. the least squares residual) may be stationary and hence the estimation in (12) and (13) may be super-consistent. The test for the presence of this cointegrating vector is Dickey Fuller test (Griffiths, 1993, p. 701) involving a regression of the first differenced residual from (12) and/or (13) on a constant term, time and the lagged value of the residual. Rejection of the null hypothesis that the coefficient on time and the lagged residual jointly equal zero implies that the cointegrating vector — the residual — is stationary. This finding would mean that the parameter estimation of (12) and (13) are super-consistent so that the implications concerning causality are reinforced. The Dickey-Fuller F-statistics for the two regressions (using the errors from Eqs. 12 and 13) were 18.33 and 17.77, respectively, implying that the presence of a unit root in the residual can be rejected for both models. Thus, the residuals are stationary. Thus even if *RPCNET* and *RPCI* are not stationary, the least squares estimates of the models are super-consistent.

The results of our Granger causality analysis between *RPCI* and *RPCNET* are presented in Table 1. Lag lengths vary from 2 to 4. The F statistics indicate that at two lags and at three lags *RPCI* causes *RPCNET* and not conversely. Both test statistics are significant at better than the 5% level. The evidence is less clear for four lags (15.8% significance level), but that is likely due to the very small degrees of freedom involved ($n - k = 19$). Importantly, in no case is there evidence that *RPCNET* causes *RPCI.* These results suggest that regional growth in the southeastern United States causes telecommunications investment and not conversely.

Table 1. Results of Non-Causality Tests (Southeastern U.S.: 1983-1992)

H_0: *RPCI* non-causes *RPCNET*			H0: *RPCNET* non-causes *RPCI*		
Lags (*RPCI, RPCINET*)	F-Stat	Prob.	Lags (*RPCI, RPCINET*)	F-Stat	Prob
(2,2)	5.528	< 0.01	(2,2)	0.384	0.684
(3,3)	3.380	0.03	(3,3)	0.656	0.586
(4,4)	1.864	0.16	(4,4)	0.728	0.584

As an additional test for whether telecommunications investment could possibly cause economic growth, we considered a more traditional approach to the question. Here, we simply estimate a behavioral model in the spirit of the one posited by Ram (1986) — see Equations (2) - (5) — in which economic growth is determined by investment, labor supply, and government spending. In other words, we estimate

$$RPCI_t = \beta_1 + \beta_2 RPCNET_t + \beta_3 RPCNET_{t-1} + \beta_4 LABOR_t + \beta_5 GOVT_t + \varepsilon_t \qquad (16)$$

where we measured *GOVT* as the sum of real per capita spending on highways (infra-structure investment), education (human capital investment), and real per capita federal transfers and *LABOR* as state level population.[2] *RPCNET* and $RPCI_t$ are as previously

[1] R.O. Beil and J.D. Jackson (1994).

[2] Getting actual labor force participation data would have resulted in further losses of observations. Also, for a period as short as a decade, the age distribution of the population should be relatively stable so that labor force

defined. We include the lagged value of investment $RPCNET_{t-1}$ in order to recognize the fact that investment increases do not get fully and instantaneously compounded into income. If equation 16 estimates of β_2 and β_3 (either or both) are positive and statistically significant, the implication is that increases in telecommunications investment, perhaps after a lag, cause increases in per capita income. Our least squares estimates of the model are summarized as below:

$$RPCI_t = \Omega + 4.21 RPCNET_t + 3.70 RPCNET_{t-1} + \varepsilon_t \text{ ; } R^2 = 0.42, \text{ Obs.} = 46 \qquad (17)$$

where Ω is the sum of the remaining coefficients multiplied by their respective sample means. Niether $RPCNET_t$ nor $RPCNET_{t-1}$ is remotely close to being statistically significant (t = -0.50, t = 0.44, respectively). Thus, while increases in both government spending and the labor supply lead to regional growth (both are highly statistically significant), increases in telecommunications investment has no statistically discernable effect.

If we ignore the statistical implications and just concentrate on the point estimates of the parameters, this conclusion is reinforced still further. We can determine the relative magnitudes of the effects of the various variables on real per capita incomes by computing their standardized regression coefficients (Yamane, 1967, pp. 761-2). These standardized coefficients are computed by multiplying the ordinary regression coefficient by the ratio of the standard deviation of the corresponding independent variable to the standard deviation in the dependent variable. If we consider the investment coefficient that would result from long run equilibrium (where $RPCNET_t$ = $RPCNET_{t-1}$ $= \overline{RPCNET}$), the standardized regression coefficients corresponding to *GOVT*, *LABOR*, and *RPCNET* are 0.624, 0.594, 0.015, respectively. These coefficients have the following interpretation: a one standard deviation in real per capita government spending results in a 0.624 standard deviation increase in real per capita incomes; a one standard deviation increase in the labor force increases real per capita income by 0.594 standard deviations; but a one standard deviation increase in telecommunications investment results in only a 0.015 standard deviations increase in real per capita income. Put another way, the effects of the two significant variables on regional economic development are roughly forty times that of telecommunications investment.

The Granger and more traditional tests just discussed indicate that the economic activity "caused" telecommunications investment but not vice versa. This early analysis of causality had a number of shortcomings, primarily related to the data available. For example, the use of limited pooled time series-cross section data and the concomitant degrees of freedom problems (and other data limitations), we were unable to conduct many desirable statistical tests related to stationarity and were precluded from ancillary analyses that many recent applications of Granger causality analysis seem to view as required. For example, we had insufficient data to estimate an error correction version of the models, we were unable to address the question of long run causality, and we were unable to conduct an analysis to determine the optimal lag length of the various series. For these reasons, we must view our results concerning the Southeast U.S. with some skepticism. In the next sections, we turn to additional analyses void of these these problems in order to obtain further evidence.

participation for each state should be roughly proportional to that state's population (i.e., the proportion of the population between ages 18 and 65 should be stable).

5. A Causality Study for the United States

Our second study does not suffer from the data limitations and peculiarities of the first. In the section, we present causality results from a dataset of 50 years of data (1947 through 1996) on real Gross Domestic Product (*GDP*) and real U.S. telecommunications investment by telecommunications firms (*INV*).[3] Both series are included in the U.S. Bureau of Economic Analysis' National Accounts Data and Detailed Fixed Assets Tables.[4] The series are expressed both as levels and on a per-capital basis (*GDPc*, *INVc*). Due the radical institutional change resulting from the Telecommunications Act of 1996, we end the series in 1996. In our opinion, there is insufficient data available to properly assess the residual effects of the investment bubble following the Act and its eventual collapse in 2001 (Phoenix Center 2003).

We have plenty of data to perform the traditional tests for stationarity. Based on the Augmented Dickey-Fuller and Phillips-Perron tests (both with a null of non-stationarity), we find that the series are non-stationary in their levels, but stationary in their first differences. Thus, both series are I(1). Summary statistics from these tests are provided in Table 2. As prescribed, we use first differences (indicated by Δ) for the causality test. To consider whether or not the Error Correction Model ("ECM") is a more appropriate technique to the standard Granger causality approach, we evaluate whether or not the two series are cointegrated. The Engle-Granger cointegration test indicates the two series are *not* cointegrated, since the residuals from the long-run relationship are not I(0) (Enders 2004: 329, 441).[5] Thus, the standard Granger causality approach is appropriate (there is no "long-run" relationship).

Table 2. Unit Root Tests (United States: 1947-1996)

	Augmented Dickey-Fuller	Phillips-Perron
INV	1.58	2.82
Δ*INV*	-3.98*	-5.56*
GDP	3.06	8.37
Δ*GDP*	-5.08*	-4.98*
INVc	0.40	1.38
Δ*INVc*	-4.40*	-5.99*
GDPc	0.90	2.38
Δ*GDPc*	-6.07*	-6.24*

* Statistically significant at the 5% level or better.

The lengthy time series also provides flexibility in selecting lag length, a decision we did not have the luxury of making in the previous study. Because it is well known that lag length can affect the results of causality tests, the statistical evaluation of optimal lag length is a considerable improvement over our previous effort. A review of the literature quickly reveals

---

3 Some of the analysis in this section draws from Beil, Ford and Jackson (2004).

4 Investment data is reported for "Telephone and Telegraph Services" under the "Communications" heading. The data is expressed in real (1996) dollars, and we employ the data as reported. The data is available at www.bea.gov. GDP data is also in 1996 dollars. Investment does not measure the capital stock, but additions to it. This definition of investment is consistent with the current policy debate regarding policies aimed at increasing capital expenditures by telecommunications firms in an effort to stimulate the economy.

that the standard practice for selecting a lag length is choosing the lag that minimizes information criterion such as the Akaike Information Criterion ("AIC"). Implementation of this approach requires selecting a maximum lag length M and estimating regressions for all possible combinations of lag lengths up to M (i.e., M^2 regressions). From this $M \times M$ matrix of AICs, the best lag length is chosen to be that with the lowest AIC. Enders (2004) recommends beginning with a lag length of $T^{1/3}$, where T is the number of observations. Thus, we first set $M = 4$, but increase M until the smallest AIC contains only lag-lengths less than M (the final M is 6). For the AIC-selected lag lengths, we find no evidence of either serial correlation or heteroscedasticity and the error term is normally distributed (Enders 2004: 147, 338).[6]

The F-statistics of the Granger causality tests are summarized in Table 3. Results from the three smallest AIC-valued lag lengths are presented. Consistent with the previous study, the causality tests indicate that economic output causes investment by telecommunications firms. For the AIC-selected lag length (ΔGDP one lag, ΔINC five lags), the null hypothesis of non-causality is easily rejected at the 5% level with F-values of 5.03 and 4.37. Alternate lag selections are also statistically significant, although in some cases only at the 10% level. Alternately, the null hypothesis that investment by telecommunications firms does not cause economic output is never rejected. At the AIC-selected lag structure, the F-statistics are only 1.18 and 1.39, which are both well below the 5% or 10% critical values.

Table 3. Results of Non-Causality Tests (United States: 1947-1996)

H_0: *GDP* non-causes *INV*			H_0: *INV* non-causes *GDP*		
Lags (*GDP*, *INV*)	F-Stat	Prob.	Lags (*GDP*, INV)	F-Stat	Prob
(1,5)	5.03	0.03	(1,1)	1.18	0.28
(2,5)	2.76	0.08	(1,2)	0.95	0.39
(1,6)	4.54	0.04	(1,3)	1.13	0.35
H_0: (*GDPc* non-causes *INVc*)			H_0: (*INVc* non-causes *GDPc*)		
(1,5)	3.92	0.05	(3,1)	1.20	0.28
(2,5)	2.49	0.10	(1,3)	1.44	0.25
(1,6)	3.71	0.06	(3,2)	1.35	0.27

To further evaluate the effect of lag length on the test results, the causality tests were conducted using all lag combinations up to 5 lags (the AIC-selected lag lengths never exceed 5) for both *GDP* and both *INV* series and their per-capita versions. The null hypothesis that *GDP* does not cause *INV* was rejected 23 times, or 46% of the total tests. Alternately, the null hypothesis that *INV* does not cause *GDP* was rejected only once and only at the 10% level (2% of the total tests). We believe this test for the influence of lag length provides strong evidence on the relationship between telecommunications investment and economic activity.

For an additional test we add variables for labor and government expenditures to our dataset so we can re-estimate Equation (16) with this fifty-year time series. We define *LABOR* as civilian employment (16 years and older) and *GOVT* as real total federal and state

---

[5] We use the critical values provided by Enders (2004: 441).

[6] The tests include the Ljung-Box Q statistics, leverage effects, and White's test for heteroscedasticity (Enders 2004: 149).

government expenditures and investment.[7] The results of the regression are presented in Table 4. As before, neither of the telecommunications investment variables (t or t - 1) are anywhere near statistical significance at standard levels. The standardized coefficients for *LABOR*, *GOVT*, and *INV* are 0.79, 0.29 and -0.07 respectively. As before with the more limited dataset, telecommunications investment is found to have essentially no effect on economic activity. Labor and government expenditures are, however, highly significant and powerful determinants of *GDP*.

Table 4. Regression Results (Dep. Variable = *GDP*)

	Least Squares Estimates	Mean (St. Dev.)
Constant	-2576.2 (-7.67)*	
INV_t	0.004 (0.41)	2280.5 (14588.8)
INV_{t-1}	-0.015 (1.39)	21864.4 (14051.5)
$LABOR_t$	0.066 (9.23)*	86990.5 (22483.3)
$GOVT_t$	2.207 (5.67*	543.9 (242.9)
GDP	...	4149.4 (1879.0)
R^2	0.996	
Obs	49	

* Statistically significant at the 5% level.

6. A Causality Study for OECD Nations

In our third and final study we present causality tests for 25 countries in the Organization for Economic Co-operation and Development ("OECD"). The data for telecommunications investment (*INV*) and gross domestic product (*GDP*) for these countries spans the years 1980 through 1996.[8] Population, telecommunications access lines, and price deflators were also included in the dataset. All the data is from the electronic version of the *Source OECD Telecommunications Database*. Using the OECD Communications Outlook (2003) we adjust information to exclude spectrum auction fees. As with the United States data, we further limit the data set to the years 1980 through 1996 because of competition legislation passed in some of the markets beginning around 1996 (OECD Communications Outlook 2003). This makes the OECD data set comparable to the one used in the second study. We want to make the

[7]Both series are provided by the Federal Reserve Bank of St. Louis, FRED Database, Series SLCECA (GOVT) and CE16OV (LABOR): http://research.stlouisfed.org/fred2/.

[8] We started with 30 OECD countries using data from 1980—2001. Missing data in five countries reduced our sample to 27. We also removed Mexico and Turkey from our study because the LINES per capita and GDP per capita are much lower than those in the other countries used in the sample.

reader aware that different political regimes across the 25 OECD nations in the sample (both in policies and stability) may limit the comparability of the data across countries, but we make no adjustment for this potentiality.

To perform our causality tests with this data, we begin with mean-centered series for *GDP* and *INV* for each country. The series were also expressed on per-capita basis (*GDPc*, *INVc*). Both series are expressed in real terms using the Consumer Price Index for each country. Following Walker and Jackson (1998), we first run filtering regressions (GLS-detranding/demeaning) to eliminate country-specific trends (and further adjust the means with fixed effects) in the data. The residuals of these filtering regressions (*GDP**, *INV**) are then used for the Granger tests.

Augmented Dickey-Fuller and Phillips Perron tests applied to GDP^* and INV^* suggested both the country level and per capita data are I(0). Since the filtered series are stationary in their levels, we use the levels in our Granger tests. The results of our Granger tests for the OECD data are shown in Table 5. We report the F-statistics accompanying the three smallest values of the AIC.

Table 5. Results of Non-Causality Tests (OECD Countries: 1980-1996)

H_0: *GDP* non-causes *INV*			H_0: *INV* non-causes *GDP*		
Lags (*GDP*, *INV*)	F-Stat	Prob.	Lags (*GDP*, INV)	F-Stat	Prob
(1,2)	7.81	< 0.01	(2,1)	1.47	0.23
(1,3)	5.93	< 0.01	(2,2)	0.90	0.41
(2,2)	8.04	< 0.01	(3,3)	0.83	0.48
H0: (GDPc non-causes (INVc			H0: (INVc non-causes (GDPc		
(1,3)	4.93	< 0.01	(3,1)	2.02	0.16
(2,3)	5.08	< 0.01	(2,1)	2.06	0.15
(3,3)	5.29	< 0.01	(3,2)	1.04	0.35

As in our previous two studies, the results from these causality tests indicate that increases in economic activity cause telecommunications investment, but telecommunications investment does not cause economic activity. The F statistic for *GDP** does not cause *INV** hypothesis is 7.81, which is statistically significant at the 1% level. The null hypothesis that *INV** does not cause growth in *GDP** is only 1.47, which is not statistically different from zero. Per-capita results are also reported in Table 5. Again, we find support that *GDP** causes *INV** but none for *INV** causes *GDP**.

7. CONCLUSION

In many development theories and policy prescriptions it is suggested that increasing investment in infrastructure will lead to increases in both area wide and per capita increases in GDP. The telecommunications industry has used this perception to argue for favorable policies aimed at increasing investment in telecommunications which they claim will cause growth in the economy. These policies include subsidies, government protection from entry into the market, favored industry clauses, and tax breaks to name a few.

In this chapter we have presented findings from three separate but closely related empirical studies. The first set of data is for six Southeastern U.S. states. In the second study we present findings from a data set that includes all fifty states in the U.S. And the third study's empirical findings come from an analysis of 25 OECD nations. In all three empirical tests we find that growth in economic activity causes telecommunications investment to increase. However, we find no evidence to support the theory that increases in telecommunications investment causes growth in the economy. Therefore, confirming that telecommunications business executives are correctly moving resources to where they are most profitable. But government policies aimed at increasing these investments may only have positive results for the profits of the telecommunications industry.

In closing we would like to point out that all of our studies are conducted in developed regions. Penetration rates in all of the states and countries we investigate are very high with some approaching 100%. It is possible for third world nations, with extremely low telecommunications penetration rates, to have growth in GDP be positively effected by new investment in telecommunications. However, our results suggest developed countries would be better served by focusing policies on other forms of infrastructure such as roads, job training programs for the uneducated, and access to information. As with all empirical work, this research should be considered as neither conclusive nor incontrovertible, but as one element in a portfolio of evidence. We also not that the null of the Granger test is "non-causality," and our conclusions on telecommunications investment are based inability to reject this null. Of course, the absence of evidence is not evidence of absence, so we must qualify our findings accordingly. Alternate techniques and different data may render conflicting results. Further, investment in newer technologies (e.g., broadband and wireless internet technologies) may have more or less influence on economic growth than those available during the time periods analyzed in these studies. Generalizing the results reported here should take technological advances into consideration.

REFERENCES

R.O. Beil and J.D. Jackson. (1994). "*On the Relationship Between Telecommunications Investment and Economic Growth,*" Auburn Utilities Research Center.

R.O. Beil G. S. Ford, and J.D. Jackson. (Forthcoming). "On the Relationship between Telecommunications Investment and Economic Growth in the United States," *International Economic Journal* (Accepted for Publication December 2003).

Bollier, D. (1989). "The Importance of Communications and Information Systems to Rural Development in the United States" in Parker, E.B., Hudson, H.E., Dillman, D.A., and Roscoe A. D. *Rural America in the Information Age: Telecommunications Policy for Rural Development* (Lanham, MD: University Press of America) pp. 123-158.

Conte, M.A. and Darrat, A.F. (1988). "Economic Growth and the Expanding Public Sector: A Reexamination" *Review of Economics and Statistics*, Vol.. 70, pp. 322-30.

Cullem, C. (1988). "Direct Investment Among Industrialized Countries," *European Economic Review*, Vol. 32, pp. 885-904.

Enders, W. (2004). *Applied Econometric Time Series*. Wiley & Sons: Danvers, MA.

Engle, R. F. and C. W. Granger. (1987). "Cointegration and Error Correction: Representation, Estimation, and Testing." *Econometrica*, Vol. 55, pp. 251-76.

Granger, C.W.J. (1969). "Investigating Causal Relations by Econometric Methods and Cross-Spectral Methods" *Economctrica*, Vol. 37, pp. 424-38.

Granger, C.W.J., N. Hyung, and Y. Jeon)1988). "*Spurious Regressions with Stationary Series*." Working Paper, UCSD Department of Economics.

Greene, W.H. (2003). *Econometric Analysis*, 5th ed. Prentice-Hall: Upper saddle River, NJ:.

Griffiths, W.E., Hill, R.C., and Judge, G.G. (1993). *Learning and Practicing Econometrics*. John Wiley S Sons: New York.

Hamilton, J. (1994). *Time Series Analysis* Princeton University Press: Princeton, NJ:).

Hwa, B.C. (1988). "The Contributions of Agriculture to Economic Growth" *World Development*, Vol. 19, pp. 1329-39.

Jipp, A. (1963). "Wealth of Nations and Telephone Density," *Telecommunications Journal*, July, pp. 199-201.

Joerding, W. (1986). "Economic Growth and Defense Spending" *Journal of Economic Development*, Vol. 21, pp. 35-40.

Jung, W.S. and Marshall, P.J. (1985). "Exports, Growth, and Causality in Developing Countries" *Journal of Economic Development*, Vol. 18, pp. 1-12.

Kusi, M.K. (1994). "Economic Growth and Defense Spending in Developing Countries" *Journal of Conflict Resolutions*, Vol. 38, pp. 152-59.

Madden, G. and S. J. Savage. (1998). "CEE Telecommunications Investment and Economic Growth," *Information Economics and Policy*, Vol. 10, pp. 173-195.

NBER *The NBER's Business-Cycle Dating Procedure*, (2002). Business Cycle Dating Committee (Robert Hall, Martin Feldstein, Ben Bernanke, Jeffrey Frankel, Robert Gordon, Victor Zarnowitz), (June 7, 2002) (www.nber.org).

Noble, N.R. and Fields, T.W. (1983). "Sunspots and Cycles: Comment" *Southern Economic Journal*, Vol. 50, , pp. 251-54.

Phoenix Center. (2003). *The Truth About Telecommunications Investment after the Telecommunications Act of 1996*. Phoenix Center Policy Bulletin No. 4 (June 24).

Pierce, D.A. and Haugh, L.D. (1977). "Causality in Temporal Systems: Characterizations and a Survey" *Journal of Econometrics*, Vol. 5, pp. 265-93.

Ram, R. (1986). "Government Size and Economic Growth: A New Framework and Some Evidence from Cross-Section and Time Series Data" *American Economic Review*, Vol. 76, pp. 191-203.

Ramirez, M.D. (1994). "Public and Private Investment in Mexico, 1950—1990: An Empirical Analysis" *Southern Economic Journal*, Vol. 61, pp. 1-17.

Röller, L. and L. Waverman (2002). "Telecommunications Infrastructure and Economic Development: A Simultaneous Approach," *American Economic Review*, Vol. 92, pp. 909-923

Sheehan, R.G. and Grieves, R. (1982). "Sunspots and Cycles: A Test of Causation" Southern *Economic Journal*, .Vol. 49, pp. 775-77.

Sims, G. (1972). "Money, Income and Causality," *American Economic Review*, Vol. 62, pp.540-552.

Walker, D and J. Jackson, (1998). "New Goods and Economic Growth: Evidence from Legalized Gambling," *Review of Regional Studies,* Vol. 28, pp. 47-69.

Yamane, T (1967). *Statistics* 2nd ed..Harper and Row: New York. .

INDEX

A

B

C

D

E

F

G

H

I

J

K

L

M

N

O

P

R

S

T

U

V

W

Z